FUSEBOX:

Methodology and Techniques

ColdFusion® Edition

by

STEVE NELSON AND CRAIG GIRARD

with Additional Materials by

Nat Papovich and Hal Helms

A FUSION AUTHORITY BOOK

Produced in cooperation with

JM Publishers, Inc.

ISBN: 0-9673447-4-3

FUSEBOX: METHODOLOGY AND TECHNIQUES

Cold Fusion Edition

Printed in the United States of America.

Cover Art: **Jim Conté**, based on an original design by **Dan Bowling**.

Editing and typesetting: **S. Malkah Cohen**

ISBN: 0-9673447-4-3

First Printing: Fusion Authority, Inc., November 2000
10 9 8 7 6 5 4 3 2 1

All sales through
(718) 252-2329

ACKNOWLEDGMENTS

The authors would like to thank:

- **Judith Dinowitz** and **S. Malkah Cohen** of JM Publishers, Inc. for their publishing and editorial expertise;
- Technical Editor **Nat Papovich** for helping us make sense;
- **Hal Helms** for allowing us to print his genius;
- **Fred Sanders** for contributing his definitions;
- **Dan Bowling** and **Jim Conté** for their work on the cover design;
- **Shawn Epling** for assistance with several of the internal graphics;
- The **Instant Knowledge Team**, **Gabe Roffman**, **Kevin Myers**, **Josh Diehl** and **Fred Sanders** for starting fUseML;
- **Michael Dinowitz** of Fusion Authority and House of Fusion for putting this book under the Fusion Authority Book imprint;
- **Allaire™ Corporation** for creating ColdFusion®.

The authors acknowledge the contributions of other **writers** on the topic of Fusebox who have shared their insights with us: **Eron Cohen**, **Tom Langer** and **Michael Smith**.

There have also been many **readers** who kindly commented on the book while it was under development: **Carl Conner, Tobe Goldfiger**, **David Huyck**, **Nancy Leiby**, **Jeffrey Marsh**, **Bill Poff**, **Joe Schuch** and **Corey Snow**, plus several more who have chosen to remain anonymous. In many cases, their commentaries represented hours of thoughtful, detailed analysis and yielded valuable insights into the growing and evolving Fusebox phenomenon.

We are grateful for the additional **tech support** provided by **Michael Slatoff** and the staff members of **AGS**: **Al Stahl**, **Ken Cratty**, **Heath Livermore** and **Michael Munshaw**.

And of course, the myriad contributions of **the members of the Fusebox Organization** and **participants on the Fusebox lists** in assisting in the development of Fusebox cannot be measured.

STEVE NELSON would like to thank his wife and best friend in the world, **Nicole**, for all her love and help getting him through rough times; his parents, **Sue and Larry**, for their constant encouragement; his nephew, **Clayton**, for having the best toothless smile; and all the folks at Allaire for creating ColdFusion.

CRAIG GIRARD would like to thank his parents, **Mary and Pete**, without whom he would be lost; **Cindy Mazza** for the love and support to write this book; **Ellen Hoch** and **Raymond MacElroy** for having confidence in him; **Eddie Guerra** and **John Paul Wagner, Jr.** for an RIT experience he will never forget and friendships that will last a lifetime; and **Bill Mallonee**, **Doug Pinnick**, **Ty Tabor** and **Jerry Gaskill** for the music.

TABLE OF CONTENTS

FOREWORD

"There are two ways of constructing a software design: One way is to make it so simple that there are obviously no deficiencies, and the other way is to make it so complicated that there are no obvious deficiencies. The first method is far more difficult."

-C.A.R. Hoare

When I was a boy, I read a story involving something called "Ever So Much More So" powder. It did what it advertised — took a thing and made it "ever so much more so". If something was sweet, it made it sweeter. If something was hot, it made it hotter. I've often thought the effect of the Web was like someone sprinkling this magical powder on the world economy. It magnifies the properties of the systems it touches — and in doing, so brings things, both good and bad, into sharp focus. It places in our hands, as developers and as humans, great power.

Today, though, things are very different. Now, unexpected, unanticipated behavior in the software *we* write is the chief factor in an astonishing figure that repeated studies confirm: *70% of corporate software projects are either abandoned or declared as failures*. As our economy transitions fully into one based on software and the information it manipulates, this alarming number threatens to become far more than an embarrassment. The very health of the economy may be endangered if this situation continues.

We can use the power of the Web to benefit many — if we can bring down that 70% failure rate. But doing so means we must give up on the cherished notion of the software cowboy, riding the range with his or her favorite code editor … .

Our roles are too important; the stakes are too high. Mountain Dew, pizza, and long nights must yield to more powerful tools if we are to reliably produce software of predictable quality. Certainly, we need the latest advances in software languages and compilers, but that alone is not sufficient. We need better ways of working — ways that will reduce the complexity in our software systems and let groups of developers combine to produce great software. We need methodologies that support cooperation among developers who do not live in the same time zone — or even on the same continent. We need a way of working that will allow all of us to perform at the skill levels we presently have, so that each of us can make a contribution to the effort.

This small book is a major contribution to this effort. When Allaire™ Corporation's ColdFusion® first "caught fire" and thousands of new developers were still struggling between the differences in lists and arrays, Steve Nelson and Gabe Roffman began creating just such a methodology. They called it Fusebox, a worthy pun on the language it was originally intended for — ColdFusion. Today, Fusebox has itself caught fire as the preferred methodology for ColdFusion development — and it is making inroads in other languages as well.

Writing software is no easy matter. In fact, it may well be the most complex feat that we humans attempt and even sometimes succeed at. One reason — I think the chief one — is that any software beyond the most trivial involves the interaction of many separate, discrete pieces — "moving parts", to use the mechanical engineer's vocabulary.

Systems that involve such intricate interactions of components are labeled "complex", a technical term used by those who study such things. One of the unique things about complex systems is that behavior arises **out of the system itself** that was neither planned for nor anticipated. Complexity theorists call this "emergent behavior"; software engineers use the more terse word "bug".

This isn't to say that complexity is necessarily bad. Many games are, at their heart, complex systems, and we delight in their challenges. A game such as chess, with only 32 "moving parts" yields patterns of such complexity that it has virtually defined the summit of human mental calisthenics. Only recently have the most powerful computers been able to challenge their carbon-based competitors — and then only with extensive help from humans. Still, a Rubicon of sorts was passed when Deep Blue, the IBM supercomputer, in its historic chess match with Gary Kasparov, made moves of such subtlety that its own creators were taken aback. What they were experiencing was the surprise — and thrill — of emergent behavior in a system of their own creation.

The notion of emergent behavior in software holds an intriguing promise for the future of programming. Many have lamented that software so little resembles a true engineering discipline, despite heroic efforts along these lines. It may well be that in the future, software will become less like engineering and more like ranching. Our software "creations" may acquire a "mind of their own" — and programming may involve the selection and reproduction of programs to solve problems, especially if the complexity of the problem defies the rigid nature of algorithms and control structures.

If this occurs — if the experiments in "software genetics" currently under way in universities and research laboratories bear fruit — we may someday see the snake of complexity swallow its own tail. We may use the very features of complexity that today frustrate our efforts to solve problems unsolvable by any other means. One thinks of the words of the humorist Will Rogers: "If stupidity got us into this mess, then why can't stupidity get us out?"

I am therefore heartened by the emergence of such tools as ColdFusion and Fusebox. Developers who were willing to mine the sparse documentation available on ColdFusion discovered a rich ore of pure gold. Development cycles became shorter, bugs (those *emergent behavior* characteristics of complex systems) became fewer, predictability in schedules increased. But, admittedly, such mining was not for the faint of heart, and all of us involved in the movement listened repeatedly to the plea, "Where can I get a course on Fusebox?"

Happily, this book is the answer to that question. Steve Nelson and his co-author, Craig Girard, have taken a systematic approach to Fusebox that will make it accessible to anyone interested in learning. It is written in plain English and it is aimed squarely at developers working in the real world. If you have wished for a way to make your own development simpler, surer and more successful, you have come to the right source. As well, I can think of no better investment you could make in your own career than to become skilled in the techniques provided by this book.

– Hal Helms

INTRODUCTION

A Brief Outline of the Problem

Writing large web applications can be quite a complex task. Not only do you need to make sure the application does what it is supposed to do, it needs to look the way the client wants it to look, and you need to do this in a timely fashion. This often means managing multiple developers. It is very common for a large application to be built by numerous people, i.e., Michael takes Section One, and Cindy takes Section Two, Bill takes Section Three, and so on. The next issue comes after the sections are created: How are these going to be brought together?

Beyond this, you also need to make sure that the application lasts, meaning that, in a year, the next group of developers to inherit this application will have some way to understand the code. Is there a common methodology each section was written to? Or were all three sections written differently? Whose methodology was "best"?

First, a Definition

Within this book, we constantly refer to Fusebox as a "methodology", which *dictionary.com* defines as

> **meth•od•ol•o•gy**
>
> 1.
>   a. A body of practices, procedures, and rules used by those who work in a discipline or engage in an inquiry; a set of working methods: The *methodology* of genetic studies; an opinion poll marred by faulty *methodology.*
>   b. The study or theoretical analysis of such working methods.
>
> ***Usage Note:*** *Methodology* can properly refer to the theoretical analysis of the methods appropriate to a field of study or to the body of methods and principles particular to a branch of knowledge.

Fusebox fits this definition perfectly. It is a body of practices, procedures and rules used by those who work in web development. It is also the study or theoretical analysis of such working methods. There is a core set of recommended Fusebox techniques that, if strayed from, could mean that "technically" you are not developing in Fusebox. However, it is not an exact science. Many developers use Fusebox methodologies as a base and then add their own styles on top of them. Many share their findings with the community of Fusebox developers: If the technique gains popularity, it may become part of the core methodologies.

The Fusebox Solution

Let's look at the situation practically. Would you decide to build a house without first determining how many bedrooms, bathrooms, etc. you need, where they should be and what doors lead where? Would you start construction without drawing up blueprints to show the contractors exactly what goes where? Of course not. Then why would you try to build an application without a thorough understanding of what the client REALLY wants? And why would you start writing code before you've thought out the flow of information and actions and made sure it can work the way both you and your client envision?

The real issue at hand is not which methodology is best. The issue is how we can turn unorganized code into organized code. Once we're in agreement on how the code is best organized, we can figure out how to optimize it. Once all the code is organized in the same way, no one in the team will need to think about the architecture of the application. They will skip that step and attempt to solve the more important problem of what the application is going to do.

Fusebox attempts to do one very simple thing:
Create an architecture for any web application.

The Need for (Development) Speed

Fusebox can help address another serious issue. Most internet companies consider reducing costs by speeding up web application development a hot topic. Too many companies are running out of money and being forced to go out of business because of sluggish development. The easy answer for developers is to blame the management and say that it was not their fault that the company went under. But this isn't helpful.

When companies are run solely on investment money with little or no "real" money coming into the business (most dot-com companies fit the bill), they only have a limited amount of time to get the business off the ground and the product to market. If they are too slow, they are threatened by the competition and (maybe) their investors. The times of investors throwing money away on dot-coms is over. Investors will no longer tolerate chronic losses. They are in their business for profit, and businesses MUST begin being profitable.

What Can We Do?

Many dot-coms do have an actual revenue stream, although their expenses seem to dwarf this income, making it look like a pittance. This will only be tolerated for so long; investors will shut the business down. We, as web developers, can help this problem by reducing our expenses. Good web developers do not come cheap; most of our expenses go directly into our pockets through salaries. For us to reduce our expenses, we need to speed up our development times.

The era of consuming months or years in development of a custom software, utilizing dozens or hundreds of programmers is over. We tested and proved the possibilities of this new paradigm in our work on **ValueMusic.com**, discussed as a case study/tutorial in Chapter 9. **It is indeed possible to build large web applications in a matter of weeks.** We were able to build full new sections in a matter of days, sometimes in just a few hours, fully specified and designed, with very few bugs. **This is the future of Fusebox development.**

Let's Answer Some Questions

Q) What is "Fusebox"?

A) Fusebox is a methodology. It is a set of best practices, procedures and rules. It's not a product that you buy or software that you need to install. Fusebox is a way of organizing a web application in such a way that it makes it easier for the programmers to understand. As much as it is a way to organize code, it is a way to organize your thought processes in regards to system development. Once you become familiar with Fusebox, the way you think about application structure will change.

Q) How complicated is the Fusebox Process?

A) The Fusebox Process is as much a way of thinking about your application as it is a methodology. There is an internal logic and considerable flexibility built into it. A basic understanding of the Fusebox logic process and core conventions can give you all you need to start working in it.

In addition, a beautiful thing about Allaire™ ColdFusion® (CF) is that it is simple, meaning that the language contains no complex processes, yet it achieves apparently simple results. With a basic understanding of databases and HTML, you can learn and understand how the language works virtually overnight. Although one of the "problems" with ColdFusion is that it lacks a structured approach to build large applications, this isn't a fault in the language. It is something that is up to the programmer. The Fusebox Methodology helps solidify the architecture of a ColdFusion application by offering guidance on how to organize web applications.

Q) Who should read this book?
A) Any web application manager or developer. This Fusebox implementation guide is based on Allaire's ColdFusion Application Server, and therefore will be immediately valuable to the ColdFusion developer. However, Fusebox was created for easy portability to other web scripting languages, such as ASP, Perl or PHP. As of this writing, a Fusebox version for PHP is nearing completion, and an ASP version is also in the works. The guidelines presented in this book will be beneficial to web developers, no matter what language they use.

Q) Can my little ten-file application really benefit from Fusebox?
A) Fusebox applications do not have a specific size where they work best. Whether your application only consists of ten files or 2,000 files, the Fusebox architecture will help you organize your application. In fact, a small application is an excellent learning ground for mastering the Fusebox methodology and techniques.

Q) Fusebox looks at the application in depth. Why is such a level of detail so important?
A) Creating specifications and designs for large applications is a complex process. It takes time to figure out exactly what you and your client want an application to do before you can begin building it. The Fusebox process avoids the common problem of not completely thinking the application out before it is handed to the developer to build.

One of the beautiful aspects of Fusebox is that it creates a structure that can be understood by both programmers and non-programmers. That means that the process of writing specifications can be greatly simplified.

Q) How else does Fusebox help the development team?
A) The building of a large application is seldom done by only one person. Management of a team can be incredibly difficult unless there are guidelines about how the team is going to work. Extending this to the next level by adding temporary people to the project like consultants and contractors makes the project even more difficult to manage. Fusebox's modular nature, dedication to code reuse and self-explanatory naming systems therefore become a real boon, plus offering guidelines for how to deal with application management in multiple-developer team environments.

Q) How does this relate to the "real world"?
A) Throughout this book, we discuss how we use the Fusebox Methodology to create sites both large and small. Also we provide code samples and case studies so you can get a better idea of the code involved.

Q) Who or what is "Fusebox.org"?

A) The Fusebox Organization is a non-profit group of developers that maintains a web site dedicated to the advancement of the Fusebox Methodology. **Fusebox.org** *(http://www.Fusebox.org)* is community-driven through discussion boards and mailing lists which allow users to suggest new ideas to add to the Fusebox Methodology or question the current concepts.

Q) Is there a Fusebox Seal of Approval or Certification of Compliance?
A) No. Fusebox is not a product and the Fusebox Organization has no real powers. Fusebox is simply a collection of ideas, each of which will help organize your code and system development process. You can adopt as much or as little of the Fusebox Methodology as you want, without fear of not being "fully compliant".

There **is a "Fusebox Inside"** sticker available as a voluntary advertisement, which we encourage you to use.

After having read this book, you will have an understanding of the concepts of a proven methodology for designing, organizing and developing web applications. Providing you understand Fusebox is a methodology and not an exact science, this book will inspire ideas, allowing you to create more dynamic, scalable systems. Once you are inspired, please share with the rest of the world your new-found knowledge through the **Fusebox mailing list**, available at **House of Fusion** (*http://www.houseoffusion.com*).

CHAPTER 1:
The Fusebox Concept

Defining the Problem

As programmers, we know the excitement found in writing code. We are crafts people in the world of ones and zeros. Once a project is finished, we sit back and view our creations like proud parents, amazed at what we have brought into the world.

We also may be familiar with the headaches of code that was written without a plan for the future. Undocumented code can be confusing to decipher; unorganized code can be impossible to maintain. At some time in every programmer's life, it becomes clear that standards need to be applied when developing, to help us stay sane and to facilitate a change of project ownership.

> **WANTED:**
>
> - **Longevity**
> - **Adaptability**
> - **Scalability**

There are hundreds of computer languages in use today. Compiled, 4th generation, interpretive, scripting – no matter the type of language, there comes a time when the community using the language decides to apply standards to them.

The rising demand for software applications built for the World Wide Web created many new computer languages. Web application servers, like Microsoft's Active Server Pages, Allaire's ColdFusion, PHP and others, were created, each with their own strengths and weaknesses. The first web applications were simple, fast and easy to build. Programmers did not worry about maintenance or reuse of code, because they could quickly and easily write it again if necessary. But, as time went on, web application servers became more powerful and capable, and the demand for high-end applications served over the web increased.

Today, web languages are nearly as powerful and complex as any computer language on the market. Increased popularity of a language means applications are more apt to stay in use for long periods of time, ushering in the need to update the existing application. It also means larger applications will be written, leading to teams of programmers working together.

This trend points to one thing: The need for a universal web application standard. Software languages existing before the birth of the web show us the great benefits to be gleaned from implementing a standardized programming practice. The use of such a standard has many benefits, including:

1. Giving programmers a common ground for understanding each other's code.
2. Decreasing development time.
3. Decreasing debugging time.
4. Faster and simpler updating.

Enter Fusebox

The web application development community now has a standard, the Fusebox Methodology. This has been proven to reduce and even eliminate the problems associated with unorganized code.

The Fusebox Organization was established in 1997, by Steve Nelson and Gabe Roffman. Both accomplished ColdFusion programmers, the two then shared an office in downtown Charlottesville, VA. They decided to create a standardized way of coding so that, when they completed an application, the code is its own documentation. They also decided that the method would work with any web application language and not just their personal favorite, Allaire ColdFusion.

Drawing ideas from Object Oriented Programming, Steve and Gabe came up with a methodology for developing web applications. Each application is broken down into hierarchical directories, each building off the one above and having its own set of actions to perform. Each directory is driven by a common file that the application parses to complete the requested action. This file accepts all the commands of the user and calls the files needed to complete that command. The name "Fusebox" was applied to the new methodology because they realized that the structure of the application resembled a common household fuse box.

After hashing out hundreds of ideas, they felt the web application community as a whole could benefit from their inventions and discoveries. They also knew that the more people used Fusebox, the more it would mold into a tighter specification, drawing from the experiences of the community at large.

The Fusebox Organization introduced a web application methodology primarily for ColdFusion development that it felt could benefit the ColdFusion community at large. It quickly grabbed the attention of a core group of ColdFusion developers, who tested it, proposed changes, and re-tested the specification repeatedly. The result: An open-source, universal, standard methodology for ColdFusion development, spread worldwide by word-of-mouth.

The need for information, examples and tutorials about Fusebox led to the creation of the Organization's website, ***http://www.fusebox.org***. The site contains two Fusebox white papers, basic and advanced Fusebox techniques, and ColdFusion code examples written to Fusebox specifications. The Fusebox Organization has made this available to the ColdFusion community free of charge.

The demand for Fusebox knowledge also led to the creation of an Internet mailing list, currently being hosted by **House of Fusion** (***http://www.houseoffusion.com***). This list creates a forum for anyone using the Fusebox specification to post their successes, failures, questions and knowledge accumulated while using the specification. This mailing list is also the venue for suggesting updates for the Fusebox specification.

As of early 1998, Fusebox was going strong, but it still had never been tested on a large-scale application. Then Steve and Gabe landed a contract to develop **eBags.com**. This became the first large scale web application to implement Fusebox methodologies. The site went up just a few months later, proving Fusebox could handle large applications with lots of traffic.

Two years later, the site is still up and successful. The code has been handed over to other developers who have been able to add to and update it without a problem. Steve and Gabe have accomplished their goal. The Fusebox Organization has created a universal standard for writing web applications, and found a way for the code itself to be its own documentation.

CHAPTER 2: Basic Fusebox Methodology

Overview

Defining the Terms

In the first chapter we discussed the need for organized code, especially when working in groups. We discussed the history of the Fusebox Methodology, and the introduction answered a few commonly asked questions. In the introduction, we also defined "methodology" and noted that Fusebox fits this definition perfectly.

With all that in mind, let's define a few terms and gain an understanding of Fusebox. This chapter will begin to lay the foundation for you to build on. Remember our analogy to designing and building a house. There is the home itself, and there are the circuits that power it. Fusebox uses a similar structure.

Home Application

Briefly put, a **home application** is the overall application, or the root directory of your application. It is usually the first place to which a user goes when on the site (i.e., **http://www.mysite.com**). The home application is generally named after the system you are creating, although it does not need to be. The home application is a container for other applications, called **circuit applications**. We will go into this in more detail in Chapter 5.

Circuit Application

Circuit applications are sub-applications of a home application, or sub-directories of a root directory. Each directory is its own application and is said to "extend" the home application. Each sub-application has its own functions and responsibilities and should be designed and built with minimal dependencies on the home application. The home application, together with its circuit applications, create the whole application. (See Chapter 5.)

Here's an example of an e-commerce site making use of home and circuit applications. The site contains various home and many circuit applications. **Http://www.mysite.com/search** allows you to search for products, while **http://www.mysite.com/info/testimonials** allows users to view, add, edit and delete testimonials. Unless the user looks at the URL, they may never be aware that they have been using several applications.

This is similar to a real life home. Whether a person plugs a television into an outlet in the kitchen or the living room, they still get power, because they are in their home (assuming they paid the power bill).

Introducing the "Fusebox"

Let's extend the household fuse box metaphor. Every household contains a fuse box. This fuse box controls the flow of electricity through a house. The electricity does not flow randomly, but instead is controlled by the fuse box. The fuse box uses fuses to moderate the electricity in each circuit. Each circuit has its own fuse and can function independently of all the other rooms. When one circuit's fuse blows, the rest of the house still has power.

The Fusebox Methodology shares this concept. A web application's ***index.cfm*** file acts as the fuse box. This file controls the Fuseactions (requests to the server) and Fuses (individual files), and determines the flow of the application. The application's "Fuses" are the files that are plugged into the Fusebox, the *index.cfm* file, to complete an action.

Each directory in an application contains **one** *index.cfm* file. These files have one task: Processing Fuseactions. Remember that a household's electricity flows through the fuse box, through the fuses and into separate rooms of the house. Each *index.cfm* file directs the programming flow the same way: Every action requested by a user is routed through the *index.cfm* file. The *index.cfm* file evaluates the Fuseaction being requested and invokes the Fuses necessary to complete the Fuseaction. (For a sample *index.cfm* file, please see the diagram in Chapter 4.)

Introducing the Fuseaction

What Is an Action?

Whenever a user interacts with a web application, the server performs an **action**. This action is whatever the user is allowed to do. They may want to add an item to a shopping cart, delete an item from a shopping cart or purchase the items in their shopping cart. Each *action* is the user commanding the server to do something, or a single command to the server.

The Internet is a stateless environment. In other words, the user does not stay connected to any server as they use the Web. When a user makes a request of the server, the user is logged in, the server processes the request, returns the output to the user, and logs the user out. Because of this, an action must be sent to the server with every request. If an action is not sent, the server will not know what to do.

Typically, actions are defined by the particular page being requested. The particular page the user is viewing usually contains a hypertext link or form action pointing to the next file in the flow of the application. If a user was removing all the items from their shopping cart, a typical Universal Resource Locator (URL) may look like this:

http://www.fusebox.org/deletecart.cfm

Fusebox defines a way to organize all the "actions" of an application, called "**Fuseactions**".

What Is a Fuseaction?

One page of an application may link to one or more different actions, via the same *index.cfm*. An action can be sent to the server three different ways:

- part of a URL string:

```
index.cfm?fuseaction=showUser
```

- a form field (variable):

```
<input type="hidden" name="fuseaction" value="showUser">
```

- or browser cookie variables.

The Fusebox Organization recommends sending actions to the server in either form or URL variables, because these are the only variables that are specific to each page.

Fusebox defines each user action as a **Fuseaction**. The term "Fuseaction" is a reserved word in the Fusebox Methodology, intended to be unique and descriptive. Its purpose is to command the server and give the programmer a quick description of what it does. The processing of each Fuseaction is made up of one or more "Fuses".

Introducing the Fuse

Continuing our metaphor of the household fuse box, houses have fuses that can trip or blow, which handle different circuits. Similarly, a web application has different components to control different functions. One file may display a form for the user to enter information, another may enter that information into a database and another may send an e-mail. Each file the Fusebox calls, i.e., any file included by the *index.cfm*, is called a Fuse.

However, a bunch of Fuses just bouncing around a Fusebox isn't going to do us much good. In order to make any use of our Fuses, we need to organize them.

Types of Fuses

The Fusebox Specification defines six (6) principal types of *Fuses*.

> **Application Files** ("*app_filename.cfm*") are files that pertain to an application or applications as a whole. Two of the most important types of Fusebox application files are:
>
> > ***App_globals.cfm*** contains information that is needed globally for the home application and all of its circuit applications. For example, if a variable defining the datasource of a database is required by a home application and its circuit applications, this variable is set in *app_globals.cfm*.

App_locals.cfm contains information that is specific to a circuit application. One *app_locals.cfm* file is created for each *index.cfm*.

Display Files use the prefix notation *"dsp_filename.cfm"*. These files "return", or display, information to the user. They can contain CFML and HTML, along with other client-side processes like JavaScript and XML. These files could be used for displaying the results of a database query or presenting the user with a form. Display files should contain no CFML processing that isn't dependent on or embedded in the rendering of the page. Using CFML in display files is certainly acceptable for correctly formatting the <CFOUTPUT> of a query, but long tracts of CFML should be avoided in these files and instead placed into an action file (see below).

Action Files use the prefix notation *"act_filename.cfm"*. These files do not display any information to the user. They are used for many different purposes, but are most commonly used to change information on the server. Action files can contain CFML and SQL, but not HTML. These files are never seen by the user. SQL in an action file could run a *select*, *insert*, *update* or *delete* query as well as call a stored procedure from a database. The CFML could be used to change other data, such as writing to a file, making changes to the data in an LDAP server, or performing an HTTP call.

These files are not limited to database changes. They can be used for doing those tasks that do not fit particularly well into a display file, including large chunks of error checking in the form of CFML conditional logic.

Query Files use the prefix notation *"qry_filename.cfm"*. These files contain select-only SQL queries or stored procedure calls. They are usually reserved for queries referenced in multiple files. Instead of rewriting the query each time, the file is included when needed, using the <CFINCLUDE> tag. These Fuses should not be dependent on any other templates for processing and should only contain the SQL call and any CFML dependent on that call. Try to avoid writing more than a few lines of CFML other than the <CFQUERY> or <CFSTOREDPROC>.

Redirection Files use the prefix notation "*url_filename.cfm*". These prevent a user from repeatedly resubmitting information to a form because s/he has hit the "reload" button on the browser. These files are generally simple, containing only a single <CFLOCATION> in them, but may occasionally have multiple <CFLOCATION> tags, as needed. With <CFLOCATION> tags in their own files, your <CFCASE>

statements in the *index.cfm* file only contains references to include appropriate files.

ColdFusion Custom Tags (CF/CFX Tags): These files are ColdFusion extensions. See your ColdFusion manual for more information. Fusebox does not disallow or specifically address these extensions.

Conclusion

This chapter continued the explanation of the common terms and definitions used within the Fusebox Methodology, begun in the Introduction.

Fusebox is a **methodology**, as we defined it, for the web development community. It is a body of practices, procedures and rules to organize your code. Many developers begin with the basic Fusebox techniques and eventually add their own methods and procedures on top of that foundation.

Each application has a **home application** and can have one or more **circuit applications**. Each application contains an ***index.cfm*** file: This file is the **Fusebox** and controls the flow of the application. Each call to the application goes through a Fusebox, which processes the requested **Fuseaction** by calling the **Fuses** required to complete it.

Before we discuss how to put all this together into an application, let's take a look at what needs to happen **before** you start coding.

CHAPTER 3: Before You Even Get Started

The Difference Preplanning Makes

Since the creation of computer languages, code has always followed what is called the "software development life cycle" (SDLC). The SDLC is the path a software application takes from its inception to design, development, testing and deployment. There are three paths that software projects follow:

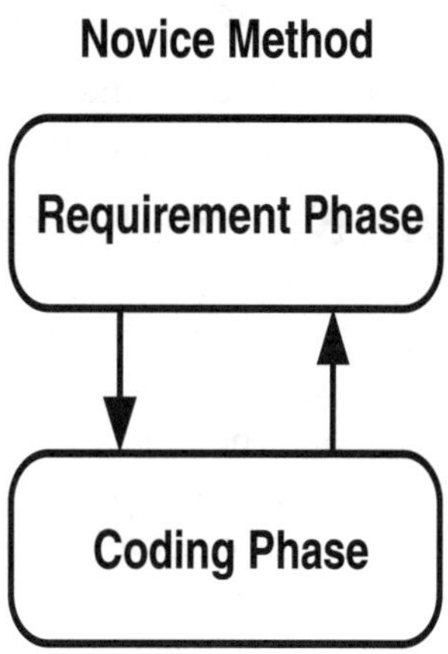

The Novice Method: This SDLC usually consists of only two phases: The Requirements Phase and the Coding Phase. This is the path almost every programmer has experienced. It is also the leading cause of stress and disappointment in inexperienced programmers.

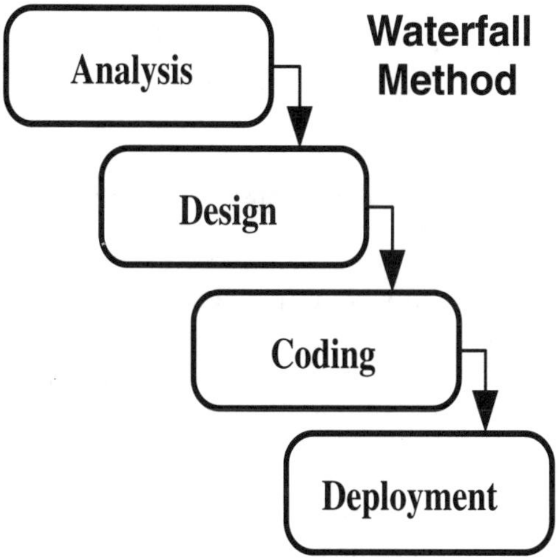

The Waterfall Method: This SDLC consists of four phases: Analysis, Design, Coding and Deployment. These phases are followed in a waterfall-like fashion from top to bottom. The Waterfall Method is a step up from the Novice Path in that it adds the very crucial Analysis and Design phases.

The Spiral Method: This SDLC consists of the same five phases as the Waterfall Method (Analysis, Design, Coding, Testing and Deployment). The difference is that these phases are in constant communication with one another, and it is common for development to go from Analysis to Design and back again, each time tightening up the specifications. This type of interface occurs between all the phases.

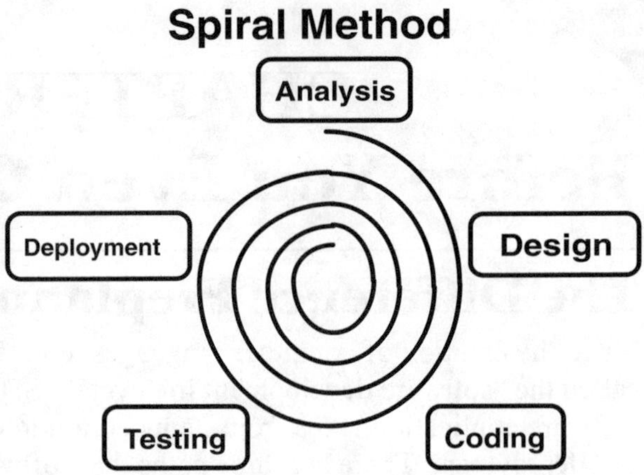

To further understand the triumphs and pitfalls of the various methods, let's look at a few real world examples:

The Novice Method

The Novice Method is a situation everyone will probably recognize. First, a person in authority decides a software application is needed. The requirements of the application are usually written out on a notepad, or better yet a napkin. These requirements are then expressed to the programmer(s). (Often a team of programmers will be involved, each in charge of one piece of the puzzle.) Taking what was told to him or her, each programmer begins to pound away at the keyboard. A while later, a functional application has been finished.

The programmers are quick to show the application to the person in authority, only to find it wasn't quite what the creator of the requirements had envisioned. So the programmers go back to the code and make the changes requested. (This scenario alone could go on forever, but we will move past it.) Finally, the programmers have given the person in authority what was desired and all is well.

Somewhere along the line, enhancements are always requested. This is when the programmers go back to the code and ask themselves "What did I do here?" They then proceed to rummage through lines and lines of code, possibly separated into many different files. The need for a file system and code organization becomes apparent.

The programmers then proceed to add comments and little reminders to themselves about what the code is doing and how it works. This works well, and the programmers walk away feeling good about what has been accomplished. Now, every time they are asked to add to the application, they read the comments, recall what has been done, and add the new section of code to complete the given task.

As time goes by, the original programmers move onto other projects and a newcomer is brought in to maintain the code. The newcomer is quick to read the comments, only to find that the hieroglyphics left behind are not helpful. They are not entirely useless, but in too many cases, can only be deciphered by the original author.

The newcomer struggles on and, after a while, is capable of understanding the programmers' comments and portions of the code enough to understand the concept of the application. The newcomer is asked to create a new section for the application and has enough understanding of the code to add to it. In other words, he or she knows what variables are needed in the new section, which variables to accept and which ones to return.

But the code is still very difficult to understand, due to the complexity of its flow. The flow of the application can be called its "code trail". This code trail starts with one file, then calls another. That file in turn calls another and so on, until the action of the application finishes, way down the road, in a file relatively unrelated to the first.

The unfortunate day inevitably arrives when the newcomer has to correct an error in the application. The complexity of the code trail greatly increases the time it normally takes for the bug to be found, fixed and returned to the user. The newcomer struggles with the code until he or she decides the previous programmer was an incapable idiot, and the new programmer proceeds to rewrite the code the way he or she feel it should be written. Then this newcomer moves on, another person assumes the role of newcomer, and the SDLC starts over again.

The Waterfall Method

A customer requests a software application. A group of analysts, usually consisting of a facilitator, a note taker and a modeler, sets up a meeting with the client, usually with just those in charge at first. The purpose of the meeting is to get an initial idea of how the present system works, what they are looking for in a new system and which people will be involved with the system.

The facilitator's job is to direct the meeting, ask appropriate questions to get desired information and keep the meeting from getting off track. The note taker's task is obvious: To write down pertinent information presented during the meeting. The modeler's job is to create visual representations of the business processes discussed.

This is usually done using **Unified Modeling Language** (UML) or a Visio-type modeling tool. The UML is a modeling language for diagraming software systems. Used widely in object-oriented development, the UML is the collection of modeling practices by Grady Booch, James Rumbaugh and Ivar Jacobson. Its use in Fusebox is described at length in **Appendix B: fUseML**.

Several meetings now take place, each building on the meeting before, each tightening up the application's requirements. Some meetings focus on the business processes, others on the users involved with the application. Ideally, selected users themselves are involved at relevant stages. These meetings are known as the **Analysis** or **Specification Phase**.

Once the requirements are clearly defined and the models have been made, the programmers begin the **Design Phase**. They plan out how they will write the code to satisfy the specific requirements of the system. From the models, the programmers are able to define what existing code can be re-used and what new code needs to be written.

The **Coding Phase** is next. The goal is to spend as little time as possible coding and more time on the previous two steps. By using the design sheets created during the Design Phase, this phase should be completed relatively quickly and easily. The programmers are able to set into place the reusable code previously identified and create the new code from the design sheets.

Once the application has been written and can be demonstrated, the application moves into the **Testing Phase**. In this phase, testers will attempt to "break" the application simply by using it like a normal user. Testing ensures that errors are caught by internal users **before** the application is sent to the end-user.

The last phase in this method is the **Deployment Phase**. This phase consists of placing the code on the devices that have been specified as needed by the application. In the web application world, this means moving the application to production servers. As long as the application has gone through the other phases, this phase should be relatively simple.

The Spiral Method

The **Spiral Method** uses the same processes as the Waterfall Method. However, during the Spiral Method, the phases are revisited and refined, creating "versions" of an application. Each version is a tighter, more accurate application than the previous version.

Each version will repeat all five steps of Specification, Design, Coding, Testing and Deployment. Each version will attempt to fix problems from the previous version(s), along with adding new features that the users felt were left out from the previous versions. By using the Spiral Method, an application will become closer and closer to exactly what the application should do. The Waterfall Method essentially stops with Version 1.

The idea behind the Spiral Method is that, at every phase, the project team is in constant communication with one another to create a well-tuned application.

Why Fusebox?

So where does Fusebox lend a helping hand in all this? It's fairly easy to understand how Fusebox assists the Coding Phase of all the methods. But, because of the modular nature of its architecture, Fusebox aids in the Analysis and Design Phases as well. Unfortunately, many software shops do a poor job of determining what they're trying to accomplish before beginning to write code. This causes problems down the road. By not thinking through and writing down what the application is going to do first, the programmers, database designers, graphic artists and clients do not fully understand one another. Each one thinks the others know what they want, when they're really envisioning different things. Creating specifications is a good way to clarify and solidify the requirements and goals of the system.

Specifications are the first step of the Spiral Method. The specification defines what the client wants. Remember, it is possible to create bad specifications. Just thinking about ideas may have been enough for a very small team, but once you start increasing the size of your team and the size of your application, you can run into problems if ideas are not well organized and carefully documented.

FUSEBOX CAN HELP.

Building a Fusebox Specification

Fusebox was designed to be easily understood by the developer. Developers are beginning to realize that, because of the way a Fusebox application is structured, it can be easy for the client to understand how the application works. Such understanding can be accomplished by using the analysis phase to create a specification document with only the circuit applications (each directory) and Fuseactions required. These two areas of Fusebox can be described without the need for technical jargon. For Fuseactions that contain a display for the user, a specification should attach drawings or, eventually, full HTML documents or Photoshop mock-ups (still no CFML).

Begin building a Fusebox specification by starting with the main group of people that will be involved in **creating** the application. Schedule a few uninterrupted days with a whiteboard. Getting people all in the same room to create the specification and prototypes is generally the hardest part of building any application. Be aware of this problem ahead of time, and schedule appropriately. Also, review the key people involved, especially the facilitator and note-taker. Make sure everyone understands his/her role and importance to the process.

> **Note:** You don't have to spend $80-100 on a whiteboard from an office store. If you go to any large hardware store, you can purchase a 4' by 8' shower

board for about $10, which can serve the same purpose. Look in the plumbing section. You will also need paper to record the final form for each process.

Whiteboard ideas should not be permanent – they should be free flowing. Don't be afraid to erase the group's ideas often and start over. This will force repetition which drills the ideas into everyone's head. Start by focusing on the user's experience.

The navigation model is what needs attention first, not the look and feel of the site. Don't worry yet about breaking the actions down into the different circuit applications.

Attempt to use the whiteboard to draw the layout of every page that you can think of. Continue doing this until there is too much information to fit on the whiteboard.

Now, the note taker writes down all the ideas, in preparation for the first draft of the specification.

Time to Write Draft 1 of the Specification

A specification does **not** involve technical jargon: Simple English (or the language of your choice) is best.

Some Fuseactions have a display to the user, others do not. For Fuseactions that do have a display to the user, the specification should include the drawings from the whiteboard discussion. Copying the drawings from the whiteboards onto a sheet of paper is fine, although these layouts should eventually become HTML prototypes (with no CFML) of what the user sees.

This is where specification and design begin to mix. The creation of HTML prototypes does not require a large amount of technical knowledge. Given the right WYSIWYG tools, any competent web surfer can turn a drawing into an HTML prototype. This step will prove whether or not the page layout is feasible, which allows the developer to understand what the client wants.

Client sign-off on this stage is essential. **IT IS MUCH EASIER, LESS COSTLY AND LESS STRESSFUL TO MAKE CHANGES DURING THE SPECIFICATION AND DESIGN PHASES THAN TO CHANGE THE CODE LATER.**

Building a Fusebox Design

It is important to understand the difference between specification and design. The specification is the "What" (what the client wants). The design is the "How" (how you will build what the client wants). This is crucial to fully understanding the Spiral Method used in Fusebox.

Again, it is extremely important that you understand the difference between specification and design. If necessary, read the above paragraph again.

Once you understand the difference, it will be very easy to see how Fusebox fits into the Spiral Method. Think of the Design Phase as creating a Fusebox application with all the technical jargon that was left out of the specification. You're still not using any code, only technical jargon.

The best place to start the design is to write out a list of all the files necessary for each of the Fuseactions that were created in the specification. Use as much technical information as you need. Remember: The file information does not need to be shown to the client. All the client cares about is what they want done, not how you will accomplish it. Don't forget the difference between the "What" and the "How".

Also, keep in mind that the Design Phase should not contain any actual code. It should be written in easy-to-read, everyday language. The design should also explain some of the steps the application will perform in certain areas (processes, not code).Your client should be able to follow the user's steps through the application and understand the input/output needed at each step.

Taking Advantage of Fusedocs

This is the stage at which the wise designer will begin to incorporate the Fusedocs techniques outlined by Hal Helms in **Appendix A: Fusedocs**. This technique of commenting assures that you will be able to keep track of each step of development and be able to hand it off to your successor with complete confidence.

Using the Fusebox Naming Conventions

Be sure to name each file necessary for the Fuseaction with the **proper Fusebox naming convention**. Remember the file naming conventions from Chapter 2 that you use in the design of a Fusebox application. In most cases, you will find that these are the three most important:

> ***dsp_filename.cfm*** is a **display file** that contains information displayed to the user. This file never updates data on the server side, and should not contain large blocks of pure CFML logic.
>
> ***act_filename.cfm*** is an **action file** that will update data on the server side or run any other action that does not contain output for the user to see.
>
> ***qry_filename.cfm*** is a **query file** that will contain one or more database queries or stored procedure calls. These are kept separate from the display files to enable reuse of the queries in multiple display files. These are usually Select SQL queries, because they are reused in different parts of the application more often than ordinary insert, updates or deletes.

Now Do the Specification and Design Phases All Over Again

Once both the specification and the design have been written, sit down and do the whole process over again. Review the updated specification with the client. Try to figure out where ideas had been left out. Review what is not technically feasible in the given time frame and figure out different solutions to those problems. This is the spiral method, except that, for the first few versions, you should not include coding. Skip over that phase until you have done a few versions of the specification and design.

It is never smart to begin coding directly after the first specification and design have been written. Doing so will only cause major amounts of time delays in the end. Even if the application is small, spending a few more days repeating the Specification and Design Phases will save you from major problems and delays further down the road.

Do I Really Need To Spend Time Writing a Specification and Design?

Surprisingly, many programmers do not write any type of specifications. Even fewer fully design the application from the specification. This is sloppy and causes the following problems:

- Not writing specifications will almost inevitably cause the client to make many change requests. Numerous change requests will cause major tension between the client and the developer. This story is all too common, but has a fairly simple solution. Tension occurs because the developer and the client did not agree in advance on what they feel the application should look like and do. Writing good specifications that involve both the developer and the client, using non-technical terms, will **resolve many change requests BEFORE the application gets coded**, thus saving countless hours of changes to the code.

- Writing specifications helps **prevent changes to the requirements** of the application once coding has begun. If the client proposes a change during the Coding Phase, the entire series of Specification and Design Phases will have to occur again. The client knows that this can consume a lot of time and (time being money) will be less apt to propose such changes "on-the-fly".

- Not writing designs from your specifications will slow down the Coding Phase tremendously. Designing an application can be a frustrating task for an anxious developer, because it feels like unnecessary work. After designing many applications, however, you will find that you can **figure**

out problems ahead of time, when time is cheaper. Once the Coding Phase has begun, changes to the requirements of the application can be very expensive!

It is hard to attempt to figure out how an application is going to work without writing any code, which is why creating a specification for an application is an art, not a science. The more thought that goes into what each of the files must do, and how they interact and combine to satisfy the user's expectations, the less time it will take to write the code.

CHAPTER 4:
Basic Fusebox Techniques

Chapter 2 acquainted us with basic Fusebox methodology and terminology. Now let's take it to the next step and discuss basic Fusebox techniques. These techniques build the foundation of the Fusebox Methodology. A developer can use these nine simple steps and be using the Fusebox Methodology effectively.

Basic Technique 1: The Fusebox

The "Fusebox" in the Fusebox methodology is the application's *index.cfm* file. The *index.cfm* file controls all of an application's Fuses and is where each Fuseaction is defined. The *index.cfm* file determines what Fuses make up each Fuseaction. Let's take a look at a sample *index.cfm* file.

The *index.cfm* file is the file that controls our application. Therefore, it must know how to process each of the Fuseactions it receives from the user.

As shown in the figure, the main part of the Fusebox is a <CFSWITCH> / <CFCASE> statement to process Fuseactions. First, we set the <CFSWITCH> tag to evaluate the variable "*attributes.fuseaction*". When a <CFCASE> tag finds a case that equals the value of the *attributes.fuseaction* variable passed into the Fusebox via a form or URL variable, it runs the code in that <CFCASE> statement. Here, the two Fuseactions listed are "*welcome*" and "*some_other_page*". (The second name indicates that a Fuseaction can be any action within your application.)

Another <CFSWITCH> statement inside a Fusebox may look like this:

```
<CFPARAM NAME="attributes.fuseaction " DEFAULT="showUsers">
<CFSWITCH expression="#attributes.fuseaction#">
    <CFCASE value="AddUser">
    <CFMODULE TEMPLATE="act_adduser.cfm" firstname="Steve"
    lastname="Nelson">
        <CFINCLUDE TEMPLATE="url_showusers.cfm">
    </CFCASE>
    <CFCASE value="showUsers">
        <CFINCLUDE template="qry_getusers.cfm">
        <CFINCLUDE TEMPLATE="dsp_listusers.cfm">
    </CFCASE>
</CFSWITCH>
```

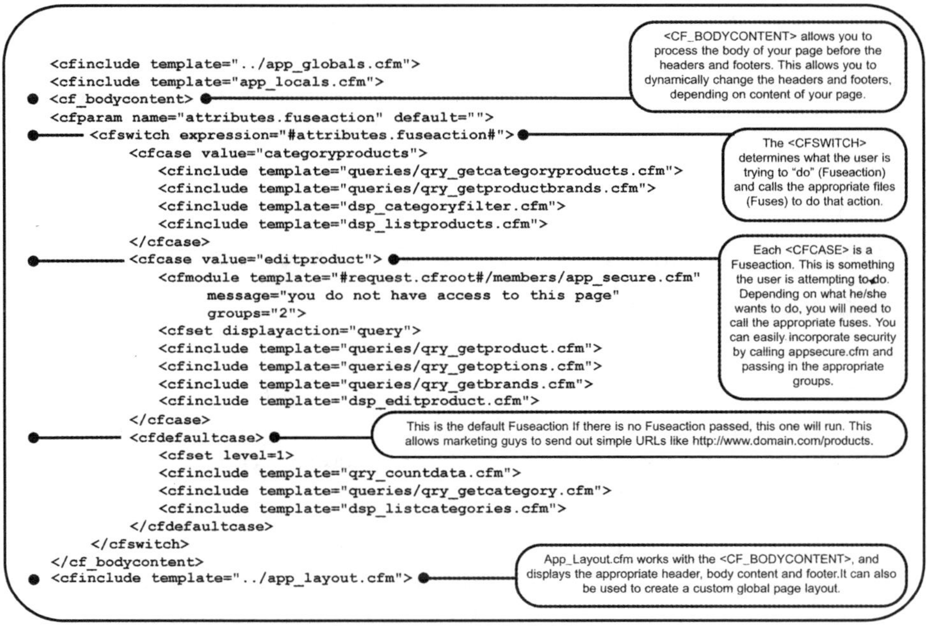

SAMPLE INDEX.CFM FILE

This Fusebox contains two actions: **addUser** and **showUsers**. The <CFPARAM> tag ensures that the variable "*attributes.fuseaction*" will always exist and will have a default value of "*showUsers*". If the user pointed directly to the Fusebox and did not include the *attributes.fuseaction* variable, the default Fuseaction will be run. In the case that the Fuseaction "*addUser*" was sent to the server, the Fusebox runs the file *act_adduser.cfm*, then redirects to the *showUsers* Fuseaction.

Basic Technique 2: The Fuseaction

Every call to an application requires a Fuseaction. The Fuseaction value is stored in an attributes-scoped variable called *attributes.fuseaction*. The Fusebox will use this variable to determine which Fuses are needed to complete a task.

If no *attributes.fuseaction* variable exists, then the default page will be displayed. The default value for *attributes.fuseaction* is set using the ColdFusion <CFPARAM> tag:

```
<CFPARAM name="attributes.fuseaction" default="DisplayProducts">
```

This tag tells ColdFusion to look for *attributes.fusaction*. If no *attributes.fuseaction* variable exists, create one and give it a value of "DisplayProducts". ColdFusion ignores this tag if the variable already exists, and the value of *attributes.fuseaction* remains as is.

Note: Originally, we said that the <CFPARAM> tag used to default the Fuseaction should be placed within the *app_locals.cfm* file. Some developers prefer to add this tag in their *index.cfm* file, instead. Both techniques are correct. Both follow valid Fusebox Methodology, and the choice is up to the developer.

Basic Technique 3: Passing the Fuseaction

As stated above, every call to the application requires a Fuseaction. If the default action is not desired, the Fuseaction must be passed to the server. This can be done using a URL parameter or a form field variable. (Cookies are distinct between browsers, not page requests, therefore cookies do not make a good medium for passing actions.)

A **URL parameter** is a variable that gets attached to the end of a page request's Universal Resource Locator (URL). When that URL is requesting a ColdFusion file, the ColdFusion Server will convert the URL parameters into variables a CF file can understand. A URL parameter may look something like:

```
http://www.fusebox.org/index.cfm?fuseaction=delete
```

In this case, the variable is "*fuseaction*" and its value is "*delete*".

A **form field variable** is a variable passed by an HTML form to the server when the user submits the form. A form field variable may look something like:

```
<input name="fuseaction" type="hidden" value="delete">
```

The variable in this example has the same name and value as the URL parameter; it is simply passed to the server in a different manner.

If the application is being called with the use of the <CFMODULE> tag, it may look like:

```
<CFMODULE template="/yourdirectory/index.cfm" fuseaction="delete">
```

Again, the application being requested is sent a variable named "*fuseaction*", having a value of "*delete*".

The only difference in the processing of the variable "*fuseaction*" in these three examples is in their scope. Variables passed on the URL string are in the URL scope. Variables passed in a form field are available in the form scope. Finally, variables passed to a <CFMODULE> are available from within the module via the attributes scope.

Basic Technique 4: The Fuses and Their Prefixes

One way Fusebox helps developers organize their code is with the use of "Fuses". A Fuse is a file. There are six (6) types of files, each having its own prefix, as outlined in Chapter 2. The purpose of the prefix is to allow the programmer to have, at a glance, an understanding of what the file can and cannot do, as well as where to find it in the application's directory structure.

Let's review each type of Fuse, discuss its prefix, and examine some code.

Application files are files that pertain to the application itself, at either the home or circuit level. These files all use an "*app_*" prefix. The two most important types of Fusebox application files are:

> ***App_globals.cfm*** contains information that is needed globally, for every page of the application. For example, if you set a variable for the datasource of a database that is used in many of your smaller applications within your larger application, that variable would be set in this file.
>
> ***App_locals.cfm*** contains information that is specific to a particular circuit application and not general enough to be used globally throughout the application. An example might be setting a default *attributes.fuseaction* value. For every *index.cfm* file, there is one (and only one) *app_locals.cfm* file (and vice versa).

Display Files are used to display information to the user. They use a prefix of "*dsp_*" and are the **only** files that contain information that the user will see. They commonly contain CFML and HTML (or any other display format) used to retrieve the information needed for display. Display files are NOT used to change data on the server side. They **only** display information to the user.

dsp_showUsers.cfm

```
    ...<CFINCLUDE template="qry_GetUsers.cfm">

<table>
<CFOUTPUT query="GetUsers">
    <tr><td>#username#</td></tr>
</CFOUTPUT>
</table>
    ...
```

Action Files are the files that actually "do" something with the data and take a prefix of "*act_*". Action files are commonly used to perform database updates (to insert, update and delete data within a database), call stored procedures or change other data, such as writing to a file or making changes to the data in an

LDAP server. Action files are not limited to database changes; they can also be used for doing tasks that do not fit particularly well into a display file. For instance, sending e-mails is commonly placed in an action file. Action files never display any information to the user.

act_emailUser.cfm

```
<CFQUERY name="GetUser" datasource="#attributes.DSN#">
     SELECT * FROM tblUsers
     WHERE userID = 1234
</CFQUERY>

<CFMAIL to="#GetUser.email#" from="fusebox@fusebox.org"
subject="Fusebox techniques ">
     Dear #GetUser.username#,

     Fusebox helps organize your code!

     Fusebox
</CFMAIL>
```

Query Files have a prefix of "*qry_*". Queries or stored procedure calls that are used repeatedly by different circuit applications or Fuseactions are placed in a file of their own and called using <CFINCLUDE>. Doing this speeds up development time when an update needs to be made to the file. The developer does not need to change every file containing the query, just remove or change the one file.

qry_getUsers.cfm

```
<CFQUERY name="getUsers" datasource="#attributes.DSN#">
     SELECT * FROM tblUsers
</CFQUERY>
```

Redirection Files have a prefix of "*url_*". After a user has submitted information to a form and the data they have submitted has been processed, it is important to send the user to another Fuseaction to display a message to them. This ensures that, if the user hits the "reload" button on their browser, they will not continue to submit the form data.

These files are generally simple, containing only a single <CFLOCATION> in them, but they may occasionally have multiple <CFLOCATION> tags, depending on what needs to happen. By placing these <CFLOCATION> tags in their own files, your <CFCASE> statements in the *index.cfm* file will only contain references to include appropriate files, which makes the *index.cfm* file much easier to read.

URL_showUsers.cfm

```
<CFLOCATION url="index.cfm?Fuseaction=showusers&#urltoken#">
```

CF/CFX ColdFusion Custom Files use a prefix of "*CF_*" for extension files written in CF, and "*CFX_*" for extension files written in another language, such as C++ or Java. For more information on CF extension files, see the ColdFusion user manuals included with ColdFusion Server.

Basic Technique 5: Calling the Application

An application is always called through the *index.cfm* file. In other words, **the only file a user should ever call is the *index.cfm* file**. By using a central file, we increase the level of understanding and organization in our applications. We don't need to think about which file to start with when debugging an application. We know it will be the *index.cfm* file.

The *index.cfm* file was modeled after languages such as C, where each application has a main file, which calls on other functions as needed to complete the task.

Basic Technique 6: Point All Links and Form Actions to the *Index.cfm* File

All links and form actions will point to the *index.cfm* file. This can done through various techniques:

Universal Format (recommended method for easy handling):

```
<a href="index.cfm?fuseaction=registration">Register</a>
<form method="post" action="index.cfm">
```

Relative Format:

```
<a href="../../registration/index.cfm?fuseaction=registration"> Register</a>
<form method="post" action="../../registration/index.cfm">
```

Absolute Format:

```
<a href="/user/registration/index.cfm?fuseaction=registration"> Register</a>
<form method="post" action="/user/registration/index.cfm">
```

Different Server Absolute Format:

```
<a href="www.domain.com/user/registration/index.cfm?
fuseaction=registration">Register</a>
<form method="post" action="www.domain.com/ user/registration/index.cfm">
```

Each of these circuit applications will most likely require more than one file. So each of the circuit applications will be given its own directory.

Basic Technique 7: Variable Scope

ColdFusion allows for **variable scoping**. Variable scoping uses **dot notation** to specify the range, or "**scope**". This means that, to scope a variable, we simply have to add the appropriate scope name before the variable name, separating the scope and variable names with a dot. A number of variable scopes exist, including the attributes scope. Each scope has its own characteristics and range within a CF application.

In Fusebox, all variables capable of being changed by a user or the application need to be scoped with the "*attributes.*" prefix.

To understand why we do this, it is helpful to understand the <CFMODULE> tag. A typical tag call using <CFMODULE> may look like this:

```
<CFMODULE TEMPLATE="act_AddUser.cfm"
     USER="Joe Smith" ACCESSLEVEL="1">
```

In this example, the file *act_AddUser.cfm* is the tag we are calling. "*user*" and "*accesslevel*" are two programmer-specific attributes that will be sent to the tag as it is called. In order for the tag to make use of the two attributes, it must reference them using the "*attributes.*" prefix. The *act_AddUser.cfm* file references these variables, using *attributes.user* and *attributes.accesslevel*. Any reference to "*user*" and "*accesslevel*" from within *act_AddUser.cfm* will result in an error. Only *"attributes.user"* and *"attributes.accesslevel"* will exist inside the tag.

If we now refer to all our user-changeable or public variables using *attributes.variablename*, we have enabled our application to act as a **standalone application** or a **CF tag**. (This is a very important concept to understand, as it is exactly what Fusebox applications are trying to accomplish.)

How do you convert an application's variables to the attributes scope? The Fusebox Organization has provided a custom tag to perform this feat. The file ***formURL2attributes.cfm*** is a Fusebox reserved file (custom tag). This file is included in an application's *app_globals.cfm* file like so:

```
<CF_FORMURL2ATTRIBUTES>
```

This code will check and see if the user is requesting the application through a tag or as a standalone. If the application is being called as a standalone, the variable *attributes.fuseaction* will not exist, and the *formURL2attributes.cfm* file is called.

If the application is being requested as a tag, it will convert all form and URL scoped variables to the attributes scope. Then the "parent" application can pass these values into the "child's" tags/applications. We'll discuss this concept further, shortly.

What's in a Name? The FORMURL2ATTRIBUTES.CFM File

As its name suggests, the file *formURL2attributes.cfm* converts all form and URL variables to attributes-scoped variables. Fusebox does this so that every application can also be a CF tag, turning entire tag libraries into a single CF tag. Thus, **Fusebox applications are essentially tag libraries** which, through the Fusebox techniques, have been **simplified into a single tag**.

Since Fusebox applications can be both a “Tag Object” (called as a tag from another CF application) or a “Web Object” (called as a standalone application through a URL), there needs to be a way to handle variables for both types.

The easiest way to do this is by standardizing on scoping all variables within a Fusebox application to the attributes scope, then changing all form and URL scoped variables into attributes-scoped variables. By doing this, a CF application can be called as either a tag or directly from a browser, and it will work both ways, which is very cool.

Place the *formURL2attributes.cfm* file in your /CFUSION/CUSTOMTAGS directory. Then call this tag, <CF_FORMURL2ATTRIBUTES>, as the first line in your *app_globals.cfm* file. The following is the code for the <CF_FORMURL2ATTRIBUTES> tag:

```
1   <CFSETTING enablecfoutputonly="yes">
2   <CFIF isdefined("cgi.query_string")>
3       <CFLOOP list="#cgi.query_string#" delimiters="&"
        index="valuepair">
4           <CFSET URLName = "#ListGetAt(valuepair, 1, "=")#">
5           <CFIF NOT ISDEFINED( 'ATTRIBUTES.' & URLname )>
6               <CFSET SetVariable("caller.attributes.#urlname#" ,
                "#evaluate("URL."&"#URLname#")#")>
7           </CFIF>
8       </CFLOOP>
9   </CFIF>
10  <CFIF isdefined("form.fieldnames")>
11      <CFLOOP list="#form.fieldnames#" index="field">
12          <CFIF NOT ISDEFINED( 'ATTRIBUTES.' & field )>
13              <CFSET SetVariable("caller.attributes.#field#" ,
                "#evaluate("form."&"#field#")#")>
14          </CFIF>
15      </CFLOOP>
16  </CFIF>
17  <CFSETTING enablecfoutputonly="no">
```

Let's examine this file to see what it does. Line 1 simply tells ColdFusion not to output any white space. The tag really begins with Line 2. This checks to see if the CGI variable *“cgi.query_string”* exists. This is the variable that stores all of our URL variables.

If it exists, we then do a <CFLOOP> over the *"cgi.query_string"* variable. You will notice that the delimiter gets set to the "&" (ampersand) character. That is because a *"cgi.query_string"* variable will look like this:

fuseaction=AddUser&Firstname=Joe&Lastname=Smith

By setting the delimiter to "&", instead of its default "," (comma), we have broken the *"cgi.query_string"* variable into the following value pairs:

Fuseaction=AddUser

Firstname=Joe

Lastname=Smith

Now the <CFLOOP> will run through Lines 4 through 7 three times, once for each value pair. Line 4 uses the ListGetAt() function to filter out the URL variable name and store it into the variable "*URLname*". Line 5 then checks to see if a variable named "*attributes.URLname*" exists ("*URLname*" being the value of the variable "*URLname*" set in Line 4). If the variable does not already exist, it is created in Line 6. This process repeats for as many value pairs as are defined in the "*cgi.query_string*" variable, or once for each URL variable that exists.

Now, Line 10 checks to see if there are any form field variables defined. If the user has submitted information to a server through a form, the variable "*form.fieldnames*" will exist. If it exists, we do a <CFLOOP> over the variable, leaving the delimiter at the default of ",", since the variable contains a comma-delimited list of a form's input field names. The variable "*form.fieldnames*" looks like this:

fuseaction,firstname,lastname

The <CFLOOP> will execute three times in this case, each time checking to see if the variable *"attributes.field"* exists, where *"field"* is the value of the index variable *"field"* created in the <CFLOOP> in Line 11. If the variable does not already exist, it will use the SetVariable() function to create one and assign it the value of that form field.

There you have it. It's that easy. We now have all of our variables in the attributes scope, and we can develop applications that are also ColdFusion tags.

A Brief Review

Let's just take a minute to recap our basic concepts:

Basic Technique 1: The Fusebox

Use the *index.cfm* file as your master controller for the application, located in its own master directory.

Basic Technique 2: The Fuseaction

Break each action into its own Fuseaction, in its own subdirectory.

Basic Technique 3: Passing the Fuseaction

Pass the Fuseaction, using a URL parameter or a form field variable.

Basic Technique 4: The Fuses and Their Prefixes

Differentiate between the different Fuses and their functions, making use of Fusebox file-type prefixes to identify the type of file and giving each one a descriptive name that identifies its function.

Basic Technique 5: Calling the Application

Always call the application **from** the *index.cfm*, which directs all action within the application.

Basic Technique 6: Point All Links and Form Actions to the Index.cfm File

All links and form actions must point to the *index.cfm* file, via Universal Format (recommended method for easy handling), Relative Format, Absolute Format or Different Server Absolute Format.

Basic Technique 7: Variable Scope

Take full advantage of Fusebox and CF by scoping all variables capable of being changed by a user or the application with the "attributes." prefix.

Putting It All Together: Hello World!

Now that we have reviewed the basic Fusebox techniques, it's time to try our first application. Like every good programming guide, we will start with the "Hello World" application. This will allow us to put into practice what we have just learned. We have labeled the techniques as they are being used for your reference.

First, let's look at the code, then we will talk about it.

INDEX.CFM: Basic Technique 1

```
<CFINCLUDE template="app_globals.cfm"> <!--- Basic Technique 2 --- >
<CFPARAM name="attributes.fuseaction" default="hello"> <!--- Basic
Technique 3 --- >
<CFSWITCH expression="#attributes.fuseaction#">
    <CFCASE value="goodbye">
        <CFINCLUDE template="dsp_goodbye.cfm">
    </CFCASE>
    <CFCASE value="hello">
        <CFINCLUDE template="dsp_hello.cfm">
    </CFCASE>
    <CFDEFAULTCASE>
        <CFINCLUDE template="dsp_hello.cfm">
    </CFDEFAULTCASE>
</CFSWITCH>
```

APP_GLOBALS.CFM: Basic Technique 2

```
<CF_FORMURL2ATTRIBUTES> <!--- Basic Technique 7 --->
```

FORMURL2ATTRIBUTES.CFM: Technique 7

```
<CFSETTING enablecfoutputonly="yes">
<CFIF isdefined("cgi.query_string")>
    <CFLOOP list="#cgi.query_string#" delimiters="&"
    index="valuepair">
        <CFSET URLname = "#LIstGetAt(valuepalr, 1, "=")#">
        <CFIF NOT ISDEFINED( 'ATTRIBUTES.' & URLname )>
            <CFSET SetVariable("caller.attributes.#URLname#" ,
            "#evaluate("URL."&"#urlname#")#")>
        </CFIF>
    </CFLOOP>
</CFIF>
<CFIF isdefined("form.fieldnames")>
    <CFLOOP list="#form.fieldnames#" index="field">
        <CFIF NOT ISDEFINED( 'ATTRIBUTES.' & field )>
            <CFSET SetVariable("caller.attributes.#field#" ,
            "#evaluate("form."&"#field#")#")>
        </CFIF>
    </CFLOOP>
</CFIF>
<CFSETTING enablecfoutputonly="no">
```

DSP_HELLO.CFM: Technique 4

```
<html>
<body>
<h1>Hello World!</h1>
</body>
</html>
```

DSP_GOODBYE.CFM: Technique 4

```
<html>
<body>
<h1>Good-Bye Cruel World!</h1>
</body>
</html>
```

Congratulations, you have now written your first Fusebox application. Let's take a walk through to see what was done here.

The first file is our Fusebox, the *index.cfm* file, and will be the file that is called by the browser. The first thing this file does is include the *app_globals.cfm* file. This file is being called to include all of our global variables. *App_globals.cfm* checks to see if the variable *attributes.fuseaction* exists; if it does, this application was called as a CF tag and *app_globals.cfm* does nothing.

In this case, no *attributes.fuseaction* exists, so *app_globals.cfm* calls the <CF_FORMURL2ATTRIBUTES> tag. <CF_FORMURL2ATTRIBUTES> then converts all our form and URL variables to attributes scoped variables.

Control is then passed back to the *index.cfm* file, which uses <CFPARAM> to set the value of *attributes.fuseaction* to "hello".

Next, we enter into the <CFSWITCH> statement, where <CFSWITCH> is evaluating the variable *attributes.fuseaction*. The first <CFCASE> has a value of "hello", which is equal to our current Fuseaction. Having found a match, CF executes the code in between the <CFCASE> statement. In this case, it includes the *dsp_hello.cfm* file.

Dsp_hello.cfm is a display file that outputs a HTML file that reads "Hello World!".

Control is then given back to *index.cfm*, which breaks out of the <CFSWITCH> statement and is complete.

Just in Case: The CFDEFAULTCASE Statement

Notice that our <CFSWITCH> statement contains a <CFDEFAULTCASE> tag. If a user does not specify a Fuseaction they will be sent to the <CFDEFAULTCASE> and that code will be run. This technique will make the marketing department happy, since it allows for easy to read URLs, such as *http://www.valuemusic.com/products*. (**Note:** No additional text, such as *"index.cfm?Fuseaction=listproducts"*, has been attached to the end.)

Now let's look at some more complex techniques.

CHAPTER 5: Advanced Fusebox Techniques

Fusebox is striving to be a framework that works for any web application. The end goal is that, regardless of what the application does or who will be using it, the framework for building the application will be the same. The basic Fusebox techniques may be enough to get the beginner started, but it is not enough of a framework to build ANY web application.

To achieve that bold end, the Fusebox Organization has created advanced techniques for dealing with common problems when building a web application.

These are not the only solutions to these problems, nor are they the only problems you might face. The Fusebox Methodology has been designed to be expanded and modified to suit **your** needs, as well as the needs of your project. With this flexibility in mind, the Fusebox mailing list, hosted by House of Fusion (***http://www.houseoffusion.com***), is continually discussing new and improved Fusebox techniques.

Overview of Complex Techniques

Web applications are rarely simple. The basic Fusebox techniques do not solve many of the problems we are faced with when building large web applications. To attempt to make Fusebox work in any web application, Fusebox needs to be able to recognize the types of problems web developers face when building applications.

The Four Main Types of Common Problems

In general, programmers face four common problems:

COMPLEXITY: If your application is larger than one directory of files, you may slowly begin to feel overwhelmed by the size of your application. Fusebox will help by breaking your large application down into smaller applications, then assisting with putting the pieces back together.

SPEED: By using a few common techniques in everyday practice, you can tremendously improve the speed of your application.

REUSABILITY: Reusing code is not a new concept in programming, but it is an incredibly important concept. Generally, code reuse in a web application is done sloppily. The Fusebox techniques will offer solutions to reusing entire applications, individual files, forms and user processes.

PORTABILITY: ColdFusion offers the ability to move code to many of the most popular operating systems. Therefore, portability is not a Fusebox concern. Fusebox is more concerned with how we can go from a development server environment to a production server environment with the greatest ease and safety.

How Do We Deal With Complexity?

When you begin a project, it may feel overwhelming in size. It may feel as though it will take months or even years of development with many programmers to accomplish the task. Making this type of complexity into a simple task is Fusebox's greatest achievement.

Advanced Technique 1: Define your Home Application

The first step to reducing the complexity of your application is understanding the end goal of your "home" application.

The **home application** is the overall application, such as: ***http://www.ValueMusic.com***. It is made up of many circuit applications, tied together with a common interface.

The user does not realize they are using multiple circuit applications. They are under the impression they are using the site "ValueMusic.com", which they are.

The entire site is made up of many circuit applications that do various specific tasks, such as browsing products, renting instruments, gathering information about the user, displaying product details, executing the purchase, etc. Yet, to the user, whether they are searching for a tuba or entering a credit card for a purchase, they are still in the home application.

This is similar to a real life home. Assuming they paid the power bill, it doesn't matter whether a person plugs a television into an outlet in the kitchen or in the living room. It still gets power, because it is in the home.

Advanced Technique 2: Break Your Home Application Into Many Circuits

Once you understand what your home application is attempting to do, determine what the various circuit applications will do that will be involved in your home application.

A **circuit application** generally consists of a single directory of files that perform a few related tasks. An example of this is the **SecretAgents.com** member registration process: *http://www.SecretAgents.com/members/*. The member registration has multiple Fuseactions, but all of these Fuseactions are focused around doing membership tasks, such as creating accounts, logging in, logging out, etc.

It is important to realize that a circuit application may contain bugs. However, if it does, it is possible to remove the buggy circuit application from the home application without bringing the rest of the home application down.

It is also possible to go in the other direction. When a new circuit is added to the home application, it can be added without affecting other circuit applications.

On the other hand, be careful: When excessively reusing code, this statement may not be true. If one circuit application calls a query file from another circuit application and the circuit application containing that query is removed, it **will** affect the other circuit application. This is where documentation comes in.

Because web applications are not static, it is important to be able to add new features or remove old features from the site without affecting the entire site. Using Fusebox to build your large-scale applications will prove to be especially helpful when it comes time to upgrade the application.

Advanced Technique 3: Break Your Circuit Into Many Fuseactions

Once you understand what your various circuit applications are, determine what "Fuseaction" each of these circuit applications will have.

The **Fuseaction** will tell the circuit application what the user wants to do. Which Fuseaction the user is attempting to accomplish will determine which files are needed to process the appropriate Fuseaction.

Each Fuseaction is a single case statement in the <CFSWITCH> inside the *index.cfm* file.

Advanced Technique 4: Break Your Fuseactions Into Fuses

Once you understand all the various Fuseactions that comprise a circuit application, you need to determine what Fuses are required to process this Fuseaction.

A **Fuse** is a single file that uses the Fusebox naming convention. It is called through either a <CFINCLUDE> or a <CFMODULE> statement, from within one of the Fuseaction <CFCASE> statements. A Fuse is **never** accessed directly through a URL, such as:

http://www.secretagents.com/members/act_deleteuser.cfm

This particular case would be a security hazard. Such problems are prevented by the code in the *application.cfm* file, discussed in more detail in Chapter 7, The Importance of Forcing Users to Go Through *index.cfm* Files.

Instead, a Fuse is only accessed through the *index.cfm*, such as:

```
<CFCASE value="deleteuser">
    <CFINCLUDE template="act_verifyuser.cfm">
    <CFINCLUDE template="act_deleteuser.cfm">
    <CFINCLUDE template="url_viewuser.cfm">
</CFCASE>
```

This ensures that a user calls all the necessary files that are needed for the code inside that Fuse.

Advanced Technique 5: Tying Circuit Applications Together with the Home Application Files

The home application is made up of many circuit applications, so when writing a Fusebox application, it is important to be able to tie everything together. Remember that the home application is nothing more than a concept. It is the result of multiple circuit applications.

You can also think of the home application as a **directory structure** on your ColdFusion server. By putting all of your circuit applications in the same root directory and its subdirectories, that entire directory structure makes up the home application.

The root directory of your home application contains the *app_globals.cfm* file, which centralizes the calls to other global application files (*app_files*). These *app_files* will all be stored in the root directory of your home application.

Remember: The root directory of your home application may hold these *app_files*, but the root directory itself can also be a circuit application. If you take a look at ***http://www.ValueMusic.com***, you will notice that a few of the links go to ***http://www.ValueMusic.com/index.cfm***. The root directory is itself a circuit application, containing tasks that are globally important.

A Quick Look at Some Additional Fusebox Application Files

In addition to *app_globals.cfm*, there are several other application files in the Fusebox toolbox. Here are a few you will find yourself reaching for quite often:

App_locals.cfm: Each circuit application contains an *app_locals.cfm*. This file is necessary for variables which exist inside of a single circuit application and is important when creating Fusebox custom tags. For example, if you have a datasource which is specific to that single circuit application, but different from the "*mainDSN*" which is common in all other circuit applications, you could set that value in this file.

App_server.cfm: This file becomes very important when you are ready to scale up to clustered servers. There will be certain variables which may have different values in the various servers in your cluster, such as variables (i.e., the IP address of that machine), or certain datasources may be different on different machines in your cluster. When using source control, it is best not to add this to source control, so that the file does not get deployed to every server.

App_secure.cfm, app_login.cfm, app_logout.cfm: These files allow for security checks and can be called in any circuit application. They will be better explained in the Chapter 7: "Securing a Fusebox Application".

Advanced Technique 6: When to Use Which Types of Links

Your directory structure must be set up to be able to handle multiple circuit applications, since you will eventually need to link these together. This can be done so by using the different types of links described in the **Basic Techniques** of Chapter 4. Use the **Universal Format** as much as possible (i.e., point links and forms directly to *index.cfm*).

The universal format is especially important when creating reusable custom tags out of your Fusebox application. By using this format, you can call your Fusebox application as a <CFMODULE>, and the links and forms will still work.

There will be cases in which you cannot use the universal format, such as when building global navigation. If you have navigation which exists on every page (or many pages), you want to be sure the link points to the appropriate directory, regardless of which directory the user is currently in. In these cases, we recommend using the **Absolute Format** (i.e., *#Request.WebRoot#/directoryname/index.cfm*) in your menus. This will allow you to use the same menu on multiple circuit applications, while still leaving the links intact.

Advanced Technique 7: Common Global Variables

ColdFusion has many different scopes of variables. Some remain in RAM (server/application/session); others exist only on a specific page instance (attributes/variables/request/url/form/caller/) For most global variables, we will use the "*request*" scope.

The **request scope** is similar to the "*application*" scope, except that it does not remain in memory like application-scoped variables do, which means it does not require a <CFLOCK> tag around them. Request-scoped variables also exist at every level of a custom tag. So if one custom tag calls another custom tag, the request-scoped variable will exist in both of them.

Global variables can be very useful but can also pose a danger if one area sets a request-scoped variable that is named the same thing somewhere else. You might then end up with unexpected results.

Some Fusebox global variables are not required, by any means, but are very helpful in solving common problems and are highly recommended. These variables should exist in the *app_server.cfm* file, since you may need to change the values of them on each machine in the cluster when in a clustered environment:

Request.CFRoot: This is the mapping set in the */cfide/administrator,* which points to the root directory where your *app_ files* are. This allows for absolute paths inside the <CFINCLUDE> and <CFMODULE> tags.

Request.WebRoot: This is the mapping set in the web server administrator. This mapping is useful for global navigation. For example:

```
request.webroot="www.secretagents.com"
#request.webroot#/members/index.cfm
```

This allows you to move to different servers by changing only a single variable.

Request.ImagesRoot: One way to easily improve your web sites performance is to move all of your images off of the ColdFusion servers and onto separate servers. Images require a good amount of disk access, which will slow a server down. This variable will allow you to start with images on the CF server. Then, when you expand, you can separate the images by simply changing this single variable. For example:

```
<img src="#request.imagesroot#/site/logo.gif">
```

Request.SSLRoot: Secured Socket Layers (SSL) can degrade the performance of your web server because of the authentication process. You will want to use this only when necessary.

If you need to secure certain pages of your application, point them to:

```
<a href="#request.sslroot#/checkout/index.cfm">
```

When developing your secured application, you may not have an SSL certificate on your development server. This variable allows you to quickly switch between secured pages and unsecured pages.

Request.Protocol: When dealing with secured pages, you need to secure the images and other embedded files on that page. This variable will allow you to dynamically change *request.imagesroot* to *https://*, when necessary.

```
<CFSET request.protocol = "http://">
<CFIF CGI.server_port IS 443>
     <CFSET request.protocol = "https://">
</CFIF>
<CFSET request.imagesroot=
"#request.protocol#www.secretagents.com/images">
```

Request.MainDSN: Changing datasource is fairly common: By using this variable in the datasource of every <CFQUERY>, you can quickly change the datasource of each <CFQUERY> in your home application just by changing the one value:

```
<CFQUERY name="Myquery" datasource="#request.maindsn#">
```

Request.Timespan: One of the biggest performance boosters is to cache your queries, using either application variables or the "*CachedWithin*" attribute in <CFQUERY>. *Request.timespan* allows you to quickly reset when the query should get the latest data. This is important when trying to keep your data in cache in sync with your live data.

Request.URLToken: You can get a small performance gain by switching from *Client.URLToken* to *Request.URLToken*. You might as well get the performance boost.

Advanced Technique 8: <CFAPPLICATION> and the Issue of Cookies

<CFAPPLICATION> offers a way to turn on session, application and client management. The <CFAPPLICATION> tag should be placed in the *app_globals.cfm* file.

Your application should especially make use of application and client variables. These two types of variables offer a variety of excellent techniques. However, when using client variables, be sure to store them in a database, instead of the registry.

This tag allows you to specify the datasource that should hold the client variables.

<CFAPPLICATION> helps to solve the problem of cookies. There are a number of web users that do not use cookies. They might think cookies are a security concern, or they may be at a public terminal, and don't want the browser to store their identification or personal information. For Fusebox this is okay; we have a solution.

The only cookie variables you should ever use are for session identification purposes, mainly CFID and CFTOKEN (which combine to form URLTOKEN).

These variables uniquely identify a user's browser. If you need to store more user-specific information, use client variables. They are more secure, offer larger storage space and are simpler to work with than cookies.

Even though the only values you should need to store in a cookie are CFID and CFTOKEN, you still should allow your user to choose whether cookies should be set. In the <CFAPPLICATION> tag, you should set the attribute *SetClientCookies* to "*no*". This will prevent CFID and CFTOKEN from being automatically set as cookies. When a user logs into the site, you should present them with a checkbox that asks if they want to set the cookie. If they check *"yes"*, **then** set *Cookie.CFID* and *Cookie.CFTOKEN*.

You can still use client and/or session variables without cookies by passing CFID and CFTOKEN in the URL. This technique is a little more complex than simply using cookies, but it is worth understanding the concept, so that you can implement it for a cookie-free environment. If you only rely on cookies to store CFID and CFTOKEN and the user turns off cookies, then the user's client and/or session variables will be reset or lost on every page view. This technique prevents that loss from occurring.

#request.URLToken# —> No Cookies

Here's an example of the relevant code:

```
<CFOUTPUT>
     <a href=index.cfm?fuseaction=myfuseaction&#request.urltoken#>some
     link</a>
</CFOUTPUT>

<form method="post" action="<CFOUTPUT>index.cfm?fuseaction=myfuse-
action&#request.urltoken#</CFOUTPUT>">

<CFLOCATION
url="index.cfm?Fuseaction=myfuseaction&#request.urltoken#" add
token="no">
```

What Can You Do to Rachet Up the Speed?

Advanced Technique 9: For Speed Freaks

How can we speed up our Fusebox applications? People are often concerned that Fusebox will slow their application down. However, this should not be an issue. Most likely, the only difference between the way you are building your applications now and the Fusebox techniques is by adding a few useful application-wide files. Sure, adding a couple extra <CFINCLUDE> tags will slow your pages down by a few tenths of a millisecond, but since an average page can take anywhere from 50-500ms to load, you should be looking elsewhere to speed up your pages. This section will focus on ways to cut major processing time.

You can get a very minor increase in speed (about 1-2 milliseconds) by using <CFINCLUDE> instead of <CFMODULE>. This technique is not critical, but can be helpful. Here, it is important to remember to treat each of the included files as if they are being called from <CFMODULE>. The reason for this is that Fusebox applications are designed to be called from the *index.cfm* file using <CFMODULE>, thereby turning an entire application into a multi-file, multi-action custom tag. By using <CFINCLUDE> in your *index.cfm* instead of <CFMODULE>, you can slightly speed up processing while still getting the same effect.

This means that you should use the attribute- and caller-scopes when possible within every Fuse (*act_*, *dsp_*, *qry_*, *url_* and *app_* files), just as if you were creating a standard custom tag.

Advanced Technique 10: Write Exploded Benchmarking Info

In early versions of ColdFusion, it is possible to get the execution time of the entire template by going into the ColdFusion Administrator's "Debugging" settings (located in the "Miscellaneous" section of the left-hand navigation). There, you can display a variety of information useful for debugging purposes, including lists of all instantiated variables and SQL query information. This offers developers the ability to pinpoint which templates are causing bottlenecks.

Fusebox applications attempt to simplify large applications by breaking them down into smaller applications and then breaking those down into many files. Being able to see the execution times of each of these files is very useful. If a Fuseaction is processing slowly, you need to know exactly which template is creating the slowdown.

In ColdFusion Version 4.5+, it is possible to obtain a detailed view of the execution times of each included file by checking the "Detailed View" checkbox on the debug settings tab in the CF Administrator.

Advanced Technique 11: Caching Queries

Query caching is an advanced technique and should only be attempted if you've mastered the rest of the Fusebox concepts. This technique can give incredible performance improvements to your application, but only if used properly.

In your <CFQUERY> tag, there is an attribute known as "*CachedWithin*". This attribute takes a timestamp of when is the next time the query should be run.

Utilizing this technique eliminates unnecessary, repetitive calls to the database. The first user that runs the query will make a call to the database, then store the returned recordset in memory associated with the specific query name. ColdFusion will then use the recordset stored in memory instead of re-running the query each time the information is needed.

Cached queries can produce performance improvements of up to twenty (20) times faster than not using cached queries, and sometimes even faster than that. For example, you may have written a query that takes 200 milliseconds to run. When run from memory, that same recordset will only take 5-10 milliseconds to return. This is a very noticeable difference and will scale your application to many more users without having to add more expensive hardware.

On the Other Hand

Query caching **can** cause problems if it is not done correctly. Here is the process when done well:

1) Change data (insert, update or delete ANY data)
2) Refresh the associated cached queries

Sounds simple, right? Well, if data in the database changes and the query stored in memory is not refreshed, you will have data integrity problems.

Here's an example of how caching can backfire. Let's say you have an e-commerce site that sells widgets. Let's also say that on Monday morning, your widget retails for $50. You write a cached query to retrieve the cost of the widget from the database. That afternoon, your company decides that they will make huge amounts of money if they change the price to $100. So you go into the database and change the price to $100, but **don't** refresh the query that you wrote in the morning. The query will automatically refresh after a given time period, of course, but let's say you have set the *"CachedWithin"* attribute of the <CFQUERY> to once per day, which is very common. Monday afternoon rolls around and a user sees that widgets are selling at the fantastic price of $50 and so decides to buy 1,000 of them. By Tuesday the query is automatically refreshed, but this mistake cost the company $50,000, or an unhappy customer.

But Don't Let That Stop You

Don't be too fearful of using query caching. Yes, it is entirely possible to let the refreshing slip, but as long as you do it correctly, you will **save** money, not lose it. And yes, it's even possible to do query caching when scaling to multiple servers. There is more information about doing this technique on the **www.Fusebox.org** site.

One other potential problem with refreshing has also been addressed by the Fusebox Organization. As mentioned above, the variable *#Request.Timespan#* is set in your *app_server.cfm* file. This allows you to quickly reset the timespan for the entire home application by simply changing that value. To use this technique, simply place this variable into the *CachedWithin* attribute in <CFQUERY>:

```
<CFQUERY name="myquery" cachedwithin="#request.timespan#" ......>
....
</CFQUERY>
```

How Can We Reuse Our Various Pieces of Code?

Reusing code is an important concept that is used very effectively in Fusebox, at many levels. Fusebox enables you to reuse circuit applications, entire multi-step processes, queries, actions and display files.

Advanced Technique 12: Reuse Circuit Applications

Fusebox techniques offer a unique method of integrating multiple ColdFusion applications together with ease. ColdFusion offers the ability to turn a **single** ColdFusion file into a ColdFusion tag. Fusebox offers a technique for turning **multiple** ColdFusion files into a single ColdFusion tag.

Some of the built-in ColdFusion tags, such as <CFFILE>, offer something a little different than the other tags: an "*action*" attribute. <CFFILE> can do *action="read/write/append/upload/move/copy/rename/delete"* Each of these actions requires different parameters, but they are all focused around manipulating files.

Fusebox offers this same functionality when creating custom tags. Fusebox uses the attribute "Fuseaction", but it serves the same purpose as the "action" attribute in a tag like <CFFILE>.

This technique simply requires you to call the *index.cfm* file as a <CFMODULE>. It's important to use <CFMODULE> instead of <CFINCLUDE>. Otherwise, the variable *#attributes.Fuseaction#* could affect other areas of your application. <CFMODULE> will keep these variables local to that one *index.cfm* file.

Here's an example:

A user submits a form which goes to

www.mysite.com/index.cfm?fuseaction=RegisterUser.

The *parent index.cfm* file accessed looks like this:

```
<CFSWITCH expression="#attributes.fuseaction#">
    <CFCASE value="registeruser">
        <CFINCLUDE template="act_adduser.cfm">
        <CFSET request.redirectuser="no">
        <CFMODULE template="/newsletters/index.cfm"
            fuseaction="sendEmail"
            Email_id="4"
            toAddress="#attributes.toAddress#">
        <CFINCLUDE template="url_thankyou.cfm">
    </CFCASE>
```

```
    <CFCASE value="thankyou">
        <CFINCLUDE template="dsp_thankyou.cfm">
    </CFCASE>
</CFSWITCH>
```

This *index.cfm* above does not actually send any email. In fact, the developer doesn't need to know all the intricacies of how the "*SendEmail*" Fuseaction works. He or she simply needs to know what it does and what attributes it requires. This is similar to the fact that you do not need to know **how** <CFFILE> works to be able to use it to write files.

Here, the parent *index.cfm* calls the child *index.cfm* (its own Fusebox), which may reside in a different directory, to perform the action for it. The child *index.cfm* may look something like this:

```
<CFSWITCH expression="#attributes.fuseaction#">
    <CFCASE value="sendEmail">
        <CFINCLUDE template="qry_checkforemail.cfm">
        <CFINCLUDE template="act_saveemail.cfm">
        <CFINCLUDE template="act_sendEmail.cfm">
        <CFINCLUDE template="url_emailreceipt.cfm">
    </CFCASE>
    <CFCASE value="email receipt">
        <CFINCLUDE template="dsp_receipt.cfm">
    </CFCASE>
</CFSWITCH>
```

The Fuse *act_SendEmail.cfm* is the action file that actually sends the email that the user requested of the parent application. But note that this Fuseaction, "*SendEmail*", does a few other things, too: It checks to see if the email already exists in the database. If not, it saves the email. The program's flow-of-control to the child application was transparent to the developer. All the developer needs care about is that there is a need to send a user an email.

Note that there is a *url_* file in the *SendEmail* Fuseaction. Also note the request variable "*RedirectUser*", which was set by the previous *index.cfm* file. That was done because this *index.cfm* file is being called from another *index.cfm* file. Here, we simply want to run the "*SendEmail*" Fuseaction and not redirect the user to the "*EmailReceipt*".

This may be a little confusing, so let's look at the *url_EmailReceipt.cfm* file more closely:

```
<CFPARAM name="request.redirectuser" default="yes">
<CFIF request.redirectuser>
    <CFLOCATION URL="index.cfm"?Fuseaction=email
receipt&#request.urltoken#">
</CFIF>
```

This allows us to **not** redirect the user if that will send the user to an undesired Fuseaction.

We use a request variable here instead of an attributes variable for security reasons. This way, the user cannot hack the redirect by setting this value as a URL variable.

When using this technique of reusing an entire circuit application, be sure to point all HTML links and HTML forms to the parent application, using the Universal Format. That way, the parent application will coordinate whatever action is to be done:

```
<a href="index.cfm">
<form ACTION="index.cfm">
```

Advanced Technique 13: Reusing Multi-Step Processes

You will soon find yourself relying on the ability to reuse multi-step processes. The most common example of this is a user registration/login process. With the Fusebox tag <CF_RETURNFUSEACTION>, you can create a **single** method of registering a new user, regardless of how many steps this process takes. This tag also provides a single method for a returning user to login and reuse this entire process anywhere it is necessary for a user to have a "*User_ID*".

Let's look at a **forums application**: Users who have not logged in may be allowed to read messages. However, if they wish to post their own message or reply to another message, it will be important that they state who they are, so that the messages can be associated with specific users.

When the user attempts to write a new message, the application will check to see if the input contains a *#client.user_id#*. If not, the application will redirect the user to the */member/index.cfm*. This will happen regardless of whether s/he needs to login or to register a new account. The user can remain in the members application as long as s/he needs. When the user is done (i.e., finished creating a *#client.user_id#*), s/he will be returned back to the "*WriteMessage*" Fuseaction in the forum. This technique keeps the user focused on what s/he was doing originally, while allowing the use of the functionality of another application.

The syntax for this technique is quite simple. In the Forums application, set the URLs of both where the user needs go and where s/he should be returned when s/he is done with that application.

Forums Application:

```
<CFSWITCH expression="#attributes.fuseaction#">
    <CFCASE value="read thread">
        <CFINCLUDE template="qry_getthread.cfm">
        <CFINCLUDE template="dsp_readthread.cfm">
```

```
    </CFCASE>
    <CFCASE value="write message">
        <CFMODULE template="#request.cfroot#/app_secure.cfm"
            message="You must login or create an account to write a
            message">
        <CFINCLUDE template="dsp_writemessage.cfm">
    </CFCASE>
</CFSWITCH>
```

***app_secure.cfm*:**

```
<CFIF not isdefined('client.user_id')>
    <CFSET client.message="#attributes.message#">
    <CF_RETURNFUSEACTION
        action="set"
        returnurl="#cgi.path_info#?#request.attributeslist#"
        gotourl="/members/index.cfm?fuseaction=login form">
</CFIF>
```

Members Application:

```
<CFSWITCH expression="#attributes.fuseaction#">
    <CFCASE value="registeruser">
        <CFINCLUDE template="dsp_registeruser.cfm">
    </CFCASE>
    <CFCASE value="saveuser">
        <CFINCLUDE template="act_saveuser.cfm">
        <CF_RETURNFUSEACTION
            action="return">
    </CFCASE>
    <CFCASE value="login form">
        <CFINCLUDE template="dsp_loginform.cfm">
    </CFCASE>
    <CFCASE value="login">
        <CFINCLUDE template="qry_validateuser.cfm">
        <CFIF validateuser.recordcount>
            <CF_RETURNFUSEACTION
                action="return">
        <CFELSE>
            <CFINCLUDE template="url_loginform.cfm ">
        </CFIF>
    </CFCASE>
</CFSWITCH>
```

If the user is not logged in, *app_secure* will send them to the login form:

```
gotourl="/members/index.cfm?fuseaction=login form"
```

Once the user has successfully logged in or created an account, he or she will be sent back to the Forums application:

```
returnurl="#cgi.path_info#?#request.attributeslist#"
```

Advanced Technique 14: Reuse Those Forms!

When capturing user input, we need to present the data in three different ways:

1. We need a blank form for a user to enter new information.
2. We need a pre-populated form that displays a user's previously supplied information and prompts for any required data that is missing.
3. Lastly, we need a form to edit what the user has already entered into the database.

The programmer will commonly use three different display files with three different forms. A more efficient way to code this would be to use **only one form** and just change the data that is displayed under the different circumstances. This technique eliminates the need to edit all three files every time the form changes.

Start by thinking of a form as having three settings:

Blank: This setting clears the form and prepares it for new data.

Form: This setting means the user entered something incorrectly. Instead of making the user retype all the data, the form fields are filled in with what the user typed in previously, while also flagging the error(s).

Query: This setting is used when a user is editing a record in a database (i.e., to change a password). This means the user should run a query to obtain the existing values to populate the form.

Call your form as a series of CF tags, using <CFMODULE>, and pass it an attribute named "*Action*", with a value of *BLANK*, *FORM* or *QUERY* and an attribute of "*FIELDLIST*", consisting of the list of elements on your form. Your <CFMODULE> tag would look like this:

```
<CFMODULE TEMPLATE="dsp_MyForm.cfm"
    Action="blank"
FIELD LIST="firstname,lastname">
```

The *dsp_MyFile.cfm* would look like this:

```
<!--- This form has two text fields: Firstname and lastname. Here is a list of
all the fields --->
<CFIF ATTRIBUTES.Action IS "Blank">
    <CFLOOP LIST="#attributes.fieldlist#" INDEX="counter">
        <CFSET SETVARIABLE("#counter#", "")>
    </CFLOOP>
```

```
<CFELSEIF ATTRIBUTES.Action IS "query">
    <CFQUERY NAME="getContact" DATASOURCE=
    "#attributes.ContactsDSN#">
        select #field list#
        from Users
        where Users_id = #attributes.users_id#
    </CFQUERY>
    <CFLOOP LIST="#attributes.fieldlist#" INDEX="counter">
        <CFSET SETVARIABLE("#counter#", "#evaluate("GETCONTACT."
        & "#COUNTER#")#")>
    </CFLOOP>
<CFELSEIF ATTRIBUTES.Action IS "form">
    <CFLOOP LIST="#attributes.fieldlist#" INDEX="counter">
        <CFSET SETVARIABLE("#counter#", "#evaluate("FORM." &
        "#COUNTER#")#")>
    </CFLOOP>
</CFIF>

<FORM method="post" action="index.cfm">
<INPUT NAME="fuseaction" TYPE="hidden" VALUE="processForm">
    <CFOUTPUT>
        <INPUT type="text" name="firstname" value="#firstname#">
        <INPUT type="text" name="firstname" value="#last name#">
    </CFOUTPUT>
</FORM>
```

By modifying the above code for "*Action IS query*", the same effect can be achieved even if the form values are not all from the database. You may have to build a custom loop and form value-setter on a per-form basis. However, this will still save you time over making two or three templates.

Advanced Technique 15: Reusing Display Blocks

A technique that is incredibly useful when building large-scale applications or when working with multiple developers is the "Display Blocks" technique. A display block is a special display file that can be freely reused in multiple places. A display block is a section of a web page, not an entire web page. It does **not** begin and end with HTML></HTML> because the display block will be included within another display file that **does** contain those tags.

Many large e-commerce sites use display blocks extensively. For example, a home page for a bookstore may include a "Bestsellers" and "Editor's Picks" section, or even a menu on the left-hand side. These are all blocks. The CFML code for these sections is in a separate file, separate from the body of the page.

By keeping each section in its own file, we are able to develop each of the blocks one at a time, while also being able to reuse the blocks on other pages.

Each block is self-contained. If it requires a query file to display properly, that file is included (using absolute path format) at the top of the blocks file.

Two things to note about blocks are the **forms** and **links**. When display files are reused in this format, it is very important that the links be either universal URLs ("*index.cfm*") or absolute ("*/directory/index.cfm*"). It is important that links and form actions not be relative URLs, because this limits the reusability of the block.

Using the block concept reduces the frequency of rewriting a display file. This reusability is powerful. A directory named "*Blocks*" is created off of the root directory of your application, where global display blocks are stored. Display blocks all begin with *dsp_*, just like a standard display file. If you are building an e-commerce site that has a secured administrator section, you may want to have a second blocks directory that exists within the secured section of your site.

Advanced Technique 16: Reusing Query Files

Like the display blocks technique, query files can be reused. A directory named "Queries" is created off of the root directory of your application, where global query files are stored. Global query files will begin with *qry_*, just like standard query files.

These global queries can be called from anywhere in your application, allowing the best possible reuse of queries. Instead of rewriting the <CFQUERY> statement each time, simply <CFINCLUDE> the desired query file.

Advanced Technique 17: Reusing Action Files

Just as the "Queries" directory is used for global queries, the "Actions" directory is used for global actions. These actions can be anything that may be used in multiple places throughout any of your circuit applications. Centralizing the location of these files gives greater control over the total application.

Advanced Technique 18: Reusing Global Navigation Using <CF_BODYCONTENT>

This tag is implemented by wrapping it around the <CFSWITCH> statement of your application's *index.cfm* file. The purpose of this tag is to capture a Fuseaction's output and store it in a request variable, so that it can be accessed at a later stage in the application.

The tag is implemented like so:

Example *index.cfm* file:

```
<CFINCLUDE template="app_locals.cfm">

<CF_BODYCONTENT>
    <CFSWITCH expression="#attributes.fuseaction#">
```

```
        <CFCASE value="cart">
            <CFINCLUDE template="dsp_cart.cfm">
        </CFCASE>
        <CFCASE value="checkout">
            <CFINCLUDE template="dsp_checkout.cfm">
        </CFCASE>
        <CFDEFAULTCASE>
            <CFLOCATION URL="index.cfm?fuseaction=cart">
        </CFDEFAULTCASE>
    </CFSWITCH>
</CF_BODYCONTENT>
</CFINCLUDE TEMPLATE="#request.CFFOOT#/app_layout.cfm ">
```

The code for <CF_BODYCONTENT> is below. The tag builds off the *ThisTag.GeneratedContent* attribute of any custom tag built using ColdFusion.

```
<CFIF not thistag.HasEndTag>
    <CFSET thistag.generatedcontent="">
    You must have an end Tag
    <CFABORT>
</CFIF>

<CFPARAM name="request.headerfile">
<CFPARAM name="request.footerfile">
<CFPARAM name="attributes.showbody" default="yes">

<CFIF len(request.headerfile)> <CFINCLUDE
TEMPLATE="#request.headerfile#"> </CFIF>
<CFIF attributes.showbody>
<CFOUTPUT>#request.bodycontent#</CFOUTPUT> </CFIF>
<CFIF len(request.footerfile)> <CFINCLUDE
TEMPLATE="#request.footerfile#"> </CFIF>
```

The tag first tests its own execution mode. This refers to which end of the tag is currently being interpreted. If the beginning tag, or <CF_BODYCONTENT>, is being interpreted, its execution mode is "*start*". If the ending tag, or </CF_BODYCONTENT>, is being interpreted, its execution mode is "*end*".

<CF_BODYCONTENT> waits until the execution mode is equal to "*end*", then it stores the content that has been generated between the opening and closing tag into a request variable, *Request.BodyContent* by default. It does this by accessing *ThisTag.GeneratedContent*, which is a ColdFusion reserved word. Reserved words are words (variables) that are used by the web application server itself and cannot be changed explicitly by the user.

ThisTag.GeneratedContent holds all the output that occurred inside the opening and closing tags. <CF_BODYCONTENT> references it at the end of its execution, so that it can capture all the output generated during its life span.

The beginning of <CF_BODYCONTENT> contains an error check. Since this tag requires the use of an end tag, it tests this value by running *ThisTag.HasEndTag*. If the tag being executed has an end tag, then *ThisTag.HasEndTag* is equal to true. If it is false, it raises an error.

You may be asking yourself, "Why would I use this tag?" There are two advantages:

Advantage 1

Many times we find ourselves needing to place the output of our Fuseactions in the middle of different design schemes, or we may wish to prepare for the future, when the design department may want to change the look and feel of the HTML around our Fuseaction. We can plan for this scenario by placing the output of the *Request.BodyContent* variable between our header and footer files. This can be accomplished like so:

```
<CFINCLUDE template="dsp_header.cfm">
<CFOUTPUT>#request.bodycontent#</CFOUTPUT>
<CFINCLUDE template="dsp_footer.cfm">
```

This makes it very easy for us to sandwich the output of our Fuseaction in between our surrounding HTML. This is a lot easier to understand, update and debug than a large HTML file.

Note: The newer version of <CF_BODYCONTENT> no longer requires the *app_layout.cfm* file. This functionality is built directly into the new <CF_BODYCONTENT> tag.

The <CF_BODYCONTENT> tag will first include the *#Request.HeaderFile#*, then display the body of your page (*Request.BodyContent*), then display the *#Request.FooterFile#*. You can change header and footer files from within the body of your page.

You also should set default values for *Request.HeaderFile* and *Request.FooterFile* from within your *app_globals.cfm*. It will be pretty rare that you'll need to change these values, so you won't need to write the default values over and over.

Advantage 2

The second advantage in using <CF_BODYCONTENT> comes when calling a Fusebox application as a custom tag. Normally, this returns a full page from the tag; when output together with the present Fuseaction, this would result in a page inside of a page, like the screen shot below.

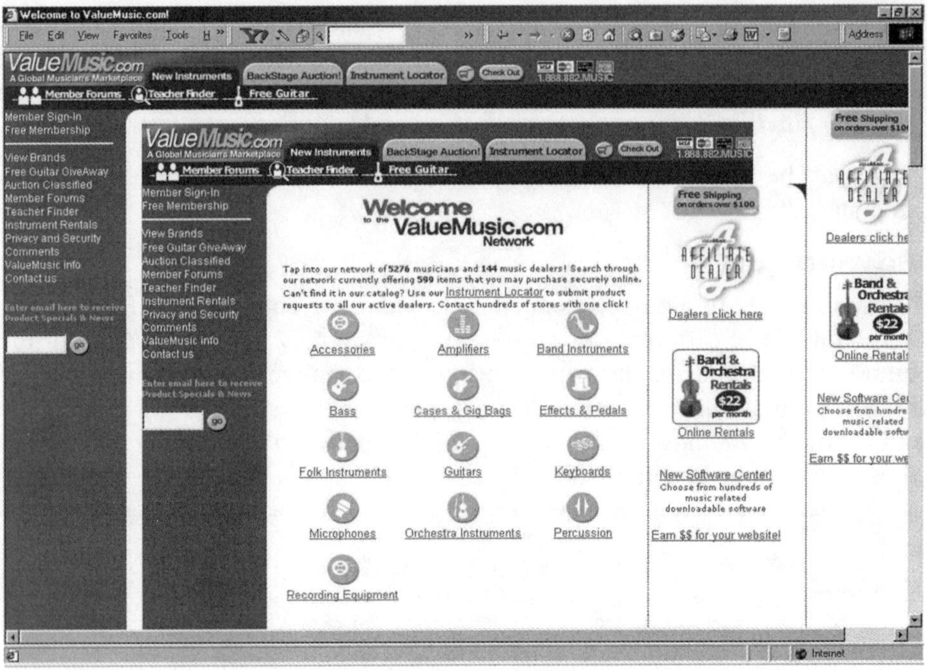

PAGE INSIDE A PAGE

By applying <CF_BODYCONTENT> in conjunction with *app_layout.cfm*, we gain complete control over our HTML output. A complete universal page layout is possible, designed as a unit, not just pieced together.

How Can We Optimize Portability?

Being able to go from a development server(s) to production server(s) is a vital task. Ideally, you should never do development on production servers if you can help it. If this is not an option, you should at least separate out different areas of the server for development purposes and production purposes.

There are various concerns when moving code and databases from server to server. These next techniques assist in this process.

Advanced Technique 19: Dealing with Multiple Sites on One Server

If your server contains multiple ColdFusion applications, the easiest way to manage these applications is to create a ColdFusion mapping to the root directory of each of these applications. A ColdFusion mapping is different than a web server mapping, in that it is specific to the <CFINCLUDE> and <CFMODULE> tags, not the <a> or <form> tags. This allows you to specify an absolute directory name using those two tags.

The reason for doing this is to make better use of the global blocks and queries, as we outlined above. For example, you can use:

```
<CFINCLUDE template="/ROOTMAPPING/queries/qry_somequery.cfm">
```

or

```
<CFINCLUDE template="/ROOTMAPPING/blocks/dsp_someblock.cfm">
```

anywhere in your site. This means that, regardless of what directory the calling template is in, it will be able to <CFINCLUDE> (or <CFMODULE>) the query or display block. ColdFusion mappings are set in the CF administrator.

Advanced Technique 20: Don't Use Autonumber/Identity Fields In Your Databases

When creating a database, do **not** use autonumber fields. Using an autonumber field can cause compatibility problems when upgrading or converting database systems. Instead, do the following:

1) Use a single "number/integer" data type wherever you would normally use an autonumber field.
2) Create a table titled "*UniqueID*", with one number/integer field of the same title.

To obtain a **unique row identifier**, use the following steps.

a) Query the *UniqueID* table for the current value.
b) Insert your new record into the appropriate table along with your new *UniqueID*.
c) Run a query to update the value of the record in the *UniqueID* table by 1.

This may seem a little more tedious, but believe me, it will help you in the end.

There are a number of reasons for doing this, but the main reason is that Fusebox standards are meant to allow the ColdFusion community to be able to exchange applications and databases. Databases do not have a standard "autonumber" or "identity key" data type. So by using the "number/integer" data type, an Access database structure can be easily ported to an Oracle Database, then to a SQL server database, etc.

CHAPTER 6: Testing and Deploying Fusebox Applications

In the age of the World Wide Web, companies constantly try to defy time. They have time limits placed on them, not because of personal reasons, but because of funding and market reasons. Not being the "first to market" gives your competitors the chance to gain valuable market share. A company running out of money before an application is finished is an even worse fate. The application instantly sinks into uselessness.

Identify a release date for your project and determine if these dates are reasonable. Sometimes they are not. When the time frames become unreasonable, it means the application still may be completed on schedule, but will require cutting corners to do so. We have observed that inexperienced development groups commonly cut out the specification and design phases, yet this actually causes the release date to extend. We will explain how the same problem can occur with the testing stage of a web application.

Budgets commonly dictate how much time can be spent on the various phases of development: specification, design, coding, and testing. The easiest phase for most clients to understand is the coding phase. This is because they can see a tangible application when coding is finished. On the other hand, time spent on the other three phases (specification, design and testing) feel like time wasted to the client. It may feel like little work is being accomplished, and that these phases are simply costing the company money.

Is it possible to reduce the amount of time and dollars spent by carefully following the four development phases? We think so:

TIME SPENT ON SPECIFICATION AND DESIGN MEANS LESS TIME NEEDED FOR CODING AN APPLICATION THAT RUNS WELL AND DOES WHAT THE CLIENT WANTS IT TO DO.

Similarly, **the testing phase is an investment**. You can spend either a small amount of time or a long amount of time in the testing phase. A more or less thoroughly tested application can mean more or less acceptance of the finished application. Imagine an e-commerce application where the credit card processing area is not fully tested and contains a loophole that allows a sneaky user to leave the credit card information blank, yet the order is allowed to go through to the shipping department. This could cause the company to lose countless dollars.

On the other hand, it is important to understand that a longer amount of time spent does not necessarily mean the application is more thoroughly tested. Using a concise, systematic testing process can be far more efficient than randomly testing an application for a long amount of time. Developing a testing process can be difficult. We will offer you some guidance on how to get started.

Testing a web-based application is different than testing a traditional desktop application in that fixing a bug in a production environment is far simpler than having to fix the bug on every client machine, as in traditional client-server environments. With web-based applications, the bug can be fixed on a production server, and all users will instantly see the fix.

This can be a double-edged sword, though. It is common for a bug fix to cause another bug. If a bug fix is too hastily deployed to a live production server, it can cause more problems than it is meant to fix, sometimes without the programmer even knowing.

For the testing phase to be successful, there needs to be a solid process for finding the bugs, fixing the bugs, testing the fixes and finally deploying the changes to the production environment.

After the specification and design phases have completed, there are three main groups of people involved in a web application: **Developers** (includes both programmers and graphic artists), **testers** and **end users**. Some people wear multiple hats, but in the creation of a standard application, all of these groups are necessary.

The end users tend to be the least forgiving when a server has downtime. Downtime can mean various things. It does not always mean there is a hardware problem on the server. It can mean something as simple as a spelling mistake, or a user receives an error when they attempt to finish a form, or that the server is just overloaded, along with a variety of other errors.

Testers can often over-stress a server in the testing process. When numerous users are purposely trying to "break" an application, they will try many different techniques to do so, which can cause a server to be over-stressed. This commonly interrupts a developer who is creating something new, along with an end-user who may be using the application.

Setting Up a Testing Environment

Because there are three groups of **users**, the ideal testing environment also involves three groups of **servers**: Development, testing and production servers. End users use the application on production servers, programmers work on the development servers, and testers test the testing servers. The three groups never disturb each other because they work on different servers.

This is an ideal environment, but if corners need to be cut because of budget constraints, it is possible to reduce the number of servers to development and production, or to make workstations into development and testing servers, combining two servers into one. This can still cause problems when working with a group of programmers. Sometimes it just cannot be avoided.

Development servers are used to **create** the web application. An application in development is usually seen only by the programmer(s). End-users, beta testers and even clients rarely view an application on the development server. This is because an application may not be complete, only displaying error messages. It is common for a development server to consist of only a single server, although it is beneficial to also have a developer database server. If necessary, both the ColdFusion server and database server can exist on the same machine. There may only be a few developers, so a single server can handle the load. This makes development easy and inexpensive.

Testing servers are used to **verify** that the new code is ready to be launched onto the production servers. It may or may not be ok for testing servers to consist of a single server. If the development server consists of a single server, this can cause problems with production servers that consist of multiple servers. Code that works on a single server may not work on multiple clustered servers. For example, when uploading a file that is saved on the application server, the code may work fine on a single server, but once it is moved to a cluster of servers, that uploaded file may only exist on one of the machines in the cluster. When a user attempts to view the file on one of the machines the file was **not** uploaded to, they will not be able to access it. This is "bug."

If your production environment consists of multiple servers, it is best for your testing environment to be an identical mirror. This will provide for the most realistic test. Although corners may be cut here also, if you run a dozen servers in your production environment, your testing environment should contain at least two servers, to demonstrate that the application works in a clustered environment.

Production servers are used by **end-users**. They are the most important servers and should rarely if ever be rebooted or toyed with. Actually, the most common reason for production servers to have downtime is not hardware failure or operating system bugs, but because the administrators have to take them off-line for maintenance or upgrading.

One of the best ways to reduce server downtime is to use a clustering solution, a solution well supported by ColdFusion. This allows multiple servers to handle load while allowing individual servers to be taken offline and fixed or upgraded without bringing the site down.

Source Control: A Management Tool and Team Resource

Before an application even gets to the testing phase, it is possible to prepare for errors. One of the greatest but commonly underused tools created for programmers is source control. **Source control allows a team of programmers to work together without overwriting each other's code.**

This may not seem to be a significant advantage, but it is more powerful than it initially appears. Source control allows programmers to view what lines of code have changed, when they were changed, who changed it and why it was changed. This suddenly becomes a big deal in the testing and debugging phase of an application. If the application was written by one developer and handed over to another developer, source control allows the new developer to see when, where and why certain changes were made.

You can also check out entire circuit applications by checking out a folder. This allows the workload to be easily assigned to individuals in a team environment.

Source control will change the way you write your applications by forcing you to be **consistent** with how your team develops applications. It will be easier to separate out who will be working on what sections of the application **before** starting, instead of everyone working on everything. Most importantly, source control will help you stay on course by not allowing multiple people to work on the same files at the same time.

Most ColdFusion developers use ColdFusion Studio® for developing their applications. Source control integration is built directly into Studio. Because of this, your normal development workflow will not be interrupted. The only thing that will change is that, when you open up a file for the first time, you will need to "check the file out". In ColdFusion Studio, a dialog box will pop up and you simply need to choose "yes" to verify the check out. Then when you feel you've made enough changes to the file, you will need to check it back in.

> **Checking a file out** means that **you** will be changing the file and that no one else may edit the file until you are done. You can save your changes and test those changes. Once you feel you have made all the changes needed; you "check the file in".
>
> **Checking a file in** means that a new version of the file is stored in the source control database. It also means that others may now check the

file out for further editing. After a file has been checked in, the file can be deployed to another server.

An additional useful feature is that, each time you check a file in, the source control will make a copy of that version. If at any time you want to "roll back" to a previous version, you can do so without have to search through old backup tapes.

Interruptions are the biggest cause of applications not finishing on schedule. Source control can significantly improve overall productivity by reducing the amount of unnecessary interruptions. As long as the original developer makes good comments in source control, the next developer will be able to have their questions answered without having to interrupt the original developer.

Line Level Backups: A Developer's Friend

Backups are one of the most important things a network engineer can do. Without good backups, done on a regular basis, a company can lose everything it has ever worked on because of a single power surge or hard disk crash. Keeping a recent copy of the backup in an off-site location is also essential to "disaster recovery."

On the other hand, accidentally deleting a file is a common occurrence. This may not require an entire restoration or a new hard disk. Full backups are necessary to have for catastrophic failure. However, if for some reason a backup fails (which does occasionally happen!), source control can also save the day. Source control will assist you with recovering lost files by allowing you to restore the last checked in file. That way, if a backup wasn't done for a day, or maybe even a week, source control will have the most recent changes. This can be a lifesaver.

Finding and Deploying Bug Fixes

Once you have created an environment that allows testers to search for bugs and allows developers to fix them in a clean format, it is important to have a system for connecting testers and developers together. Once a tester has found a bug, they need some method of notifying the developer. Usually it takes much longer to fix a bug than it does to find a bug, so there may be a long list of bugs that need to be fixed as the tester is searching for more. It is important to have a clean way to manage this list.

Know What You're Looking For

The most common bugs can be categorized into the following types:

Hard Bugs

These are bugs which actually throw a ColdFusion error and do not allow the user to continue using the application. This is because all they see is an error message generated by ColdFusion or some other language (such as a Javascript error message). These bugs are generally obvious when generated by ColdFusion and provide a message as to why they occurred.

Having the debugging information generated by ColdFusion may be vital to being able to reproduce the error. When testing an application, hard bugs are the easiest to find and should be the first type of bug that is looked for.

Logic Bugs

These are bugs that do something which is unexpected by the end-user but are not errors to the language itself, i.e., they do not throw a ColdFusion error message. The end user may be able to continue using the application, but something has occurred which is undesired. If the error is big enough, it may be important to stop the user from continuing to use the application. For example, if a user is not sent an email receipt after purchasing a product, this could be considered a bug. Logic bugs are the most difficult bugs to find and may not be noticed until after the application has been launched.

Perfection Bugs

These are some of the most common bugs and may very well exist on every page in your application. They can be anything from spelling errors to user interface changes. They may not be errors at all, but ways to improve the experience the user has while using the application. A tester may request many of these, which will quickly eat up your time. Be sure to inform the tester(s) that, the longer you spend perfecting the application, the less amount of time is being spent actually running the business.

Bug Reporting

Once bugs have been found, there needs to be some method of notification to the developer. Hard bugs are actually the easiest to deal with because just about all the information you need can be stored without your testers or end-users telling you. ColdFusion logs all errors to its various log files, although simply looking at your CF logs may not be enough for you. Wouldn't it be better if you could track the progress of the fixes on each hard bug?

Prior to ColdFusion 4, when a hard error occurred in ColdFusion, the only thing you could do was display debugging information to the user stating that something was broken. You could not execute any CFML code (beyond <CFOUTPUT>). Beginning with Version 4 of CF, there is a new feature that allows a CFML to be run upon an error using <CFTRY>/<CFCATCH>. This means that, when a hard bug occurs, debugging information can automatically be stored in a database, along with immediately notifying the developer(s). This does not require any user intervention to be sure that you are notified when an error occurs. This is an excellent technique for maintaining a 99.9% bug free site.

As we know now, hard errors are not the only errors that occur. Hard errors are easy to keep track of because they can categorized without any intervention from the end user. Logic and perfection bugs are different. Because they are not considered "real" errors to ColdFusion, we need some way for our testers to report when something needs to be changed.

One of the simplest and most effective methods of solving this problem is to display a **"Change Request" form** at the bottom of each page for the testers of your application. Using the Fusebox security method, you can design this tool to only be viewable by users in the "testers" group. This form offers your testers a standard way to request a change to a specific page, instead of sending an email and requiring half a dozen back and forth phone calls.

The Change Request form conveys a simple request to change some text or layout on the page or to notify the developers that something is not doing what it should.

This form does not need to be ultra complex to be effective. A simple <textarea>, with a hidden form field capturing what page the user was on, may be enough. Then offer a method for your developers to view those change requests and state whether they have been finished or not.

Having bug reporting systems like this (or some other type) will save you tremendous amounts of time when attempting to rid all the bugs from your application.

Reproducing the Bugs

Finding bugs may be a fairly quick and simple task for a tester. Simply by using an application over and over will most likely generate a variety of bugs, but finding them is completely useless if they cannot be repeated.

If a tester finds a bug, s/he needs to explain to the developer exactly **how** they received the bug. Without this information, the developer cannot fix the bug.

To reproduce bugs, the more information the better. If your tester simply says "I got an error", this does not do anyone any good. A good tester can explain exactly what s/he was attempting to do when s/he found the bug. This information will allow the developer to understand what the problem is and to be able to come up with a solution.

Prioritize Your Bugs

Some bugs are far more important than others. For example:

> **Bug 1**: A user cannot complete the checkout process because of an ODBC error
>
> **Bug 2**: The word "Kat" is spelled incorrectly.

Which do you do first? What if you had a list of 100 errors like these? Bug 2 may be very simple and quick to fix, but it is not nearly as vital to the site as Bug 1.

This is a dilemma all developers face, and it is not an easy choice. It becomes even more complex when there are many bugs, all with low priorities. A good rule of thumb is that if no one is breathing down your neck to quickly fix something, do the easiest fixes first. This will reduce your overall stress level and allow you to focus on the harder fixes with less distraction.

Fix the Bug

Now comes the hard part. Once you have found the bugs, you can reproduce them, you have prioritized which bugs are the most important, and determined which ones can wait, it is time to actually **fix** the bugs. Fixing bugs can vary from being very simple to being very difficult. Sometimes it takes under a minute to fix a bug, such as a spelling error or reorganizing the layout of some of the elements on a page. Other times, it is necessary to scrap everything you've been working and start over, simply to fix a bug.

Determine If the Fix Has Caused Other Bugs

When reusing code, the way a good programmer does, it is common for a bug fix to cause an error elsewhere in your application. When code is reused, sometimes bugs may work when used in a certain way but break when reused in a slightly different manner. Prematurely launching a fix without verifying that it is solid can cause numerous problems.

Test the Bug Fix on the Development Server

Before you show the fix to a tester, try to break it yourself. This may seem obvious, but is often skipped. You may not need to spend a tremendous amount of time, but it will save your company time if you can throw errors quickly instead of handing it over to your testers and having them hand it back just as quickly because they couldn't get past the first screen.

Deploy the Fix from the Development Server to the Testing Server(s)

Before deploying your fix to the live site, it is always good to attempt to deploy the change/fix to a set of testing servers, especially if your production environment is run on clustered servers. Sometimes code that works great on a single server does not work well when run on a clustered environment.

A good example of this is with session variables. Session variables are persistent variables associated with a single user. These persistent variables are stored in the RAM of a ColdFusion server. They may work fine on single servers, but as soon as one of the machines goes down in the cluster, the user will be sent to another server, losing all of their session variables and not understanding why they are suddenly not logged in.

Deploying to a group of testing servers would have caught this problem before end-users found it.

Test the Bug Fix on the Testing Server

Simply deploying the changes to the testing server does not mean the change will work great. Often, code that works fine on your development server may not work fine on another server. There are many reasons why this may be the case. The main reason is that minor things will be different from server to server. Errors found in this step will help reduce the number of errors when deploying to the production servers.

Deploy the Fix to the Production Server(s)

Once you have tested your application on the development server and have done a test deployment to your testing server(s), it is time to deploy the code to the live site. This may be stressful because, even after all of the testing done above, there may still be minor errors once it has been moved onto the production servers.

The two most common causes of errors in this step are that either certain files were not copied over to the production servers, or the production database was not modified to the new version on the testing servers.

Test the Bug Fix on the Production Server(s)

This is the final round of testing, to ensure that everything went smoothly. It is extremely important to verify that all of the new code and database changes have transferred properly. If the previous steps of testing were complete, then this step should be quick and easy.

Remember: The reason for the many layers of testing is to make sure that your production site is **not** interrupted when new changes are made to your site.

Notify the Bug's Finder

Once a bug has been fixed or has been determined unfixable in the time frame, it is critical to notify the person who requested the bug fix. Whether they are notified by e-mail, phone, fax, or telegram does not matter. If they requested that you make the fix, it is good practice to tell them the fix has occurred.

Conclusion

Once all of these steps have been complete, you should have a rock solid application. If any of the steps are not complete, you are more likely to encounter errors in your production site. Although extensive testing does not guarantee your site to be bug free, it will significantly reduce the number of bugs.

Once your code has been tested this thoroughly, it is important to turn on the automatic error trapping, so that the developers can be notified of hard bugs. It is nearly impossible to catch 100% of the bugs in an application, so if a bug was missed, the error trapping will find the hard bugs.

Bug Detecting Tools

There are a few types of bug detecting tools available for testing a ColdFusion application. The most common ones are: Stress testing, code testing, and site monitoring tools. These types of tools are all commercially available.

Stress Testing

An example of a **stress testing** tool comes from **RadView** (***http://www.RadView.com***). This tool allows you to simulate users coming to your site. To use this type of tool, you need to create example scripts of how users use your site. Your script will work as if users are clicking links or even posting form information. Once you have set up various scripts, you can have the tool run through scripts as if there were hundreds, or even thousands, of simultaneous users. Using this tool in conjunction with the <CFTRY> tool, you can have all your errors automatically saved and categorized to a database.

A stress testing tool is very helpful for finding the obvious errors quickly. Instead of spending many days of manually clicking links and posting form information, you can spend a few hours creating your scripts and a few hours running your scripts and get a far more complete test looking for various types of errors that would be missed from manual testing. The only downside to stress testing tools is that they generally cost upwards of $15,000-$25,000.

Code Testing

If your budget cannot afford tools like RadView, you may consider **code testing**. We are currently aware of only one source for such a tool specifically for ColdFusion. Steve Nelson has created a CFML code testing tool one that is currently available for a small fee through **Secret Agents** (***http://www.SecretAgents.com***).

This particular tool works a little different from the stress-testing tool and the <CFTRY> tool. It works by physically reading your code and looking for common mistakes. This type of testing is generally very quick and easy and helps to find hundreds of potential bugs, while also alerting you to various sections of your code that may need closer attention.

For example, did you know that if you leave out a "*maxlength*" attribute on your <INPUT> tags, your application will usually throw an error? That means that, if the corresponding field in your database has a limit of fifty (50) characters, an error will be thrown the moment someone enters fifty-one (51) characters in the field. The Secret Agents testing tool will find potential errors similar to this and alert you to the problem before one of your testers or end-users comes across it.

To keep costs low and to make this tool affordable for the masses, Secret Agents is using the Application Service Provider (ASP) model. The tool is accessible on a monthly subscription basis,. ranging between $50-100/month. Go to **SecretAgents.com** for more details on this testing tool. The only perceived downside of this tool is that the text parser can be incorrect at times and may find too many bugs. This can be discouraging, and some developers do not feel they have the time to fix all the errors.

There are a few other HTML code testing tools which will do similar tests as the Secret Agents tool, specifically on your HTML code. This can be helpful to clean up your HTML, but will not help your CFML. **WebSiteGarage.com** has an excellent HTML code tester.

Site Monitoring

The last type of testing tool is a **site monitoring** tool. This can monitor your server(s) and verify that they are running correctly. When your server does have downtime, you can be notified directly to your pager or cell phone, or have it run a specific action to attempt to bring it back up automatically. There are numerous tools available to do this type of monitoring. Secret Agents will also offer this type of monitoring starting in late Fall 2000.

One thing to look for in this type of tool is that the test be done **off** your network. Sometimes errors arise in the network itself, i.e., a bad router or hub. If you are testing within your own network and a router is dead, you may never know that your site is down.

Keeping Within the Budget

If you have a budget to meet on your project (as most of us do), use as many of these tools as you can. Each will save you tremendous amounts of time, which quickly will prove to pay for the cost of the tools. However, these tools do not replace good old-fashioned manual testing. Get your end-users, clients, coworkers, friends and family involved in trying to find the logical and perfection bugs. The level of thoroughness depends on how much time and how many testers you have. The more users you have trying to find bugs, the faster you will find them.

CHAPTER 7: Securing a Fusebox Appplication

One common web application question is, "How can I create secured sections of my site?" This may seem like a straightforward question with a single answer, but it is not. There are numerous ways to secure a web application: Some are simple, others are more complex. But security is a basic component of any web application. There is and will always be a need to create secured areas of an application, which is why we will describe some of the challenges associated with securing an application, and some potential solutions.

Let's face it: **Security through obscurity just doesn't work.** For example: Storing the private tools on a separate server with no domain name and accessing it through a simple IP address, i.e., an obscure URL, is not a good idea. Sooner or later, if the information is important enough, someone will figure out where the obscure information is and will be able to access it. The minute you need to demonstrate your application and the person to whom you are demonstrating it sees the IP address, your private site is no longer secure. If the information you will be publishing on the web is important, read this chapter thoroughly.

Existing ColdFusion Security Options

There is a tag built into the ColdFusion server called <CFAUTHENTICATE>, but to be honest, we have not yet encountered a single CF developer who has made this tag and its associated functions work correctly. This is a problem. For a generic login application to work, it must be easy to set up and administer. More importantly, it must be easy to integrate into an application.

Creating a generic login application is quite complex. Writing a generic login application that is open enough to work in any application is not an easy task. We will attempt to show a solution that has worked for us numerous times, but may not work in all situations. This particular solution is not a mandatory part of the current Fusebox specifications. It is merely a collection of suggestions.

There are a few different concepts to understand before looking at how you can secure a web application:

a) Securing your web servers from non-web-based attacks;
b) Understanding the three main types of users;
c) Understanding groups of users;
d) Storing user security information;

e) *App_Login.cfm* and *App_Secure.cfm*;
f) Defining the five main areas of a secured web application;
g) Understanding the importance of forcing users to go through *index.cfm* files;
h) Keeping the user's focus after they have logged in;
i) Integrating existing user data;
j) Creating backup plans for when someone does get in.

Securing Your Web Servers from Non-Web-Based Attacks

ColdFusion can run on NT, Solaris, HP-UX, and Linux, with just about any database, on just about every platform, and just about any mail server, LDAP server, FTP and a few other things. Being able to secure your web servers from backdoor intruders that are attacking through non-web-based attacks is beyond the scope of this book. It is, however, a primary responsibility of your server administrator, so let's move on.

Understanding the Three Types of Users

Let's take a look at "who" will use a web application. Step back away from the groups of users that may look at your specific application and look at the different types of users who may use ANY Fusebox application. There are three (3) main types of users to pay attention to:

1. **Public Users** (You know nothing about them.)
2. **Registered Public Users** (They have a *#client.user_id#* or similar unique identifier.)
3. **Registered Private Users** (They have a *#client.user_id#* and a *#client.user_groups#*.)

Public users are users whom your site knows nothing about. These users are completely anonymous to your site and in general are not given very many privileges on a web site. Because you do not know who they are, you cannot connect them to any records in the database until they tell you more information and obtain some sort of identifier connecting only that user to that user's data.

Once a public user has freely registered some information (this is completely up to you) and they have been given a *#client.user_id#* through the registration process (a variable that connects them to their information), they become a **Registered Public User.** This user may be given access to some areas of a site along with being allowed to do certain things, but because they are still not truly known, other than filling out various forms, registered public users should not be able to edit data other than their own.

For example, you don't want anyone in the world to fill out some information about who they are and immediately be able to edit the prices on your product data. This would be absurd. Tasks such as editing data should only be done by users who have been given this privilege.

To do these types of tasks, a user must belong to the appropriate group of users who have been given permission to do so. After a user has registered and has been given a *#client.user_id#*, you may want to assign that user to a particular group(s) of users. By assigning them to various groups of users, you will grant them access to certain areas of the site that can only be viewed by those groups of users.

Once they have been assigned to one or more groups, they should have a variable called *#client.user_groups#*. This should be a list of all the groups to which they belong.

Once they have both a *client.user_id* and a *client.user_groups*, they are now a **Registered Private User**.

How users are assigned to the various groups necessary for your site is completely up to you. Groups of users are different in every application, which is why this method of security will work in ANY Fusebox application.

Understanding Groups of Users

Before any web application is secured, the most important thing to do is to identify the "groups" of users that will be accessing the different areas of the application. Groups of users are people who need to access the same sections of a site.

For example, in an e-commerce application, you may have a "product administrators" group, and a "customer service" group. People who answer other peoples' questions concerning their orders do not have a need to edit the products in a site. And conversely; the product administrators do not have a need to access user information. In addition, there are cases where both groups may need to access the same area, such as a product administrator who must be able to view a single user's order history, or to add/edit frequently asked questions about products.

User groups is an important concept. No section of a web application should be secured to individual users, because this is not a scalable solution. Having to edit code for every single user is a management nightmare and very error-prone. Dealing only with groups of users is the better solution. Each user can be classified as belonging to a specific group and your security measures can be applied en masse.

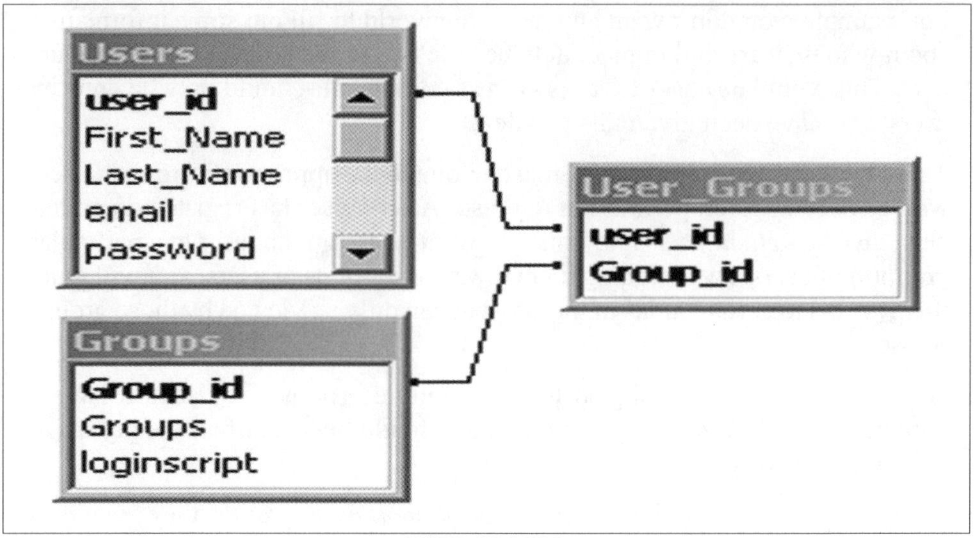

USER GROUPS

Storing User Security Information

There are two commonly used methods of storing user security information: In databases and in LDAP directories. Most web developers are already familiar with databases, and unless you have reasons not to, Fusebox recommends sticking with a database to handle your user security information. By storing security information in a database, you can easily relate various bits of data to a *user_ID* and use a single method (SQL statements) for verifying that the user may edit the data.

If your application is anything more than simple static HTML, chances are that you are already be managing a database, but **not** necessarily an LDAP server. The less things to manage, the higher level of security you will be able to achieve.

When should you use an LDAP directory? When you already have one in place that contains your user information and you are not willing (or wanting) to switch to a database to store your user information. An example of this is if your mail server, which is most likely an LDAP directory, contains your user information, and you want to tie your mail servers data directly into your application.

Regardless of how you store your user security information, this technique of securing a Fusebox application will work. Since most users will be using a database to store their user security information, we will focus on the database method from here on.

App_Login.cfm and *App_Secure.cfm*

> **Note:** While it may initially feel like *App_Login.cfm* and *App_Secure.cfm* are being dictated to you, the rules as to what they should and shouldn't do are actually more a set of concepts than a strict set of rules. If you feel you have better ideas, by all means add them into your application. After testing your ideas, if they feel sound, send them to us at **Fusebox.org**, so we can improve Fusebox. Understand that security scripts can indeed be done differently without affecting the Fusebox concepts.

App_Login.cfm is unique to Fusebox. This file is used whenever a user logs into the system or creates a new Registered Public User account. It verifies the user's identity and sets both *#client.user_id#* and *#client.user_groups#*. Whether this file checks a database or LDAP server (or some other type of storage device) doesn't matter; it is the concept of this file that matters most.

App_Login.cfm can be called from either a login script or from a registration script. With either method, the user's e-mail (or user name) and password are passed in. The file then verifies who the user is and sets the appropriate *#client.user_id#* and *#client.user_groups#*.

Here is an example of our *App_Login.cfm* file. For users to login, they pass in their email address and password. This file first checks to see if the user has a record in the users table. If not, it sends the user back to the login screen to login as someone else. If *App_Login.cfm* finds the user in the table, it sets the *#client.user_id#* variable.

Once the user has successfully logged in, *App_Login.cfm* will check to see if the user belongs to any groups. If so, a list of these groups is set in *#client.user_groups#*.

```
<!--- Set required variables --->
<CFPARAM name="attributes.email">
<CFPARAM name="attributes.password">

<!--- Check to see if the user exists in the database. --->
<CFQUERY name="checkforuser" datasource="#request.maindsn#">
     select user_id,email
          from users
               where Email="#trim(attributes.Email)#"
               and password="#trim(attributes.password)#"
</CFQUERY>

<!--- If the user was not found in the database, redirect him/her to the login
form, --->
<CFIF not val(checkforuser.recordcount)>
     <CFIF not len(attributes.Email)>
          <CFSET client.message="Please enter your Email address">
```

```
    <CFELSEIF not len(attributes.password)>
        <CFSET client.message="Please enter your Password">
    <CFELSE>
        <CFSET client.message="This Email address was not found or the
        password you entered was incorrect<BR>click the button below to
        have your <BR>password emailed to you">
    </CFIF>
    <CFLOCATION url="index.cfm?fuseaction=
    loginform&#request.urltoken#" addtoken="no">
</CFIF>

<!--- If the user was found in the table, set the #client.user_id#; they are now
a Registered Public user. --->
<CFSET client.user_id=checkforuser.user_id>

<!--- Now check for any groups they may belong to. --->
<CFQUERY name="checkforgroups" datasource="#request.maindsn#">
    select ug.group_id,g.login_script
        from user_groups ug,groups g
        where ug.group_id=g.group_id
        and ug.user_id=#val(client.user_id)#
</CFQUERY>

<CFIF checkforgroups.recordcount>
    <!--- If they do belong to groups, set the #client.user_groups# variable;
    users who belong to groups are Registered Private Users. --->
    <CFSET client.user_groups=valuelist(checkforgroups.group_id)>
    <!--- The following code is in case a certain group requires additional
    information; we may need to include another .cfm template to grab this
    information.--->
    <CFLOOP query="checkforgroups">
        <CFIF len(trim(login_script))>
            <CFINCLUDE template="#request.cfroot#/#login_script#">
        </CFIF>
    </CFLOOP>
</CFIF>
```

App_secure.cfm is a new file being introduced to Fusebox. This file is used to secure various areas of your Fusebox application. It verifies that the user has the necessary permissions to access the next set of code. If the user does not have the correct permissions, s/he is sent to another Fuseaction, which asks the user to login as someone else. Where the user is sent is up to you, as the developer.

The following code is a cross-application script that verifies that the user is logged in (Registered Public User), which we found to be a very useful. If the user is not logged in, the script sends him/her back to the login form, using the <CF_RETURNFUSEACTION>, which lets the user maintain his/her focus after logging in/creating a new account. Take a look at the code:

```
<!--- required variable --->
<CFPARAM name="attributes.groups" default="">
<!--- optional variable --->
<CFPARAM name="attributes.message" default="You do not have access
to this page">

<!--- The following code verifies whether the current user is logged in and is
at least a registered public user. If not registered, it will send the user to the
login form Fuseaction in the /members application--->
<CFIF not isdefined("client.user_id")>
    <CFSET client.message="#attributes.message#">
    <CF_RETURNFUSEACTION
        action="set"
        returnurl="#cgi.path_info#?#request.attributeslist#"
        gotourl="/members/index.cfm?fuseaction=loginform">
</CFIF>

<!--- The following code verifies that the user belongs to the appropriate
group and is a Registered Private User. The group attribute is passed into
this tag, which contains a list of all the groups that are allowed to access the
code. --->
<CFSET loginnow="no">
<CFIF len(attributes.groups) and isdefined("client.user_groups")>
    <CFSET loginnow="yes">
    <CFLOOP LIST="#attributes.groups#" index="group">
        <CFIF listfind(client.user_groups,group)>
            <CFSET loginnow="no">
            <CFBREAK>
        </CFIF>
    </CFLOOP>
</CFIF>

<!--- If the user does not belong to the requested group, s/he is sent to the
login form --->
<CFIF loginnow>
    <CFSET client.message="#attributes.message#">
    <CF_RETURNFUSEACTION
        action="set"
        returnurl="#cgi.path_info#?#request.attributeslist#"
        gotourl="/members/index.cfm?fuseaction=loginform">
</CFIF>
```

The Five Main Access Points of a Secured Web Application

Most web applications have a variety of users. Just about every web application has a "public" section. This means that users who have not logged in must be able to get to certain areas of the site without logging in. Of course, these areas of your site should not contain sensitive information.

At the same time, most, if not all, web applications do have sensitive sections which should be secured. For example, these sections may display private information or allow users to enter or edit information in a database.

There are five main ways your application can allow your users to access these secured sections:

1. Securing every Fuseaction in a given circuit application;
2. Securing every Fuseaction in multiple circuit applications;
3. Securing some Fuseactions in a circuit application, but not all;
4. Securing certain areas of a page or a single Fuseaction;
5. Securing data

The word "secure" is used very loosely here. Different users may all be permitted to access the same Fuseaction but, depending on who the user is and what that user's group is allowed to do, the Fuseaction may perform a different function for each of them.

To **secure all the Fuseactions in a single circuit application** means that, whenever a user attempts to call any Fuseaction in a single *index.cfm* file, s/he must login as a user who is allowed to access that circuit application. If the user is not allowed to access the circuit application, s/he will be sent to a login screen with a message stating that s/he does not have proper permissions. Include the *app_secure.cfm* file in the circuit's *index.cfm* file, to enable the entire circuit to be secure.

Securing multiple circuit applications could potentially be done two ways: Either include the *app_secure.cfm* file into your *app_globals.cfm* file, or include the *app_secure.cfm* file in each of the *index.cfm* files.

The first method is not recommended, for two reasons: It requires you to have a separate *app_globals.cfm* file that includes the *app_secure.cfm* file. This second *app_globals.cfm* file will be almost identical as the first, except that now you will need to maintain two separate files.

The second problem with the first method of including the *app_secure.cfm* file in the *app_globals* is that it is very error prone. You may think your circuit application is secure, when you have accidentally included the public *app_globals.cfm* instead of the private *app_globals.cfm*. It is very easy to see:

```
<CFINCLUDE template="../../app_globals.cfm">
```

and not realize that it should be:

```
<CFINCLUDE template="../app_globals.cfm">
```

(note the number of "../").

The second method, including the *app_secure.cfm* file directly in the *index.cfm* file and only having a single *app_globals.cfm* file, is the **least error prone method** of securing your entire *index.cfm* file. To do this, simply <CFINCLUDE> the *app_secure.cfm* file at the top of every *index.cfm* file, before the *app_locals.cfm* file. Call *app_secure.cfm* **after** *app_globals.cfm*, but **before** *app_locals.cfm* gets processed.

The *app_secure.cfm* file should go before the *app_locals.cfm* file simply for speed purposes. Some *app_locals.cfm* files can add tens to hundreds to, in rare cases, thousands of milliseconds to your pages. If the user is not allowed to view that page, s/he will not need the variables being set in the *app_locals.cfm* file.

Sometimes an application only contains certain Fuseactions that need to be secured. For example, in an e-commerce site, you may have a */products* circuit application which contains Fuseactions for listing, searching and viewing products. But this same circuit application also may contain Fuseactions for adding, editing and deleting products. These Fuseactions cannot and should not be accessible by the public user.

Securing individual Fuseactions within a circuit application is as easy as including the *app_secure.cfm* file as the first line in the <CFCASE> tag. Determine whether a Fuseaction can be viewed by anyone, only users who are logged in, or only users belonging to certain groups.

- If this Fuseaction can be viewed by anyone, nothing needs to be done. Treat the Fuseaction as you would normally.
- If the user needs to simply be logged in (i.e. have a *client.user_id*) call the *app_secure.cfm* file using <CFMODULE> and do **not** pass in a "groups" attribute.
- Lastly, if the user needs to be both logged in and belong to a certain group, pass in a list of groups the approved user needs to belong to.

How to secure certain sections of a page. For example, in the same */products* circuit application mentioned above, you may allow your vendors (a specific user group) to view a product and to see sales statistics on the same page as the product information that your general public (a different user group) sees. This allows you to have maximum reuse of your code. It allows you to reuse your code, simply changing the way it works depending on who the user is.

This doesn't have to be limited to display code. Action code can be secured just as easily. If there is an insert statement that you want only certain groups of users to run, then you can just as easily wrap the insert query with a <CFIF> statement checking to see if a user belongs to a certain group.

The last area of concern is **securing data**. This is not about how to keep users from hacking your database backend. This is specifically about keeping users from being able to change other user's code through the application by changing variables. If your user already has a *#client.user_id#* variable, you want only that specific user to be able to access data that pertains to him- or herself.

For example, if you passed the "*user_id*" variable in the URL instead of as a client variable, someone could very easily change "who" they are by changing the value of that URL variable.

This will more likely not be the only variable that needs to be secured, which is fine. The concept of Fusebox security is that it is designed to easily secure any application. The *#client.user_id#* will be the most commonly used variable for securing data, but you could just as easily set other client variables during logon. If a variable contains sensitive information that could change data in the database, store that variable as a client variable. When client variables are stored in a database (CF 4+), they can scale to very large numbers, while allowing for clustered servers.

Securing data in the database means only allowing users with the appropriate client variables the ability to select/insert/update/delete data. But being able to change data is only part of the problem. It will also be necessary to secure data from even being viewable. This is fairly easy to do. When running any SQL statement that needs to be secured, simply append the necessary security client variables to the query. For example:

```
Select *
    From orders
    Where user_id=#val(client.user_id)#
```

Or

```
Insert into orders(order_id,user_id....)
    Values(#max_id#,#val(client.user_id)#....)
```

The Importance of Forcing Users to Go Through *index.cfm* Files

There is one potential security hole that a programmer will quickly notice: If a user attempts to access one of the files directly, instead of going through the *index.cfm* file, (i.e., go directly to *dsp_editproduct.cfm*), he or she could bypass the security login altogether.

This is where the *application.cfm* file comes into play. *Application.cfm* is a file that the CF server runs whenever any *.cfm* file is called. In every *application.cfm* file, there should be the following lines of code to ensure that users **must** go through the *index.cfm* file:

```
<CFIF not findnocase("index.cfm",cgi.CF_TEMPLATE_PATH)>
    <CFLOCATION url="index.cfm?badfile=yes">
</CFIF>
```

The *#CGI.CF_TEMPLATE_PATH#* variable contains the server path to the file being called. For example:

C:\inetpub\wwwroot\products\index.cfm

Or

C:\inetpub\wwwroot\products\dsp_editproduct.cfm

If someone attempts to access: **www.domain.com/products/dsp_editproduct.cfm**, the three lines of code placed in the *application.cfm* file automatically sends them to the default Fuseaction in that directory.

The script is simple. All it is doing is comparing what ColdFusion template the user is accessing, and if it is not the *index.cfm* file, it redirects them to the *index.cfm* file.

Keeping the User's Focus After They Have Logged In

It is important to allow a user to maintain their focus after they have logged into a secured section of the web site. If they were browsing for products or viewing an article prior to logging on, they should not be discouraged from continuing to do so. Security is a vital area of any software that is used by multiple people, but user experience is also an important area to be considered.

Luckily, there is a very handy (and free) CF tag called <CF_RETURNFUSEACTION> that will allow you to maintain a user's focus after the user has logged in. This tag has two different actions: *set* and *return*. All the tag does is store a list of URLs (with URL variables) in a client variable separated by *#chr(13)# (carriage return character)*. When a user is ready to return back to where s/he came, the tag will select the last URL in the list and <CFLOCATION> them to that application.

In short, this allows someone to be viewing a single product, i.e.:

```
www.domain.com/products/index.cfm?Fuseaction=viewproduct&product_id=512
```

Then click the "login" link, which takes them to a three-page user registration application or to a single-page login application. When the user is finished there, he or she will be sent back to the original URL.

This way, after the user has gone through either the login process or the registration process, they are back to where they were before, but now they are simply logged in.

Integrating Existing User Data

Securing a multi-user application is nothing new. This means that, in existing companies, it is very common to have already collected user information and, in many cases, group information. If a new security method is being suggested, it is important to be able to integrate existing user information into the system.

This can be done one of two ways: Either replicate the data (i.e., copy it from a legacy database or LDAP server) or build the new securing mechanism to work off the existing legacy database or LDAP server.

The security mechanism we recommend for a Fusebox application is fairly simple, and either method described above would work. There is a preference for storing security data in a database not in an LDAP server. LDAP may be a little faster, but it is less widely used than a basic relational database. Because of this, after the security mechanism is built and handed to another developer, they will have a harder time extracting user information.

In this case, speed concerns are negligible, compared to development times. If your database cannot handle a single Select statement per logged-in user, it is time to upgrade your database software.

Unless you have no other choice, stick with a relational database.

However, a relational database may not work for everyone. A good example of when this may not work is with subscription-based sites, such as on-line image or text libraries. Sites that need to secure files that are not *.cfm* extensions may not be able to store their login data in a relational database. These types of sites tend to use the web server security to secure these files. That may require them to access an LDAP server, commonly used by web servers for handling logins.

Creating Backup Plans for When Someone Does Get In

There are a few things that you can do as precautions in case someone does get in. Not having a solid identity on the web makes it possible for a user to "spoof" another user. This simply means pretending to be someone they are not. A very simple example of this would be if someone accessed your database and published your site's user names and passwords on the Web. Because your application is looking for those two things, anyone who has those two pieces of information can access your application, at will.

Unless you have a more secure way of verifying that users are who they say they are, it is possible your user data could become compromised. There are a few things you can do to avoid this or stop it from continuing.

One very important step in this process is logging: Tracking when your users log in and log off. You can store what user is logging in, at what time, their IP address, if they have logged in multiple times from various locations, and anything else you may feel necessary. By logging this information, you can create a script that runs on a scheduled basis, comparing how often an account is accessed from various locations. That way, it is possible to check for when a user's account has been illegitimately accessed.

CHAPTER 8: Fusebox Custom Tags and Variable Scoping

Imagine, if you will, a new developer learning a new programming language. Her name is Susan. She's been focusing all her attention on memorizing the proper syntax and on debugging her first (small) application so it works correctly. After programming for a while, Susan begins to hear more experienced programmers say, "Reuse your code as much as possible." Initially, she does not understand these comments about code reuse. Susan can't fully appreciate the vehemence with which her mentors espouse writing reusable code. Then, the second application comes along, and she quickly realizes that she already wrote some code to handle a user login and some code to manage a database of products.

So what does she do?

Like any smart programmer, she'll reuse the existing code. "Good coders write good code, great coders steal great code," she thinks. To do this, she uses her favorite keyboard shortcut friend, Ctrl-C/Ctrl-V (copy and paste). This gets the job done quickly and easily, but there is an inherent problem brewing.

The harm comes when she tries to manage two applications that share some of the same code. One day, she realizes there's a much better way to handle the login process, so she makes the changes in the second application. But now the first one is out of synchronization with the second. She forgets about updating the now old application until her boss calls her up, angry as to why the second application's login process is so much faster than the old one's. Bummer.

Most of the time this isn't a big deal. If the code a developer copies is from a completely different application, the changes to the process inherent in the new piece might not be made on the original application. It **becomes** a big deal when a developer has to manage many applications. Imagine what happens when Susan has to deal with fifty different applications and be sure that the shared code is up-to-date on all of them. This is where ColdFusion custom tags save the day.

Object Oriented Programming (OOP) was designed to make reusing code easy and powerful. Languages like C++ and Java are heavily object-oriented. These languages claim this as one of their big advantages. So, hardcore programmers spend years mastering these languages. The rest of the programmers (who are less interested in being nerds and more interested in building their businesses) get stuck on terminology like "classes" and "polymorphism".

Modularity Through Custom Tags

In ColdFusion 3, Allaire offered something new to the world of web programming called "**custom tags**". Allaire's theory was that a language could have excellent methods of reuse without being as confusing as Object Oriented Programming. They thought that if developers can understand how a file is included, they should be able to understand a custom tag.

Most web application servers, such as PHP, ASP, Perl, JSP, etc., have methods of including code. Simply put, this means storing a section of your code in a file and including the code for that section in another file. This offers a way to write code once and use it again, somewhere else.

Including files like this is useful but can cause problems. Object Oriented Programming had solutions for these problems years ago. Skipping over all the jargon, these problems boil down to one point: How do you deal with variables?

Juggling Variables

Here's an example of the problem. You have a team of two developers, Joe and Bob. Joe is responsible for writing half of the application, and Bob writes the other half. They decide to reuse shared code using the above method of including files. Being programmers, they don't talk to each other much. All of a sudden, they realize their application is acting very strangely. For the most part, it's working, but every once in a while, a variable seems to have an incorrect value and they cannot explain why.

```
<!--- code_by_joe.cfm--->
<CFSET myvariable="hello">
<CFINCLUDE template="code_by_bob.cfm">
<CFOUTPUT>#myvariable#</CFOUTPUT>

<!--- code_by_bob.cfm--->
<CFSET myvariable="good-bye">
```

What ColdFusion is really seeing here is:

```
<!--- code_by_joe.cfm--->
<CFSET myvariable="hello">
<!--- code_by_bob.cfm--->
<CFSET myvariable="good-bye">
<CFOUTPUT>#myvariable#</CFOUTPUT>
```

What's wrong?

Global vs. Local Scope

Joe and Bob both set a variable with the same name. Since the second file was included, it affected the variable. In this case, all variables are "**global**", meaning that the variables exist in every file that has been included.

Global variables are not all bad; they simply may cause problems when an application gets large enough.

Allaire built a solution to this in **custom tags**. A custom tag works similarly to an included file except variables must be explicitly passed into and out of the custom tag. Variables existing inside the custom tag do not exist outside. Here is the same basic code (notice the <CFMODULE> instead of <CFINCLUDE>, which is the difference between custom tags and straight-forward including):

```
<!--- code_by_joe.cfm--->
<CFSET myvariable="hello">
<CFMODULE template="code_by_bob.cfm">
<CFOUTPUT>#myvariable#</CFOUTPUT>

<!--- code_by_bob.cfm--->
<CFSET my variable="good-bye">
```

What ColdFusion is really seeing in this case is:

```
<!--- code_by_joe.cfm--->
<CFSET myvariable="hello">
<CFOUTPUT>#myvariable#</CFOUTPUT>
```

Note that what ColdFusion really sees seems to leave out the *code_by_bob.cfm*. This is not really the case; the use of <CFMODULE> means that the "*myvariable*" set inside *code_by_bob.cfm* does not affect the "*myvariable*" in the *code_by_joe.cfm* file. Bob's variable has become a "**local**" variable.

There are three other important variable scopes to understand with custom tags:

Attributes Scope

If you want to pass variables into the custom tag, use the **attributes scope** inside the file and place the name and value in the tag call. The syntax is below:

```
<!--- code_by_joe.cfm--->
<CFSET joesvariable="hello ">
<CFMODULE template="code_by_bob.cfm"
    bobsvariable="#joesvariable#">

<!--- code_by_bob.cfm--->
<CFOUTPUT>#attributes.bobsvariable #</CFOUTPUT>
```

Caller Scope

Oftentimes, you may need to change the value of a variable that exists in the template that called the custom tag. In this case, use the **caller scope**. This scope can set variables in recursive, hierarchical parent templates like this:

```
<!--- code_by_jill.cfm--->
<CFSET jillsvariable="hello">
<CFOUTPUT>#jillsvariable#</CFOUTPUT>
<CFMODULE template="code_by_joe.cfm">

<!--- code_by_joe.cfm--->
<CFOUTPUT>#caller.jillsvariable#</CFOUTPUT>
<CFMODULE template="code_by_bob.cfm" >

<!--- code_by_bob.cfm--->
<CFOUTPUT>#caller.caller.jillsvariable#</CFOUTPUT>
```

This is a bit more complicated. Caller scope can bypass the requirement of needing to explicitly pass variables to the custom tag.

Here is an explanation: Our new programmer Jill set a variable, displayed it, then called Joe's template. Joe's template displayed her variable (even though it wasn't explicitly passed to the custom tag). Joe's template then called Bob's template. Bob's template also displayed Jill's variable.

The caller scope is useful, but it can quickly get messy if you do not know how high up the variable you need access to lives. How would Bob know that Jill's variable was two levels up? What if Jill's template called Bob's custom tag? All of a sudden it would be one level up and *caller.caller.jillsvariable* wouldn't exist in Bob's custom tag.

Request Scope

The **request scope** offers a potential solution to this messiness. Remember, we said global variables are not all bad. This is a case where you might want to use a global variable. The request scope is a global variable that will exist at every level of custom tag, no matter how many levels deep it is, and is always available as "request". Look at how much simpler this becomes:

```
<!--- code_by_jill.cfm--->
<CFSET request.jillsvariable="hello">
<CFOUTPUT>#request.jillsvariable#</CFOUTPUT>
<CFMODULE template="code_by_joe.cfm">

<!--- code_by_joe.cfm--->
<CFOUTPUT>#request.jillsvariable#</CFOUTPUT>
<CFMODULE template="code_by_bob.cfm" >

<!--- code_by_bob.cfm--->
```

```
<CFOUTPUT>#request.jillsvariable#</CFOUTPUT>
```

"*Request.jillsvariable*" is called the same way in each template, regardless of whether it was called as a <CFINCLUDE> or a <CFMODULE> nested five custom tags deep. This scope is great for storing your global information.

However, you don't want to use this scope for ALL of your variables because you will encounter the problem we faced when using <CFINCLUDE>, the double-setting of a same-named variable by two developers in different sections of the same code.

What variables **should** you store in the request scope? Variables like datasource names, web server mappings and CF server are not (or rarely) going to change across any file in the application, therefore do not need to be attributes or caller scoped. These are good candidates for request scoping.

But another alternative is to use the application scope for these types of variables.

Application Scope

The **application scope** is a fantastic place to store the types of global variables you might otherwise consider placing in the request scope. There is one great advantage of using the request scope over the application scope.

Because of the way the ColdFusion server handles these two different scopes, the application scope requires all reads and writes to the variable be **locked for single-threaded access**. This is because there is only one copy of any given application-scoped variable in the server's memory. However, if two user sessions attempt to access that application-scope variable at the same time, nasty errors could occur, and your application might crash.

Any request-scoped variable is only available to the given page request, and therefore intrinsically does not need to be locked. Two sessions never use the same request. Two users cannot make the same request. Even if two requests for the same Fuseaction or section of code occur at the exact same time, the ColdFusion server handles each one as two separate requests. No locking is needed of request scope variables.

Coordinating Request Scope Variables Through *App_globals_cfm*

Alas, there is a catch. **Request scope variables do not "persist"**, like application, server, session, or client scope variables. The way around this is to set all your application-scope variables to request-scope variables in one place: *app_globals.cfm*. Here's an example of a good way to do it:

```
<!--- app_globals.cfm --->
<CFLOCK name="application.applicationName"><!---This code for locking
is CF4.0 syntax-->
<CFSET request.StatesList = application.StatesList>
</CFLOCK>
```

Now, the contents of the persistent variable "*application.StatesList*" is available anywhere in the application, without the need for continually locking access, in the request scope.

There is one thing to note, though. If the application variable is a complex data structure like a query, array, or structure, setting it to the request scope will not produce the desired effect. The request scope only becomes a pointer to the original, application scope variable. You should use the CF function Duplicate() (Version 4.5+) to make a copy of the value and assign it to the request scope.

Before moving onto learning how to create Fusebox custom tags, be sure to play around with basic tags. Once you feel you have an understanding for how tags work, let's get a little more complex.

Creating a Fusebox Custom Tag

Most custom tags are fairly simple. They attempt to solve very small problems and are made up of a single CFML template. For the most part, these simple tags are incredibly useful, but wouldn't it be amazing if we could make custom tags from more than one file? How about a custom tag that allowed us to reuse an entire Fusebox circuit application?

With Fusebox this is possible; in fact, it's easy. You may not realize it, but the way you've been coding your Fusebox applications has already set you up to call any circuit application as a custom tag. In fact, if you've been coding according to the ideas set forth in this book, it should be as simple as calling the *index.cfm* file as a <CFMODULE>:

```
<CFMODULE template="products/index.cfm"
    FUSEACTION="reports "
    report_id="#attributes.report_id#">
```

That's really all there is to it. Just pass attributes like you would to a normal custom tag. The Fuseaction determines what you are trying to do and includes the appropriate files. Fusebox takes over from there. It couldn't be easier!

The <CF_FORMURL2ATTRIBUTES> that you have been calling in *app_globals.cfm* will change all form and URL variables to attributes-scope variables. As long as you have been scoping all of your variables with attributes, the switchover to a custom tag is a piece of cake!

CHAPTER 9: Becoming a Five-Day Fusebox Developer (FD^2)

A Brief History of ValueMusic.Com, the First FD^2 Project

Stacy's Music Store, based in Charlottesville, Virginia, has been in business for the last fifty years. In 1997, the owner, Carl Stacy, decided to take the successful musical instrument retail store his family had built and turn it into a web store. His site would differ from his competitors by pooling people-friendly music stores together into one unique e-commerce system. Thus came the birth of **ValueMusic.com**.

ValueMusic.com has gone through numerous development stages over the last two years. The impetus to the most current version was an upcoming National American Music (NAM) show. ValueMusic.com had reserved a booth, but needed a bug-free version of the site.

The first version used Microsoft™'s Active Server Pages® and a Microsoft Access® back end. The second version was built using a free e-commerce package with a Perl back end. The consultants who built these two versions were no longer available.

A ValueMusic.com investor approached Steve Nelson and a few of his developers, asking for assistance. Steve did not know Perl well enough and did not know the off-the-shelf e-commerce product at all. He also felt that finding and fixing the various bugs would take much longer than the available two weeks. With the NAM show approaching, something needed to be done.

Steve proposed his theory on speed development (which he had been working on for months but had yet to put to the test) to the ValueMusic.com team. The theory was simple:

> **Provided that**
>
> **the market for and the features of the application are already known, the correct development system was chosen, and a single, suitable developer was available,**
>
> **VERSION 1 OF ANY WEB APPLICATION CAN BE DESIGNED, BUILT AND TESTED IN FIVE DAYS.**

This concept seemed incredible at the time, due to all of the intricacies of ValueMusic.com, but Steve was confident his theory was correct. Since ValueMusic.com had no other options and just a two-week deadline, the team wasted no time and accepted Steve's "crazy" proposition.

Steve went into his small basement office on Friday and five days later came back with a made-from-scratch, working Version 1 of ValueMusic.com. This consisted of twenty-two circuit applications, and over 7,000 lines of CFML/HTML code.

This case study will show how this feat was accomplished and how a good developer can become a **Five-Day Fusebox Developer**, or as we call it, an **FD²**.

This is not for the faint of heart or for the beginner, although any developer can learn from and incorporate facets of these techniques, realizing significant improvements in productivity.

The biggest benefits will be realized by the advanced Fusebox developer who wants to go to the next level. Learn these techniques, and you will be the gladiator of web developers, an über-programmer. You will be worth a team of a dozen "regular" developers. The only place you will be paid your true worth is in the entrepreneurial environment, via stock, and lots of it.

Before the Five-Day Development Cycle Begins

Beautification Can Wait; Style Cannot

First things first. Before any coding can begin, it is important to agree upon the basic user interface for the site. The development of the user interface is **not** built into the Five-Day Development Cycle. This is the work of the graphic artists, not the application developers. The application developers may be involved at this stage, but finalizing the user interface and graphics is a subjective step and could take weeks or months to agree on. It is important to understand what area of the user interface is necessary for the application developer and what is not.

What Is Essential to the User Interface?

The most important aspect of the user interface will be **global navigation** (navigation that exists on every page or many pages), **general colors**, and **style choices** for navigation and the body of the page. Graphics are not critical, but are helpful to an understanding of what the final version will look like. Before the five-day development cycle begins, the graphic artist(s) should be able to give the developer example templates of what the various pages should look like, with and without body content.

What Is Not Essential to the User Interface?

Making the application look beautiful and having all the graphics on every page is not critical at this point. Until the developer knows what needs to be built, designing minor graphics is premature. Worrying about the detailed look of Version 1 of the application is also premature. It is common for areas of an application to completely change overnight, which means that, until the application satisfies the functional requirements, the user interface should be simple and flexible.

> **NOTE**: A Fusebox user interface framework is currently under development. If you are a graphic artist and would like to add your ideas to this collection, contact Steve Nelson at: *m@secretagents.com*.

What Does It Take to Become a Five-Day Fusebox Developer, or FD^2?

There is a serious amount of training required to get to a level where you can truthfully proclaim: "I can build ANY application in five days." However, the amount of time spent training is fairly short and the payoff is huge. Below is a list of essential prerequisite skills that you will need to become a Five-Day Fusebox Developer.

The concepts below form the basic syllabus to help you get started in your training and are not meant to be complete and absolute. It can be hard to know what to learn from any given 800-page technical book. Use this list as a guide to what to study. Learn these concepts first, then move onto the others.

The Prerequisites: Ten Key Programming Concepts You Need to Know Cold

1. HTML, especially tables and forms
2. Advanced Fusebox concepts, such as:
   a. <CF_ReturnFuseaction>
   b. <CF_ReuseForm>
   c. <CF_BodyContent>
3. Database design
4. Fusebox specification and design process
5. Form reuse
6. Complex SQL joins commonly joining 4-6 tables
7. Nested trees in a database
8. Membership, registration, and securing your applications
9. CFML
10. Snippets, hotkeys and keyboard shortcuts

plus one additional, non-programming skill:

11. Being able to think for yourself

The First Key: HTML (*especially tables and forms*)

Since HTML is the primary display language for web applications, it is vital that a Five-Day Fusebox Developer know this language hands-down. Other display languages similar to HTML are being used for different types of display, such as being able to have a display on a WML-enabled phone. WML is a little different than HTML, but the concepts are basically the same. If you know HTML well enough, picking up another markup language should be relatively simple.

The most important concepts to know in HTML are the efficient and proper use of **tables and forms**. These are not incredibly complex, but are vital to every application developer.

Tables are a great way to format a page. Although CSS is beginning to take over some of the page formatting, it is still not standard enough nor is it supported on older browsers enough to replace tables. Tables allow you to place your elements anywhere on the page.

Forms are the other critical concept in HTML that you must understand completely. Forms enable user input, which is necessary for EVERY web application that actually does anything, allowing your user to interact with the data on the server.

The Second Key: Advanced Fusebox Concepts

For more information on these concepts, review Chapter 5 thoroughly.

The Third Key: Database Design

It is sometimes possible to get a feeling for how large an application is by seeing how many tables are in its database. A small application may have a dozen tables in it; a large application may have hundreds of tables in it. The greater the count of volatile tables, the more Fuseactions and circuit applications will be needed to change that data.

You could study databases for years and years without fully understanding them. On the other hand, if you fully grasp the most-used concepts in database design, you'll have the third FD^2 key.

The most critical thing to understand about databases is how tables are related together through **primary key/foreign key relationships**. Each table has a "primary key": This is an identifier for each row or record in the database. A table may also have a "foreign key", which links tables by identifying the necessary primary key of the other table. This concept is what **normalization** is all about. An advanced understanding of the different forms of normalization is not essential.

The next important thing to understand about database design is **how the tables are joined**. There are two main types of joins: one-to-many and many-to-many. This determines how many records can be joined together between the tables.

An example of a one-to-many join is:

"ONE store may have MANY products".

An example of a many-to-many join is:

"MANY students may have MANY teachers".

If you understand the database concepts of primary/foreign keys and how tables can be joined, you can design a database, regardless of number of tables. There are many books on the market on database design. Buy the one that describes these two concepts the best.

The Fourth Key: Fusebox Specification and Design

One of the beautiful things about Fusebox is how easy it is to write specifications and designs for a Fusebox application. This is probably the most important concept in this list – not the first one to learn, but the most important. That's because, to become a Five-Day Fusebox Developer, you need to be able to write a specification for the entire application in a single day. This probably sounds ludicrous to anyone who is used to spending weeks or months building specifications and design for an application. It may sound rushed or incomplete. However, it is possible. Quickly writing specifications requires both talent and training. It **can** be learned.

To build an application, you and your client need to have a basic understanding of what the various areas of the application need to do. As the professional developer, you need to be able to fill in the gaps that the client is missing. You need to learn that when a client says:

"I want my users to be able to fill in a form and add information about themselves",

He REALLY means:

> "I want my users to be able to fill in a form to add their user information, which can be reused to edit their information. I will also need a back end tool that allows my team and I to search for users, to view and edit their information, and to delete users, if necessary."

When building a specification, it is important to be able to understand what the client wants and suggest ways to improve it. Don't be afraid of extra work at the specification stage. Developers may fear they will not be able to complete their project on time if there are added features. Adding these features during development takes a lot of time, but adding the features while designing the application will **not** take much extra time.

It is also vital that you understand the **difference** between the words "Specification" and "Design". Think of them like this:

Specification is: "What the client wants."

Design is: "How you will build what the client wants."

This means that to create a solid specification requires you, your client(s) (no more than two other people at a time), a whiteboard, and your brain all in the same room together. Turn off the phones, order pizza and spend a full day in the room together drawing simple tree diagrams like the ones described in the Specifications and Design chapter.

When you first begin attempting the Five-Day Fusebox Development cycle, specifications and design may take more than a single day. This may occur because the client has not thought about their application **at all**, or you are not able to offer any insights into their application. You **will** gain insights with experience; there is not much you can do about this until you have attempted this process numerous times. Your client, on the other hand, **can** change immediately, by coming to your meeting **prepared** for what they want to do.

The Fifth Key: Reusing Code Through Advanced Fusebox Techniques

If the word "reuse" is not continually in your vocabulary, it should be. As you build your applications, you should always be on the lookout for opportunities to reuse areas of the application. As you continue to work with your clients, they will slowly learn the word "reuse". They may not fully understand the complexity and beauty of its meaning, but they will quickly learn that it saves time, which is their money.

Understanding the advanced Fusebox techniques that permit you to reuse code is vital to being a Five-Day Fusebox Developer. It doesn't matter whether or not you use these specific techniques every day; knowing how and when to use them **does** matter.

<CF_ReuseForm>

Once you understand this tag's use, you will never write another form without it. With this tag, forms can be reused in three different ways: Inserting a new record, updating an existing record and error catching. This tag will fill in the values of each of the fields in your form, depending on where the values are coming from.

Use this tag by placing it above the *<form>* tag on your page. Pass in the action attribute (*new/query/attributes*), pass in the list of variables in your form, and pass in the name of the query to use (*for action=query*). The tag will then set the appropriate values of each of the field names you passed into the tag. Then, use these values in each of the appropriate fields in your form. (See the screen shots on pages 89 and 90.)

When a user is going to add a new record to the database, s/he needs to start with a form that does not contain any data in the fields. This is where you use "*Action=New*", setting all the fields names to NULL, i.e., <CFSET

first_name=“”> It is also important that a value for the primary key be set to NULL, as well. This will tell the next Fuseaction that it should be inserting a record into the database.

When a user is going to edit an existing record in the database, s/he needs to start with existing data already in each of the form fields. This is where to use “*Action=Query*”. It sets the values of each of the fields in your form to values imported from the database.

It is important that the value for the primary key of this record be the proper identifier for this user. By doing this, the next Fuseaction will know that it needs to update the record with that particular primary key in the database.

The last main use of this tag is for server side validation. The server side validation built into ColdFusion is very effective, but it returns a rather ugly, uninviting page, telling the user to hit the back button and fix the appropriate fields. Instead, send the user directly back to the form, filling in the values they have already entered, and indicate where they have entered incorrect information. This is where you use “*Action=Attributes*”. Your application will fill in the values of the fields with those values that exist in the attributes scope, regardless of whether you submitted the form with “*Method=Post*” or “*Method=Get*”.

First, let’s look at some screen shots:

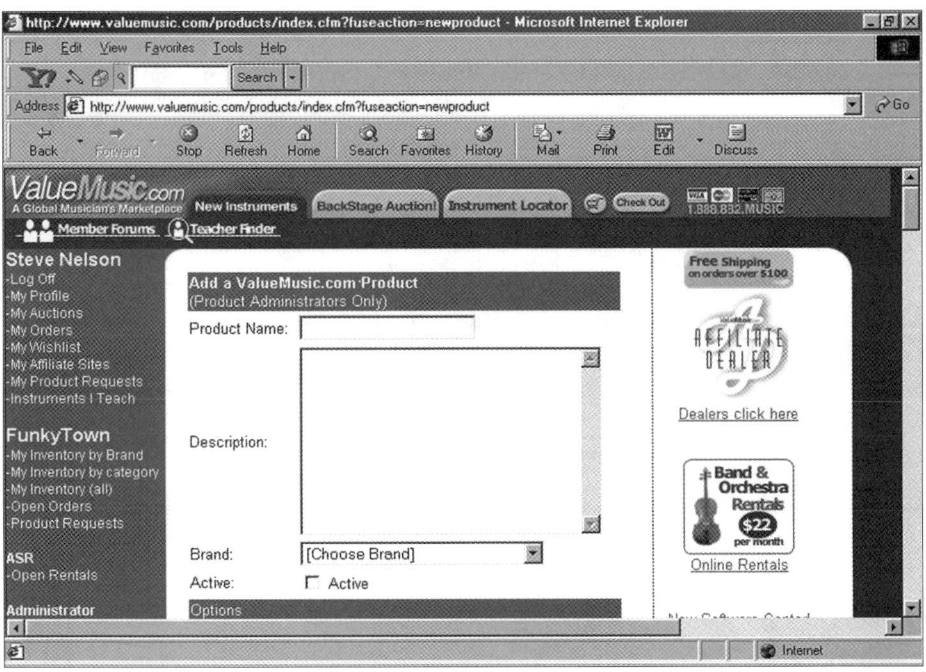

Action = New

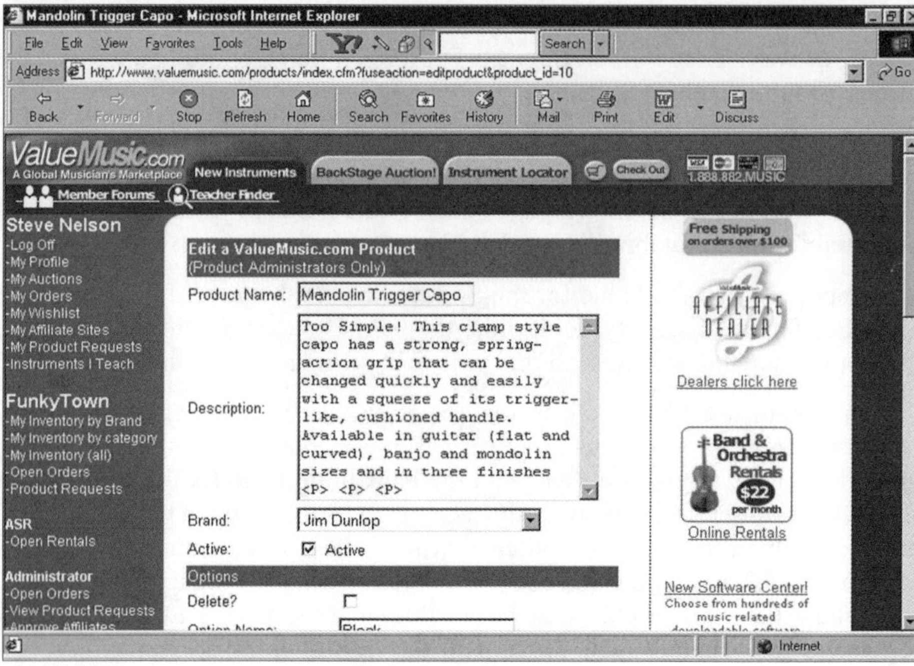

Action = Query

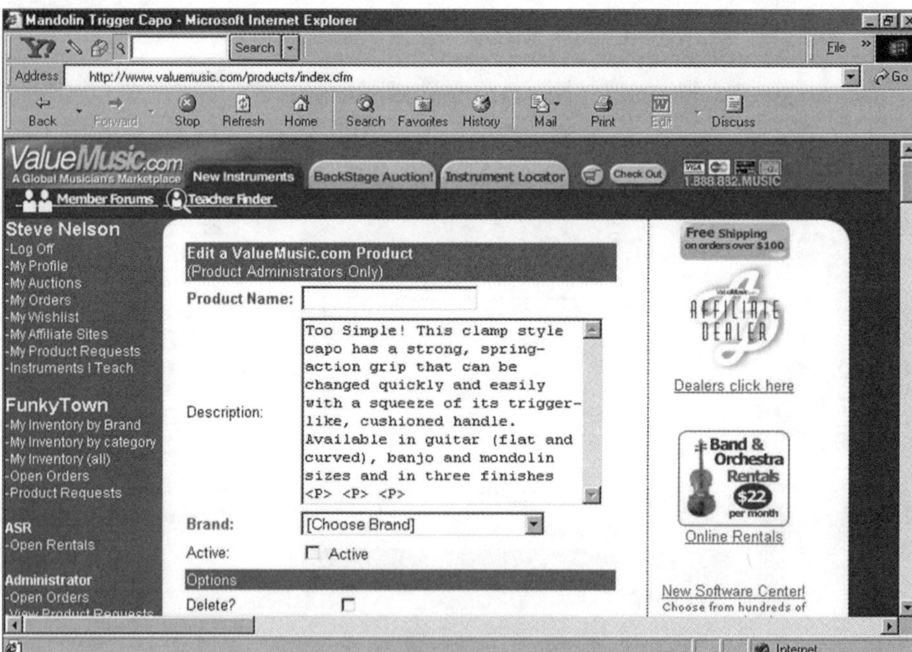

Action = Attributes

Sample Code:

```
<!--- The important thing to look at here is the use of the
<CF_REUSEFORM> tag. It creates local variables for each of the fields in
your form. Then you simply place the value in the form fields. --->
<CF_REUSEFORM
	queryname="getproduct"
	action="#displayaction#"
	fieldlist="product_name,product_description,brand_id,active,option_id,
	option_name,dealer_price, display_price,retail_price">
<form method="post" action="index.cfm?<CFOUTPUT>
#request.urltoken#</CFOUTPUT>">
	<input type="hidden" name="fuseaction" value="saveproduct">
	<CFOUTPUT><input type="hidden" name="product_id"
	value="#attributes.product_id#">
	<table border="0" width="95%">
		<tr>
			<td colspan="2" bgcolor="434eb0">
				<FONT color="ffffff"><b><CFIF len(attributes.product_id)>
				Edit<CFELSE>Add</CFIF> a ValueMusic.com
				Product</b><br>
				(Product Administrators Only)<br></font>
			</td>
		</tr>
		<tr>
			<td>Product Name:</td>
			<td><input type="text" name="product_name" value=
			"#product_name#" maxlength="50"></td>
		</tr>
		<tr>
			<td>Description:</td>
			<td><textarea name="product_description" cols="30"
			rows="10">#htmleditformat(product_description)#
			</textarea></td>
		</tr>
		<tr>
			<td>Brand:</td>
			<td>
				<select name="brand_id">
					<option value="">[Choose Brand]
					<CFSET thisbrand=brand_id>
					<CFLOOP query="getbrands">
						<option value="#brand_id#" <CFIF thisbrand is
						brand_id>selected</CFIF>>#brand_name#
					</CFLOOP>
				</select>
			</td>
		</tr>
		<tr>
```

```
            <td>Active:</td>
            <td><input type="checkbox" name="active" name="active"
            <CFIF val(active)>checked</CFIF>> Active</td>
        </tr>
    </table>
    <table width="95%">
        <tr>
            <td colspan="2" bgcolor="434eb0"><FONT color="ffffff">
            Options</font></td>
        </tr>
        <input type="hidden" name="optionlist" value=
        "#valuelist(getoptions.option_id)#">
        <CFLOOP query="getoptions">
            <tr>
                <td>Delete?</td>
                <td><input type="checkbox" name=
                "Delete_#option_id#"></td>
            </tr>
            <tr>
                <td>Option Name:</td>
                <td><input type="text" name="option_name_#option_id#
                " value="#option_name#" maxlength="50"></td>
            </tr>
            <tr>
                <td>Display Price:</td>
                <td><input type="text" name="display_price_#option_id#"
                value="#dollarformat(display_price)#" maxlength="10"
                size="8"></td>
            </tr>
            <tr>
                <td>Dealer Price:</td>
                <td><input type="text" name="dealer_price_#option_id#"
                value="#dollarformat(dealer_price)#" maxlength="10"
                size="8"></td>
            </tr>
            <tr>
                <td>Retail Price:</td>
                <td><input type="text" name="retail_Price_#option_id#"
                value="#dollarformat(retail_Price)#" maxlength="10"
                size="8"></td>
            </tr>
            <tr>
                <td colspan="2"><hr width=95% align="left"></td>
            </tr>
        </CFLOOP>
```

```
        <tr>
            <td colspan="2" bgcolor="434eb0"><FONT color="ffffff">Add
            an Option</font></td>
        </tr>
        <tr>
            <td>Option Name:</td>
            <td><input type="text" name="option_name" value=""
            maxlength="50"></td>
        </tr>
        <tr>
            <td>Display Price:</td>
            <td><input type="text" name="display_price" value="$0.00"
            maxlength="10" size="8"></td>
        </tr>
        <tr>
            <td>Dealer Price:</td>
            <td><input type="text" name="dealer_price" value="$0.00"
            maxlength="10" size="8"></td>
        </tr>
        <tr>
            <td>Retail Price:</td>
            <td><input type="text" name="retail_Price" value="$0.00"
            maxlength="10" size="8"></td>
        </tr>
        <tr>
            <td colspan="2"><hr width=95% align="left"></td>
        </tr>
        <tr>
            <td colspan="2"><input type="submit" class="buttons"
            value="Save"></td>
        </tr>
    </table>

    </CFOUTPUT>

</form>
```

<CF_ReturnFuseaction>

This tag is another prime example of the "reuse" concept. After a while, you and your client will notice that some processes can be completely reused. For example, if you write a process for registering for an account and logging in under that account, you might realize that this process can be used in multiple places. If a user is looking at a product, contemplating whether or not to buy it, then clicks the "login" button, you want them to continue focusing on the product they were just looking at. This tag makes this task very simple.

The <CF_ReturnFuseaction> tag has two actions: Set and return. The principle is that, when you set a "*returnfuseaction*", you are setting a client variable that will state, “Send the user to this page (*attributes.GotoURL*). Then, when the user is finished with whatever they are doing, return them to this page (*attributes.ReturnURL*)”.

<CF_BodyContent>

This tag was originally designed for nesting Fusebox applications together, which is a fairly rare case. However, it does have other benefits we will describe in a minute. First, take a look at **how** it makes nesting applications, which was previously a complex task, into a very simple one.

The main problem in nesting Fusebox applications is dealing with the global navigation. If you insert an entire *index.cfm* file using <CFMODULE> into another application and you have included the global navigation in each of the *index.cfm* files, you will see two sets of headers and footers. Chances are this is not what you wanted to do.

As you can see, this suddenly becomes a more complex task. To do this properly, there needs to be a way to let the inner application know that the global navigation is already turned on and that it should turn off its own global navigation, only displaying the content area of the page. The <CF_BodyContent> tag deals with this problem by processing the **body** of the page first, storing that output into a request variable, **then** displaying the header, body, and footer output. By doing this, you can affect output in the header and footer from within the body, which is normally impossible, because the header is automatically processed before the body.

While this technique of nesting *index.cfm* files inside of other *index.cfm* files is, in itself, very beneficial, this technique has other benefits. Because the body of the page is processed first, it can dynamically change information in the header. For example, if your page was displaying information about a product, you could automatically change the <TITLE> of that page to display the name of the product. Or if you wanted to highlight something in a menu, depending on a query run in the body of your page, you could do so, because the query is run **before** the global menu is created.

The Sixth Key: Complex SQL Joins Commonly Joining Four to Six Tables

Knowing and mastering specific SQL concepts is critical to becoming a Five-Day Fusebox Developer. SQL is quite a complex language in itself, but there are only a few specific techniques that you must know without thinking to become a FD^2.

Relational databases are made up of multiple tables of data. As your application grows, the number of tables will grow. You will need to know how to join all the data together. As your database design skills get better and you begin to normalize all of your tables in “third normal” form (see “Normalization” in the **Glossary**) or better, you will need to create complex SQL select statements.

The Seventh Key: Nested Trees in a Database

After you have mastered complex joins between four or more tables, the next important SQL technique to learn about is nested trees in a database. You may not commonly use nested trees in a database now, but as soon as you learn how to deal with nested data, you will begin to see how often it **should** be used.

The basic concept of the nested tree in a database is based on three fields:

- ID
- Parent_ID
- Name

With these three fields you can build a tree of data like this:

```
String Instruments
    Guitars
        Acoustic Guitars
        Electric Guitars
        Accessories
            Strings
            Tuners
    Bass
        Acoustic Bass, Etc .... 
```

This can grow to any level of depth. Being able to deal with levels of data like this allows for excellent organization of the data in your application. There are a few techniques to study when dealing with nested trees.

The first technique may be something you didn't realize you can do. It deals with aliasing the same table in a SQL select query. This can be a very effective and efficient way to deal with nested trees in a database. The only problem is that, for each level down in the tree you want to go, you need to reference another alias of the parent table.

Take a look at the Level 1 query. *#Attributes.category_id#* may be any value in the database:

```
select c.category_id,c.category_name
    from category_parents cp,category c
    where cp.parent_category_id=#val(attributes.category_id)#
        and cp.category_id=c.category_id
    order by c.category_name
```

This is fairly straightforward. This script joins *category* and *category_parents* together on the *category_id* field. It also says show all the categories that have "0" as their parent. Where "0" is the root level of the tree, it has no parents. Zero might be the answer to the age old question: "Which came first the chicken or the egg?".

You'll quickly notice that these tables are split up, because a category may have many parents, just as a child may have many parents.

The problem with this is that it does not display the categories that have children categories, and those also have children categories.

To display the next level down, we need to reference the *category_Parents* table again. To do this in SQL, you simply need to give it another name:

```
select c.category_id,c.category_name
    from category_parents cp1,category_parents cp2,category c
    where cp1.parent_category_id=0
        and cp1.category_id=c.category_id
        and cp2.parent_category_id=cp1.category_id
    order by category_name
```

This remains true because it is saying, "Show me the children of all the categories that have children that are also Level 0 parents." This will yield the next level down and can be done for as many levels as you'd like.

Aliasing tables is a topic best covered by your database documentation. In short, however, here the query is doing a self-join between the *category_id* field and the *parent_category_id* field of the same table.

This can allow for aggregate functions like *count()*. That means you can easily display the number of categories, like Yahoo! does: Art History(660); Education(79).

In older versions of CF, there is another method of dealing with nested trees, using the <CF_MAKETREE> tag. This uses ColdFusion to reorder all the nodes in your tree, so that they output a query in the order they should be displayed, when looping over the query. <CF_MAKETREE> will also specify how far to indent with each node.

These two techniques offer different solutions to the nested tree problem. They will become very important as you begin to build more complex applications.

The Eighth Key: Membership Registration and Securing Your Applications

Every application has users. There are three types of users: Public, Registered Public and Registered Private users.

Public users have not told you who they are and should not be allowed to access sensitive data, nor should they be allowed to add or edit data from the database that needs to be connected to a specific user.

Registered Public users have gone through a registration process that tells you some amount of information about them. What they tell you is completely up to you. The point of being a registered public user is that, in the future, you can connect them to data that they have created before. This user does not belong to any group and thus cannot gain access to areas of the site that are secured to specific groups of users.

Registered Private users have gone through virtually the same registration process that the Registered Public Users went through, but these users have been assigned to one or more groups that are allowed access to certain secured areas of the site.

Since many applications need some type of user registration/login process, this is one of the most important concepts to understand. This **process** should only change slightly from application to application. The **concepts** behind these three types of users will not change.

The Ninth Key: The ColdFusion Markup Language

Understanding ColdFusion Markup Language (CFML) is critical. You do not need to memorize the entire language, but it helps. To become a Five-Day Fusebox Developer, you ideally need to be able to do normal hour-to-hour work without looking in a reference manual. It's okay to check how to do certain techniques occasionally, but this should be a rare occurrence. The more time spent looking in manuals, the less time spent writing your code.

The fastest way to quickly understand CFML is to take one day off work, go to a library away from telephones and email, and read the ColdFusion Language Reference from cover to cover, memorizing as much as you can.

The Tenth Key: Snippets, Hotkeys and Keyboard Shortcuts

Allaire's ColdFusion Studio contains many opportunities for customization. The "Settings" dialog box (F8) has a tab for Code Templates that you can fill up with common ColdFusion and Fusebox code like <CFINCLUDE> statements, <CFCASE VALUE="">, etc., and access them via <CTRL>J. You can also add Snippets and assign shortcuts to them, using the "Customize" dialog box (<SHIFT>F8) and the Snippets Tab on the Resource Tab (F9). Having as many commonly-used lines of code assigned to shortcut keys will speed your development time tremendously.

Using Microsoft Windows, shifting back and forth between your development environment and the browser used to preview your work can be done via <ALT><TAB>, rather than a cumbersome mouse click. Also, your version of Windows may allow certain programs to be launched via a keystroke combination. Assigning other commonly-used tools, like Access or SQL Enterprise Manager, to hotkey is faster than having to use the mouse and the Start menu.

The more time you can spend with your fingers on the keyboard, the faster you will be able to code. Moving your hand to the mouse and back again to the keyboard can add a lot of time. Ideally, only a handful of commands during your workday will still be performed using the mouse (i.e., clicking HREF links).

The Eleventh Key: Being Able to Think for Yourself

This skill is really beyond the purview of this book. It is the honing of your basic ability to make judgments and creative suggestions to be able to come up with the right suggestions at the right time for the right application.

Building the Five-Day Application

After you feel you have a good understanding of the most commonly used techniques, it is time to begin the "practice" process of the Five-Day application. To do any large task quickly requires a very simple system:

- Do the simple areas first. This creates a reduced stress level and allows more brainpower to focus on the complex areas.
- Ignore the size of the application and focus on the generalities of "what" it needs to do. Chances are that most of the application is a composite of many simple things. Understanding that these simple things exist will make your application suddenly feel much smaller.

As soon as you see that there are only a few "hard" areas of your site, you will realize that you **CAN** build your application in five days.

This process may seem backwards from what you may have read in computer science books on software development methodologies. Most books will tell you to spend weeks or months on the specification and design area, whereas this process only spends a single day. Why is this? It is because there is a specific system to building a specification and design of your application. With lots of practice, this can be boiled down into a single day.

Preparing for Your Five-Day Development

There are certain things that need to happen before you can begin your five-day development cycle. This cycle is based on facts, not opinions. Opinions can take a long time and cannot be easily itemized.

Understanding the Application

You will not be able to build an application that you do not understand. You and your client need to have a fairly firm grasp of what the application is trying to accomplish. At this point, you do not need to have an understanding of the details, but you do need to understand the general ideas.

This step should be spent in freeform discussion between developer and client. It may take days or even weeks to complete. Be sure to cut off discussions after a certain point and move onto the next step, otherwise areas of your application will be lost in the mix.

Also remember that, while you're able to build a full version of an application in five days, you **can** also make an area wait until Version 2 or 3 or 4. It's important that the process continue flowing and does not stall on any single area.

Waiting for the Graphics

Do not spend an extremely long time on graphics before the five-day cycle has begun. For Version 1, it is essential that there be a basic style of how graphics are implemented on the site, the most important of which is the global navigation. This is the navigation that will exist on all or most pages. Having the global navigation(s) finished **before** the five-day development cycle will make it possible for the application look more like a finished product. For each successive version of your application, graphics will become more and more involved.

The Five-Day Development Cycle Begins!

Step 1) Unplug Your Phones and Disconnect Your Computer from the Internet

Distractions are the main reason we can't meet our deadlines. See for yourself: Count how many phone calls you get and how many emails you read in a day. These all add up very quickly. For the five-day cycle to work, you need to be disconnected from the world for five full days.

The next step involves two representatives of your client. They need to also turn off their phones. If they can't do that, they should not be involved in this process.

Elapsed time: 30 seconds

Step 2) Building the Hierarchical Flowcharts of Fuseactions

The first step requires **one experienced web developer** writing on **a whiteboard** with no more than **two clients** at any given time. Adding more people into the mix will only slow down the process exponentially. Decisions will take too long to make, explanations will take longer, and less work will be done. A small tight group is far better. More people's opinions can be incorporated in later versions.

This is the most important step in the entire process. This is the **structured note-taking** step. The concept here is to build flowcharts **without** all the flowchart symbols. These types of flowcharts are more hierarchies than flowcharts. The idea is to quickly understand the many processes in your application and gather enough information to get to the detailed specification step.

There should be very few symbols involved. The less symbols there are, the easier it is to explain what is going on to a non-technical person. The flow should go "down" through each process and should not connect back up to previous Fuseactions, even if it does in the real application. The reason again is for simplicity. Once loops are introduced to the flow, non-technical people may get overwhelmed. Build the loops into the "Design" step of the process (Step 5), which will not be seen by the client. The flowcharts generated during this all-day step **MUST BE SIMPLE**!

There are two main symbols in this style of flowcharts. **Boxes** represent Fuseactions and **lines** connecting the boxes represent the act of connecting Fuseactions, together with <a href> a <form> or <CFLOCATION>. At this point, it does not matter HOW they are connected, simply that they ARE connected.

Inside each box will be the name of the Fuseaction. Try to get this down to no more than about three words. Remember: The idea is to quickly get your ideas down. They need to be complete, but not perfect.

Once you understand the two main symbols and have no more than two people representing your client behind your huge whiteboard, you can begin:

Start by separating out your home application into circuit applications, each in its own box. Draw these at the top of the whiteboard with a decent amount of space between them. Each of these top boxes will represent a group of user flows (i.e., a directory of files). These boxes do not need to be connected together. In fact, connecting them will only make it harder to understand them. These top boxes are designed to make your large application feel smaller, keeping the pieces of the puzzle separate.

Once you have separated out your home application into multiple circuit applications, draw the **user flows**. A user flow is **a process the user will go through to complete a task**, made up of one or more Fuseactions. Some of the Fuseactions have a display to the user, others do not. Do not group these together into single boxes. Separate them out, one Fuseaction per box.

Connect the Fuseactions off of the top boxes that you drew earlier and begin to think out how a user would go through the various processes. For example:

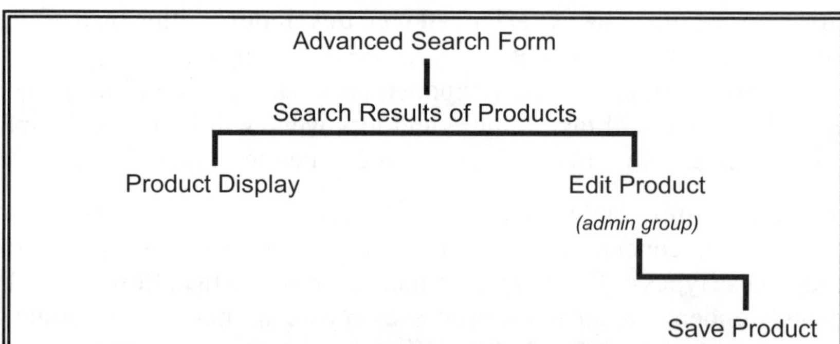

That is a fairly simple user flow. Each circuit application will be made up of many of these. With this basic information mapped out, you can understand and communicate the user's experience in a matter of minutes.

Elapsed time: 1 full day

(Going at this speed is difficult for the beginner, or for applications that have more than twenty circuit applications. The point is that you should not spend weeks or months on this stage. Do it ***quickly****.)*

Step 3) Turning Fuseaction Flowcharts into Specifications

The next step is fairly simple. This step takes your ideas from the whiteboard and puts more flesh on them. You can do this by hand or use a specification tool, such as the feature-rich application at **http://www.SecretAgents.com** (now in beta; expected release date November 2000).

This process will force you to spend time writing out in plain English (or the language of your choice) what each Fuseaction is going to do. Since you have already created the user flows, you simply need to transpose the simplistic whiteboard versions into a more detailed edition.

This step still does not involve technical explanations of "how" you will make it work. It should explain "what" the application needs to do.

Elapsed time: ½-1 day

(It is fairly easy to meet this time frame, because the hard part of deciding what the process will be is already complete.)

Step 4) Turning Fuseaction Specifications into File Design

This takes a skilled developer. In this step, you will need to explain in **technical** terms how you will build all the Fuseactions. Again, this is done by hand or by a specification tool, such as the one at **SecretAgents.com**.

Each Fuseaction will be made up of one or more files. Each of these files will explain technically how you will do what is needed to be done in the Fuseaction. The files will use the Fusebox naming convention.

If you commonly include select queries in display files, it is recommended that you break yourself of that habit and put your select queries in their own *QRY_filename.cfm* file. That way, you will quickly itemize what needs to be completed.

This step does **not** involve pseudo code. It involves explaining in plain English (or the language of your choice) just "how" you will build what needs to be built. We feel that pseudo code is a waste of time. If you can explain the code in plain English, you will be able to write the real code very quickly. You are doing the thinking now; later you will be translating your English thoughts into CFML.

The client will not see the file design. This step is solely for your purposes. The more detailed you get, the faster your development will go. After you have done this a few times, this step will go very quickly. Make the investment and get detailed with your explanations. A few sentences can go a long way once you begin coding.

Elapsed time: ½-1 day

(Using this five-day cycle, you will find that most of your application is NOT made up of complex areas. Design the simple areas first, then you can spend more time on the hard areas.)

Step 5) Build the Database

Being able to quickly build a database takes a lot of skill. In fact, you will need years to develop this skill. You won't learn it overnight. The most important things to focus on when building a database are the primary and foreign keys of each table. Once the relationships have been built, adding in the rest of the fields (i.e., first_name, last_name, …) in each table is fairly simple.

This step may involve additional conversations with your client to flesh out what data is necessary.

Elapsed time: ½-1 day

(This step may take a non-experienced database designer much longer. Don't worry. The more times you do this, the faster it will go.)

Step 6) Generate Global Files (*app_globals*, *qry_globals*, etc.)

The home application will take many different global variables. This step is relatively easy, because it's almost the same in every application. You will want to setup your *app_globals.cfm* with calls to <CF_FormURL2Attributes> and <CFAPPLICATION>, etc. You will also want to set up your *qry_globals.cfm,* which will set any memory resident queries, such as: "*select * from States*". The U.S. states are not going to change on a constant basis. Store that information in an application variable, so you do not have to hit the database every time you need that information.

Elapsed time: 15 minutes

Step 7) Generate your *Index.cfm* Files

From your Fuseaction Specification (not the file design), create your *Index.cfm* files. The specifications tool on **SecretAgents.com** will generate this code automatically for you, but it is fairly simple to just write the *index.cfm* files by hand.

Elapsed time: Less than 1 minute (using SecretAgents.com) **or up to ~2 hours** (for a very large application) **by hand**

(If you're doing this by hand, it will take longer than you think, but it is not hard by any means. It's simply a matter of how fast you can type <CFCASE> and <CFINCLUDE> statements.)

Step 8) Generate Fusedoc'd Files of Every Named File in Your Design

Create all the files that you have added to your file design. At the top of each file, create a Fusedoc (see **Appendix A: Fusedocs**, for more details), stating what the file will do and what attributes are needed, along with what variables it will return.

Elapsed time: Less than 1 minute (using SecretAgents.com) **or up to 4 hours** (for a very large application) **by hand**

(Like the previous step, it will take longer than you think by hand, but is not hard: Just a lot of cutting and pasting.)

Step 9) Write Code for ALL URL Files in EVERY Circuit Application

These are redirection files that contain <CFLOCATION> tags. They are the smallest files in Fusebox and commonly consist of a single line of code. They exist to keep the *index.cfm* file very simple and clean. These files should be called **after** you have included an action file that changes data in the database. For example, if a user adds an item to their shopping cart ("*Fuseaction=AddItem*"), they should be redirected to view the cart ("*Fuseaction=ViewCart*"). That way, if they click the reload button on their browser, they will not continually add items to their cart.

Sometimes these files will contain <CFIF> statements or even queries to determine where to send the user to, but the main goal of these files is to redirect the user to another page.

DO NOT TEST THIS CODE YET.

Elapsed time: 20 minutes-1 hour (for very large applications)

(These files do not take much skill, being simple <CFLOCATION> tags, for the most part.)

Step 10) Write Code for ALL QRY Files in EVERY Circuit Application

These files will vary in complexity. The *qry* file should contain SELECT queries and should not manipulate any data in the database. They commonly only have a single select query but may occasionally have multiple queries in them.

This is where your knowledge of the SQL language will come into play. You may need to use your knowledge of nested trees here also. Creating these files will help you redesign the database, if you realize that you cannot **get** the data that you need. Write these queries without writing how they will be displayed. Making them work together will be done later.

It is important to translate the plain English version into SQL and CFML. That is how you do this step quickly.

DO NOT TEST THIS CODE YET.

Elapsed time: 4-16 hours

(This will vary greatly, depending on your knowledge of SQL and the size of your application. However, because you are simply translating English into SQL, this step can be done quickly, even if your application is huge.)

Step 11) Write Code for ALL ACT Files in EVERY Circuit Application

The action files change something on the server side, whether it's data in the database, uploading a file to disk, or posting data to a remote server using <CFHTTP>. This is the type of code that actually "does" something. This is the meat of your application and is where your knowledge of the CFML language comes into play.

Some of your action files will be simple insert or update statements on the database; some may be a few hundred lines long, doing very complex algorithms. Do the simple ones first. Leave the more complex action files for later to give yourself time to focus on them. It is important that you translate what you described in your English version of the file in the file design into CFML. That is how you do this step quickly.

DO NOT TEST THIS CODE YET.

Elapsed time: 4-16 hours

(This will greatly vary depending on your knowledge of CFML and the size of your application. However, since you are simply translating English into CFML, this step can be done quickly, even if your application is huge.)

Step 12) Write Code for ALL DSP Files in EVERY Circuit Application

This step should be fairly easy at this point. You have already created your select statements, and you already know where each of the files point to, from your specification. Now, you simply need to build all the various forms and links into HTML.

Your knowledge of HTML and CFML will come into play here. Being able to quickly build an HTML table or form is key. Using the <CF_ReuseForm> tag will help you reuse your code, which will assist you by requiring less management of display code.

Your first version may not look pretty, but if you built a style guide before you began, it will look useable. For each new version of your application, you may want to spice up the display files, using a graphic artist. Don't let them delay your code. You can make it all work without them and add the graphics later.

DO NOT TEST THIS CODE YET.

Elapsed time: 4-16 hours

(Because you already know all the data that will be on the page, from creating the qry files, you should be able to quickly translate that into forms, links and various other display elements.)

Step 13) Run the Code and Make It All Work

After you have written all the code, it is time to make it all work. Be aware that it just won't work the first time. It is better to quickly write the code and spend a good amount of time debugging and testing your code than try and figure out all the bugs while writing the code.

This step may involve changing various pieces of code or, commonly, changing the database, because it was not designed to do what you wanted it to do. That is okay, since the bulk of the code has been written; it will simply be a matter of determining what was wrong in your logic design and fixing that.

Start by going to the default page of each circuit application and click away. Once you can click through every link and every form five times without throwing a hard or soft (logic) error, show it to your client, ready for criticism.

Elapsed time: 1-2 days

(Don't spend less than a day on this. You will save a lot of face with your client if you find the bugs before they do.)

TOTAL ELAPSED TIME: 5-11 DAYS

As you can see, large applications **CAN** be developed quickly. Although it takes a fair amount of background knowledge, once you master this development process, you can build well-designed applications quickly, with very few people.

Remember:

1. Focus on making the large problems turn into many smaller problems.
2. Solve the easiest problems first and your stress level will be reduced, giving you time to focus on the harder problems.

APPENDIX A: Fusedocs

by Hal Helms

Introduction

One of the really helpful things about Fusebox is that it supports distributed team development. Since the action flows from Fusebox to Fuse to Fusebox again, we have eliminated the dependencies between modules that make distributed development difficult in many other languages.

Without this independence between modules, making almost any change or addition to an application requires someone with an encyclopedic knowledge of the code. After all, if you don't know what other places a change might affect, only someone very foolhardy is going to plunge ahead. This often leads to tying up the most experienced developers with everything but the simplest code. The deeper into the project we get, the less that less-experienced coders in the team can help. I sometimes think of this as an inverted pyramid, where, as the project builds, the entire weight and pressure of an application gets concentrated on fewer and fewer people.

In Fusebox, we have finally acquired the ability to break up the application into many different pieces — "**severability**", as I call it. Severability benefits everyone. The customer gets the job sooner and with less stress-induced bugs. The development company lowers the cost of development by spreading the work over more (and usually less expensive) developers. The more experienced developers get to work in areas where their experience and expertise are more critical. This is usually much more satisfying work, and they can demand higher pay. Finally, new developers get the valuable experience of working on code throughout an entire application's lifecycle.

In order to gain the full benefits of severability, we need a way of communicating to the Fuse coder just the knowledge s/he needs to know to do the job. And once again, Fusebox has a solution: **Fusedoc**. Fusedoc is a method for writing documentation that succinctly states what a coder needs to know to write a Fuse.

Sorting Out the Pieces

Let's start by looking over a sample Fusedoc:

```
<!---
|| BEGIN FUSEDOC ||
|| RESPONSIBILITIES ||
I provide the user a login of both userName and password, returning to the
Fusebox with an RFA of SubmitForm. If I get a var called 'badLogin', the
user is returning to me from an invalid login.
|| HISTORY ||
Author: hal.helms@TeamAllaire.com
|| ATTRIBUTES ||
--> RFA.submitForm:  a FUSEACTION
--> [badLogin]:      a STRING
<-- userName:        a STRING
<-- password:        a STRING
|| END FUSEDOC ||
--->
```

The entire Fusedoc is implemented as a ColdFusion comment. Each Fusedoc contains *sections* that are delimited by double pipe symbols (||). Fusedoc does not try to determine what the sections should be. This depends on the needs of the developer and the project. Rather, Fusedoc provides for a way to define sections by delimiting them with pipe symbols. This provides flexibility to adapt to situations where the sections may be entirely different.

In the Fusedoc example shown above, I've outlined three sections: Responsibilities, history, and attributes. For much of the code I write, these are the only sections included. I have found that, as the amount of information increases, the willingness of coders to provide documentation — and to *maintain* that documentation — decreases. In this case, less is more.

Responsibilities: Written in the first person, responsibilities tell the programmer exactly what the Fuse's job is. Without repeating the information conveyed in the Parameters section, it should make clear to the coder what this Fuse's job is. I write these in the first person, as I find that putting myself in the place of the Fuse helps me better catch the details involved.

History: This section begins with the name of the programmer who wrote the actual code and can be expanded to add other details you find important. When edits to the code are made, you can add updates to the documentation here.

Attributes: This section lets the programmer know what parameters to expect — and what parameters are expected from the Fuse.

Here's how to read a sample line:

❶ --> ❷accessLevel: ❸a STRING ❹(allowed values) ❺

❶ Information on **where the variable is coming from**. Possible values are:

-->	explicitly passed in
<--	explicitly passed out
<->	a pass-through variable. The variable will be passed in and must be explicitly passed out without any change in the variable.
++>	persistent variable available to the Fuse (e.g. session or application variables)
<++	persistent variable the Fuse is responsible to set
+++	a file that the Fuse requires in order to run

❷ The **name of the variable** (including variable scope). Valid examples would be:

request.dsn

session.myName

application.supportEmail

[badLogin]

Since the majority of variables will be attributes-type variables (made so by the call to *FormURL2Attributes.cfm* tag in the Fusebox), you may omit the scope prefix if the parameter is an attributes-type variable. Variable names without scope prefixes are then assumed to be of type "*attributes*". Every Fuse will receive and return a Fuseaction. This is so central to Fusebox that these are understood and can be omitted from the Fusedoc.

Variables that have square brackets around them (e.g. [*badLogin*]) indicate variables that may be passed, but are not required to be — or are required only in certain circumstances. For instance, the variable *badLogin* might only be passed to the Fusebox if the exit state of the fuse was something like *RFA.failedValidation*. In that case, the Fusedoc would look like this:

<-- [badLogin]: a BOOLEAN (TRUE) on RFA.failedValidation

❸ The **datatype of the variable**. While ColdFusion is a *loosely-typed* language and does not require variables to be declared with datatypes, it is still helpful to the coder to know whether, for example, session.Customer is a STRUCTURE or a STRING.

❺ **Allowed values**. Are there any restrictions? Is there a default value? These examples show various uses of the allowed values section:

- *myQuery*: A QUERY RESULTSET (*userID, firstName, lastName*) indicates that *myQuery* will be made up of *userID* and *firstName* and *lastName*)
- *accessLevel*: A STRING (A | B) indicates that the variable *accessLevel* is *either* "*A*" or "*B*", but not both.

Additionally, there are operators[1] that can be applied:

- Optional ?
- One-or-more +
- Zero-or-more *

Examples:

- *book*: A **STRUCTURE** (*SKU, quantity, price, salePrice?*) tells us that the key *salePrice* is optional in the structure.
- *booksChosen*: A **LIST** (*book*)+ says that a list must have one book — but may have more.
- *order*: A **2D ARRAY** (*customerID, billingAddress, paymentMethod, shoppingItem**) defines an order that may not yet have any *shoppingItems* associated with it or may have several.

How Do You Eat an Elephant? One Bite at a Time

Are you overwhelmed yet? If you are, you can take comfort in knowing that everybody starts out overwhelmed. After all, you're contemplating a fundamental change in the way you code. That's pretty overwhelming stuff! I can promise you that it's worth the pain — but if you decide to go ahead with Fusebox, you'll need both reassurance *and* an implementation strategy.

As the title of this section implies, sometimes the best way to accomplish a really big task is by small steps. Implement what you understand so far. It's odd, but as you begin to implement it, you will find that you begin to understand the reasons behind the specification. And you'll be ready to implement a little more.

When I'm asked to help plan a Fusebox implementation strategy, I start by assessing the team's taste for change. Some people love change; they're energized by it in much the same way that extroverts are energized by parties and social gatherings. In that case, we move ahead very quickly.

Others of us, though, prefer change to be more gradual. When I find this, I usually suggest that we begin by adopting Fusedoc as a standard. This is an easier course to take. After all, documentation is one of those things that everyone knows they should do, but that no one has ever told us *how* to do. Fusedoc gives programmers explicit instructions about the kind and format of their code documentation.

How much detail is enough? My own test is this: Can a programmer, without knowing anything about the application other than the Fusedoc information, complete the Fuse? If so, then the Fusedoc is complete.

---

[1] These signs used aren't completely arbitrary. They are the same ones used in creating XML document type definitions (DTDs), where they serve the same purpose.

APPENDIX B: fUseML

What is the Unified Modeling Language?

The Unified Modeling Language, or the UML, is a modeling language designed to help System Architects and programmers visualize, specify, build and document business and software systems. The UML is the result of a collaboration by Grady Booch, Ivar Jacobson and James Rumbaugh, known in the industry as "the Three Amigos". For a decade or more, these three had been working separately on Object Oriented Modeling languages until the mid-1990's, when they decided to start their collaboration, forming the basis of the UML we know today.

What Is a Modeling Language?

A modeling language is the use of graphical elements such as geometric shapes, lines and pictures, to form diagrams and charts representing a system. Like any other language, it has rules that should be followed when defining the flow of a particular business system. A good visual of a modeling system is a flow chart. A flow chart uses squares, rectangles, arrows and various other shapes to represent the "flow" of a particular system.

Why Standardize?

This book has already shown the importance of universal standards in the world of web development. Standards allow new developers to easily understand an application. Standards also allow for easier debugging and maintenance. The same holds true for modeling languages, The community as a whole benefits by creating a standard.

What Types of Diagrams Can Be Created with the UML?

There are nine specified diagrams in the UML. Each one is designed to model a specific section or idea of a system.

The Class Diagram

The **class diagram** is typically used to describe objects or entities within a system. Generally speaking, systems are made up of different sections or objects that, when put together, create the system as a whole. Class diagrams help us visualize those entities, as well as their attributes and behaviors. For instance, if you were designing a bicycle, your diagram would look like this:

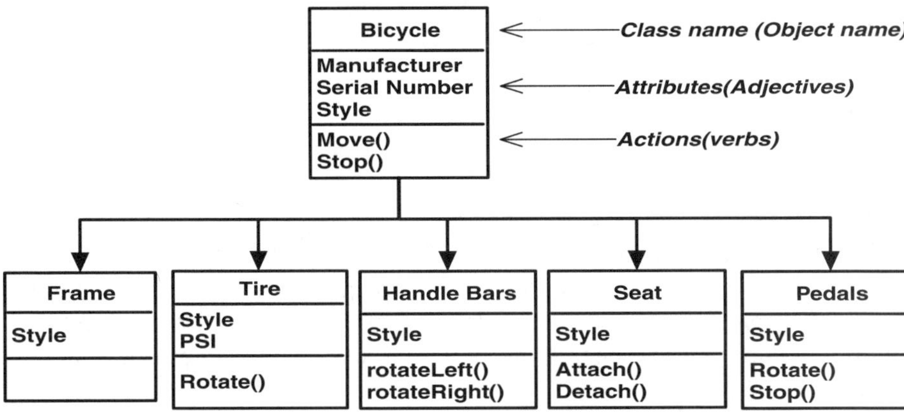

Sample Class Diagram

A class diagram is made up of three sections. The top section (the **class name**) is the name of the object. The second section holds the **attributes** of the class. The bottom section stores the **operations** or **actions** of an object.

The bicycle application, or "bicycle object", is made up of a lot of other objects. The diagram here goes on to show the **relationship** of the object to the other objects that make up the entire application. Frame, Tire, Handlebars, Seat and Pedals are all "children" of the "parent", bicycle class. You will see how this can help you build your Fusebox applications later in the JazzLoft case study.

The Use Case Diagram

The **use case diagram** describes how a user will interact with the system and can also show how the entities within the systems interact. Use case diagrams are meant to be a simple way for both programmers and clients to understand who is using the system and what actions they are performing on it.

The stick figure is the "Actor" in our Use Case. This diagram describes how a Cyclist uses the Bicycle. The ovals are the different Use Cases the actor can perform. Use Cases can also be contained within "swim lanes". Each swim lane is named after an object and contains each Use Case that is performed on that object. We'll describe and demonstrate swim lanes in the case study.

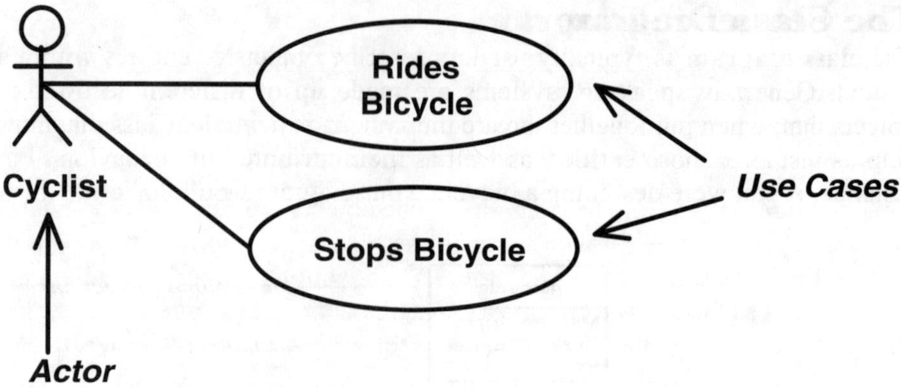

Sample Use Case Diagram

The State Diagram

The **state diagram** is used to display an object at a particular state. According to our diagram, a bicycle has two "states": stopped and moving. State diagrams are useful when showing how an action can effect the state of an object. For example, when a cyclist pedals the bike (an action), the state of the bicycle changes to "moving".

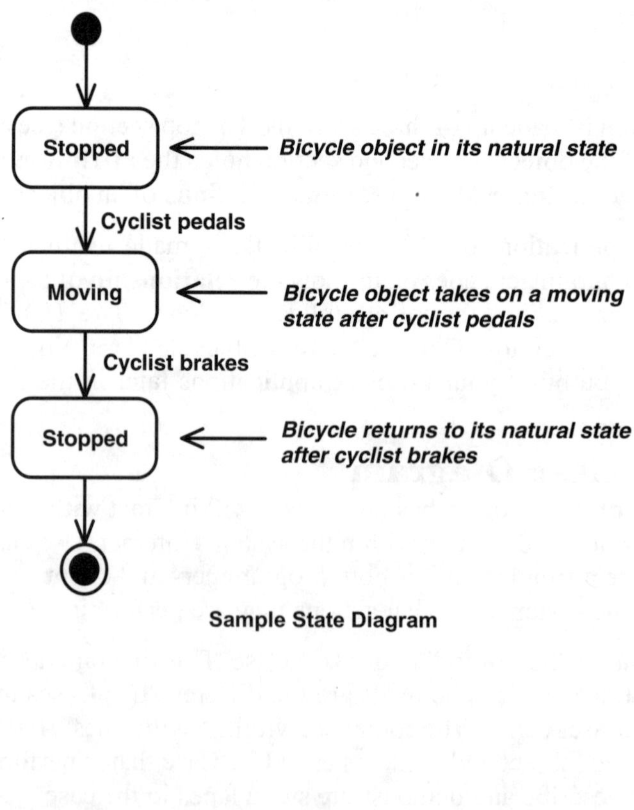

Sample State Diagram

The Sequence Diagram

This diagram describes the order of actions of an event. Each object involved in a Use Case has its own "lifeline"; messages and actions are followed in chronological order. This gives the programmer and client a way of seeing how each object interacts with other object in a given event.

This diagram is read from top to bottom. The objects are described by squares at the top. A "lifeline" (broken vertical line) is used to express an amount of time in the object life cycle. The object's "activations" (long rectangles) are used to express the amount of time a particular action is taking. The messages or actions define the interaction of one object to another and list the particular action taking place.

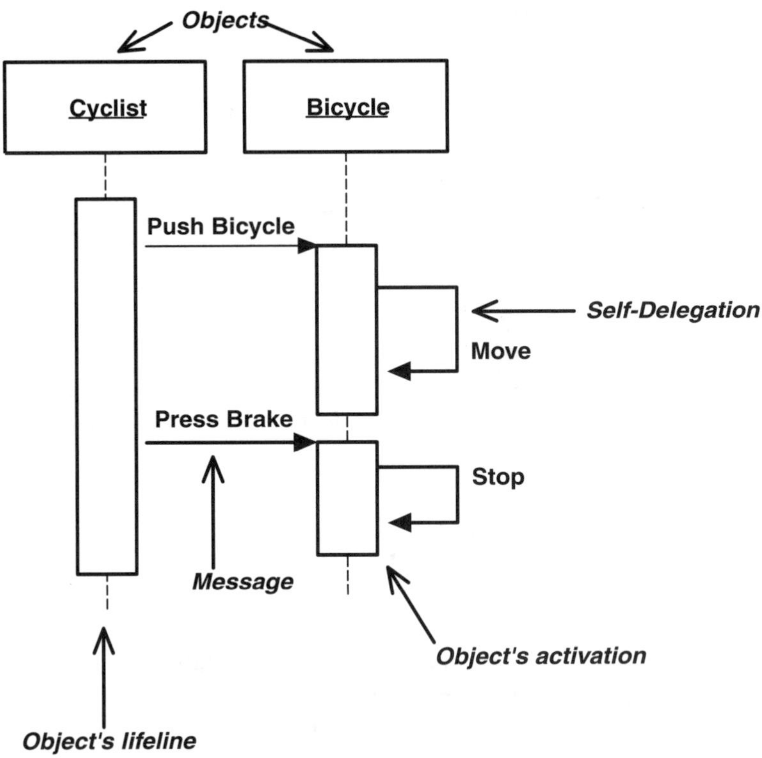

Sample Sequence Diagram

Sequence diagrams are particularly helpful in discovering the Fuseactions you will need to complete an action or event.

The Activity Diagram

The **activity diagram** is probably the closest diagram in the UML family to a traditional flow chart. Activity diagrams show the sequence of actions within an event. It can also show logic within a system. Activity diagrams are good for diagraming Use Cases. This diagram is fairly self-explanatory.

Solid dots begin and end the process flow. Ovals denote activites or actions; triangles show decisions (i.e., pedal or brake).

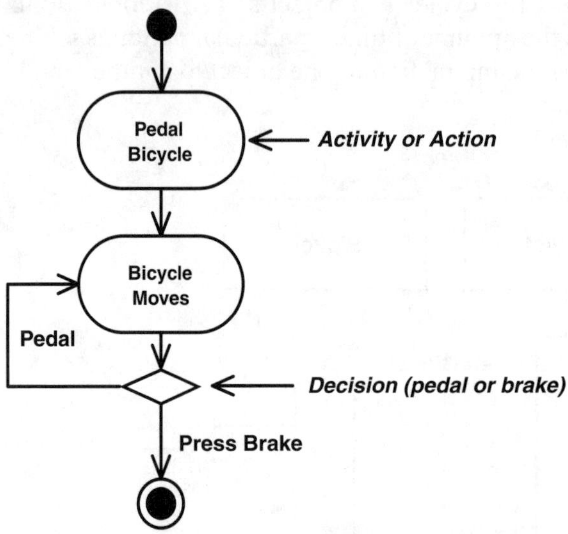

Sample Activity Diagram

The Collaboration Diagram

The **collaboration diagram** shows how the objects of a system work in conjunction with one another.

This diagram displays each object and the messages they pass to each other. A collaboration diagram is extremely useful in situations where you have multiple, distinct objects communicating with one another.

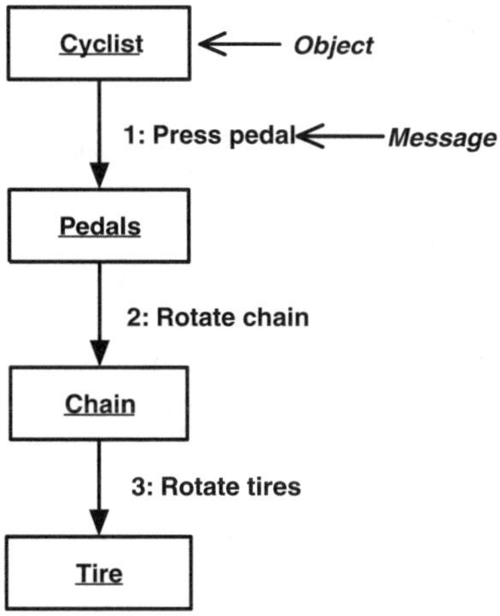

Sample Collaboration Diagram

Additional Tools

There are three other diagrams that we won't discuss in detail here:

- **The Component Diagram**: Used for designing hardware systems, describing how the different pieces work together.
- **The Object Diagram**: Used to diagram "instances" of a class. Typically used in an Object-Oriented programming environment.
- **The Deployment Diagram**: Very useful for visualizing how your code will be copied to other servers when finished. However, it is not limited to this situation.

The Analysis Document

An **analysis document** was created by Instant Knowledge to help list the purposes for each diagram type. This was defined to help the programmers and client's understand the purpose/meaning of each diagram. Each analysis document has six (6) components:

1. **What They Provide**: The purpose of these diagrams.
2. **Scope**: What objects are allowed in the diagram.
3. **Format**: What type of UML diagram to use and any other layout issues involved.
4. **Refines**: Each diagram in a UML model is supposed to validate the one before it. Any diagram, or other media, that is validated by the diagram is listed here.
5. **Refined By**: Any diagram or other media that refines this particular diagram is listed here.
6. **Notes**: Any special information we need to know about the diagram.

What Is fUseML?

Put most simply, fUseML is a form of the UML used to describe Fusebox applications in particular.

Why Use fUseML?

fUseML is a powerful tool when designing and maintaining an application, with all the tried-and-true benefits of the UML. Visually representating your application increases understanding and communication between clients and developers. It also serves as valuable documentation for future reference.

Isn't the UML Specifically for Object-Oriented Programming?

No. Although the UML was developed with Object-Orient Programming (OOP) in mind, the creators knew they would never be able to capture every situation. In the spirit of other open-source, community-driven web standards, the creators left the UML open for modifications and additions. Using the constructs of the UML, we can create most, if not all, the objects and diagrams needed to express web applications.

Why Not Create Our Own Modeling Language?

As stated above, the UML can be modified, with boundaries. But just as Fusebox is more powerful if everyone is on the same page, so is the UML. Also, the UML has been under the careful scrutiny of the entire Web for years. All the kinks are worked out; it is fully mature, unlike anything we could easily create from scratch.

How Would I Use fUseML in a Real Life Situation?

Glad you asked! The next section provides a fictional case study of ONE way the UML can be used to diagram Fusebox applications.

Where Can I Get More Information on the UML and fUseML?

There are three sites to check out:

http://www.fUseML.org
http://www.rational.com/uml/index.jsp
http://www.uml-zone.com.

How Can I Get Involved?

First, check out the website devoted to this subject: **http://www.fUseML.org**. Join the list there, then give us YOUR opinions and ideas. A standard is only as strong as its community.

A fUseML Case Study: Task Manager

Welcome to our case study on fUseML. fUseML is the use of the Unified Modeling Language (UML) to diagram Fusebox applications. This is a case study of a small application.

There are a few things that need to be understood when reading this study:

- This is a **fictional** case study of a Task Manager application.
- This is by no means meant to be a study of a GOOD task manager system. (We are not arguing design here.)
- This is meant to demonstrate using the fUseML to specify and design an application.
- The case study goes through a **complete** application analysis, meaning many of the diagrams will not directly relate to Fusebox, but are very important aspects of the specification and design phases of development.
- The purpose of including this case study in **FUSEBOX: METHODOLOGY AND TECHNIQUES** is to promote the fUseML concept and the ongoing open discussion of fUseML on the fUseML email list. We are open to and appreciate any suggestions.
- This is in **alpha** stage, a work-in-progress. It is intended to promote discussion about using the UML to describe Fusebox applications.

This case study began with the programming team at Instant Knowledge, in particular Gabe Roffman, Kevin Myers and Craig Girard.

Initial Analysis Meeting with Clients

The ABC Company has come to the conclusion that they would like to automate their current Task Manager system. Knowing Instant Knowledge has a group of web developers, ABC gives them a call.

Instant Knowledge sets up a meeting to begin understanding ABC's current Task Manager system. They send three people: A meeting facilitator, a modeler and a note taker. The facilitator immediately takes charge, and the meeting goes something like this:

Facilitator: We are here to get acquainted with your current Task Manager System. Please tell us how it currently works.

Client: Each morning the department manager writes tasks on a piece of paper. *(The note taker and the modeler are listening closely.)* The tasks are then placed in the worker's in-box.

Facilitator: What exactly does a task consist of?

Client: Each piece of paper, or task, contains a job title, description, start date and end date.

Note Taker: What is the worker's role in all this? What does he or she do with the task?

Client: Upon arrival, the worker checks his or her in-box. If he (or she) finds a task, he reads it carefully, then proceeds to complete the task. When each task is completed, the worker places it into his out-box, where the manager picks them up every evening.

Facilitator: What then does the manager do with the tasks?

Client: The manager then decides whether or not the task has been completed properly. If the manager rejects the job, then he adds a Revision to the task, and it is returned to the worker's in-box. If the job is accepted, the End Date is filled out with the appropriate date and the task is filed.

Facilitator: This has been great. I think we have all we need for now. We will set up another meeting for tomorrow.

Back at the Ranch

The group reconvene back at Instant Knowledge. There they begin to **create models** describing the business flow that was just described to them. A good way to model a business flow is to use an Activity Diagram, as outlined by the UML. Using an activity diagram allows them to describe the steps involved in the client's business process. This will also convince the client that they are on the same path, which is a major point of the diagrams.

User Interviews

Facilitator: We have created business flow diagrams of your current process. We want to make sure we fully understand how it works currently and who uses it so we can accurately determine your needs.

(The Modeler displays the diagrams to the client.)

Client: I believe you have captured the essence of our task process, I am pleased to see that. What next?

Facilitator: We now would like to get a better idea of exactly who does what in the task process. We would like to interview those involved, starting with the manager.

Client: Great, I will go get him.

(5 minutes later)

Manager: Hello, pleasure to meet you.

Facilitator: Welcome. Could you please describe your role in the task process?

(The modeler and the note taker listen intensely.)

Manager: Certainly. After arriving at the office in the morning, I head straight for the coffee machine.

Facilitator: Sugar?

Manager: Two lumps, and cream. I then look at the tasks that need to be done that day. I create a pile for each worker. If a worker has the required skill set to complete a task, I place that task in his or her pile.

Modeler: What if there are two workers with the same skills? Which one gets the task?

Facilitator: Good thinking.

Manager: When I see two or more workers have the skills required to complete a task, I find out which worker has the least amount of tasks in their pile and I place the task in that one. If all workers have an even amount of tasks in their pile, I randomly place the task in a pile.

Facilitator: How do you create this randomness?

Manager: I spin around in my office chair for one minute, then I close my eyes and place the task down on one of the piles. The one I come closest to gets the task. It's kind of like "pin the tail on the donkey".

Note Taker: I love that game.

Modeler: Good times.

Facilitator: Fascinating. Please continue.

Manager: I then deliver each task pile to the appropriate worker's in-box.

Facilitator: This information is very helpful. Could you tell us what you do at the end of the day?

Manager: I go home.

Facilitator: How about just before that?

Manager: I collect the tasks from each worker's out-box. Then I check to make sure the workers have completed the tasks successfully.

Facilitator: What indicates if the task was finished properly?

Manager: If they signed their initials on the paper.

Facilitator: Excellent. Thank you for your time. Could you send in a worker now please?

Manager: No problem.

(Enter worker)

Worker: Hey, dudes!

Facilitator: Yo. Thanks for your time. Could you give us the low down on your job?

Worker: That's cool. When I come in, I go straight to the coffee machine.

Note Taker: Popular place.

Facilitator: Easy T-Note. What happens after that?

Worker: I then go to my desk and check my in-box. If there aren't any tasks in it, I wait until a task arrives. If there is a task, I complete it, initial the task paper and place it into my out-box.

Facilitator: That's pretty straightforward. Anything else you can tell us about?

Worker: Nope, that's it.

Facilitator: Thanks for your time. We have all we need for today.

Creating the Conceptual Class Diagram

(Back at IK Headquarters:)

The note taker wastes no time creating a **Conceptual Class Diagram**. This diagram helps us to visually see the objects and classes involved in the system and what actions they can perform. The note taker begins by breaking the notes into "nouns" and "verbs".

The list of "nouns" for the ABC Task Manager project is:

> *Task Manager, Manager, Employee, Worker, Task, Paper, In-box, Out-box, Job Title, Description, Start Date, End Date, Revision, Chair.*

The note taker then creates a list of all the verbs and verb phrases from the conversation:

> *Write Task, Place Task, Check In-box, Read Task, Complete Task, Place Task, Get Tasks, Check Tasks, Reject Task, Accept Task, Add Revision, Filed, Spin Chair.*

He then creates a conceptual class diagram. The nouns become **classes**:

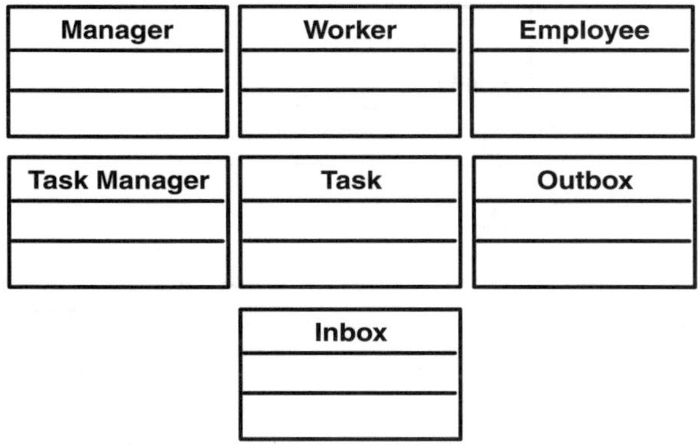

CONCEPTUAL CLASS DIAGRAM

Other nouns, such as Title, Description and Start Date, are **attributes** to a class, such as:

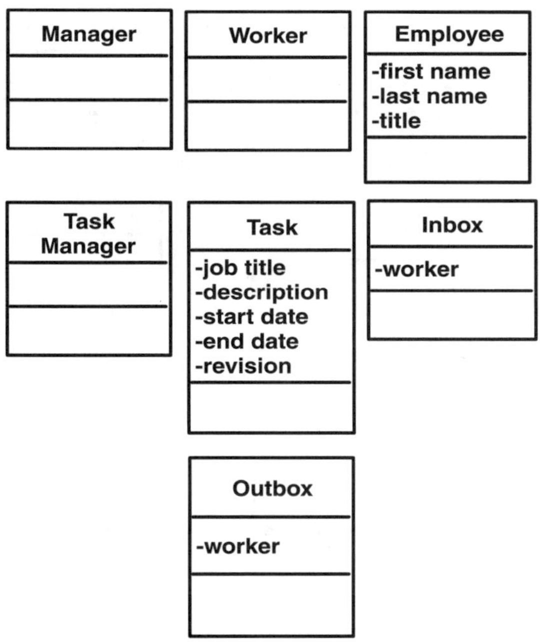

CLASS ATTRIBUTES

The note taker sits back at this point and decides that some of the classes can be grouped together. He also knows that the "verbs" extracted from the meetings become "**actions**" that the classes perform. So the note taker adds actions and associations to his diagram.

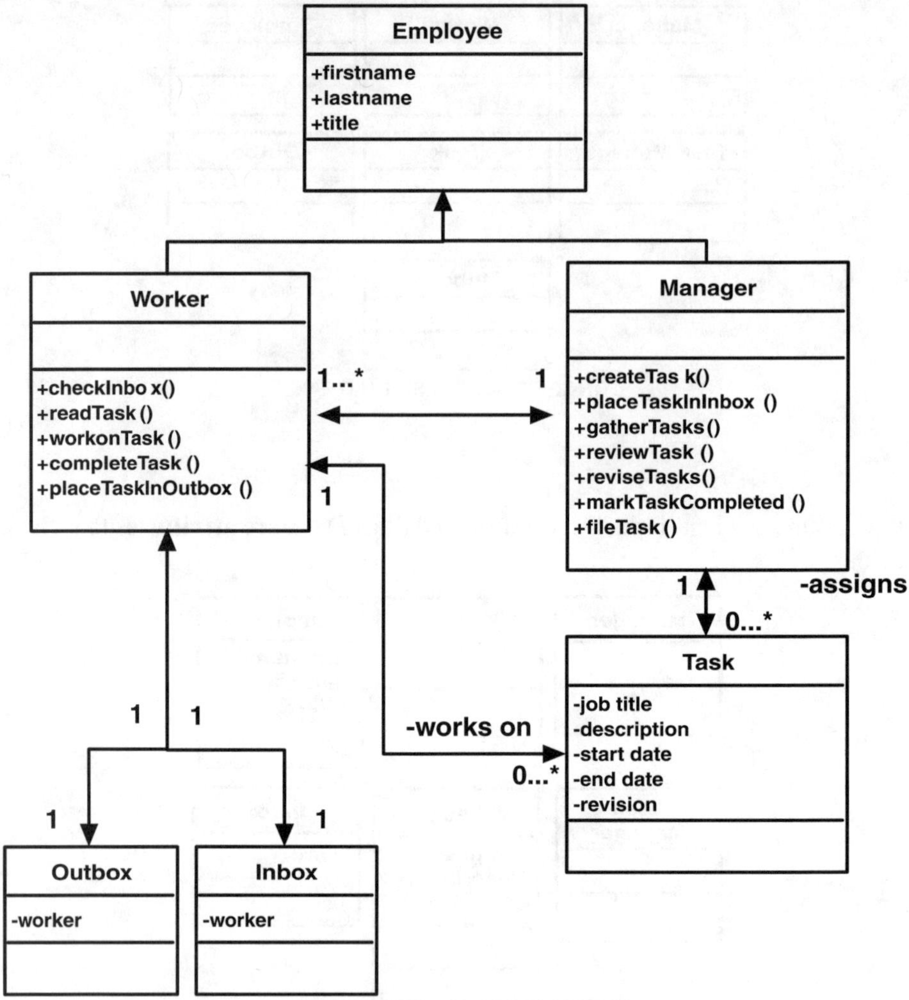

CONCEPTUAL CLASS DIAGRAM

Meanwhile, the modeler has been busy creating a new Activity Diagram to help further understand/document the way a Manager assigns tasks:

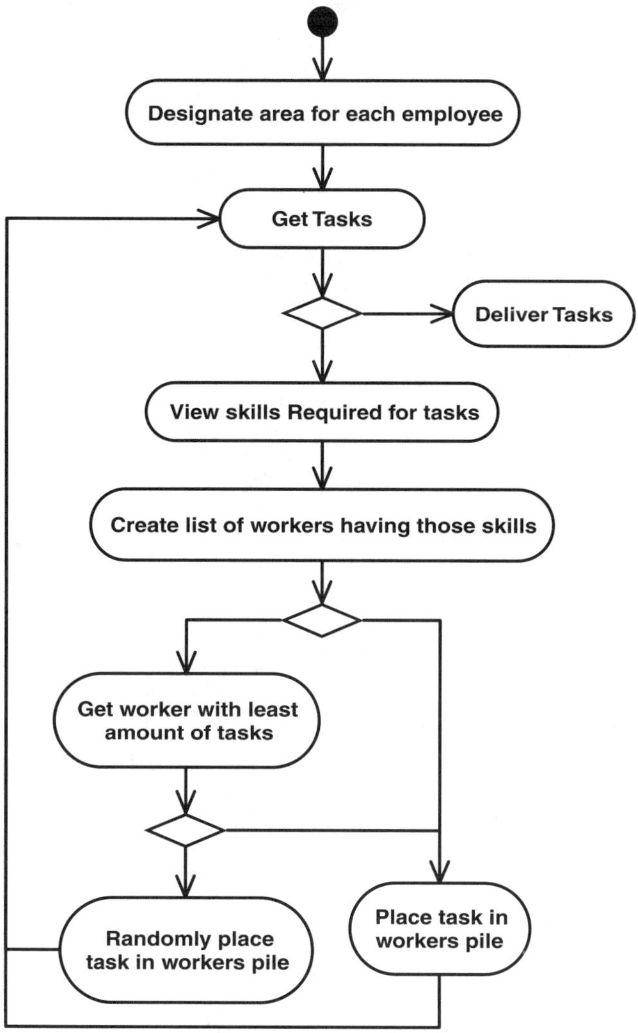

ACTIVITY DIAGRAM:
TASK ASSIGNMENT

The Pitch

The Analysts meet once again at the client's lair. This time they are here to pitch their idea for the Interactive Task Manager, or ITM.

The Facilitator: Thank you all for meeting us. We have reviewed our notes and created models to help us get a good idea of how you, the client, use your current task manager. Based on the data we have collected, we propose what we call the Interactive Task Manager, or ITM.

Client: Sounds very exciting.

The Facilitator: The ITM will allow tasks to be entered into a database and viewed through a web browser. Each employee will have their own login and status of either Manager or Worker. By creating an on-line task manager we are taking all of the paper work out of process and creating an huge database of information that can be searched.

Client: Well, I am convinced. I say it's a go! [Editor's Note: If only it were that easy, right?] What happens next?

The Facilitator: Next we would like to interview your employees again. We want to find out how they would like to use the system. This will give us a heads-up on any functionality that needs to be added to the system.

(Enter the manager)

The Facilitator: Hello, you have been filled in on the ITM, now we would like to hear how you think you would use such a system.

Manager: Well, I think the best part would be to create work sheets at the end of the week. Part of my job is creating a summary of all the tasks each employee completes throughout the week.

The Facilitator: Great idea! Anything else?

Manager: No, that's all I can think of.

The Facilitator: Thanks for your time, could you please send in your worker again?

(enter worker)

The Facilitator: You also have been briefed on ITM. Can you tell us how you would use the system?

Worker: Sure, I would obviously use it for the same tasks, such as receiving and completing tasks. But the added bonus for me is that this would eliminate tasks coming back with unfinished, as I do not have to sign the tasks anymore. My login will be sufficient.

The Facilitator: Great, thanks for your time. Client, we have most of what we need. Should anything come up, we will give you a call.

Updating the Models and Initiating Use Case

(back at IK Headquarters)

The group works together to create new models. They have new functionality now that wasn't originally discussed. This is good. It has made the last set of interviews worth the time. It is better for them to get all the intended functionality up front, rather than change it later.

With the new and old requirements understood, the group now works on diagraming the ITM system. They begin with **Use Case Diagrams**. These diagrams help the analysts understand who is involved with the system and exactly how they will use it.

The initial diagram is very simple, since we only have two people using the system. However, it still gives us a view of the system at its highest level.

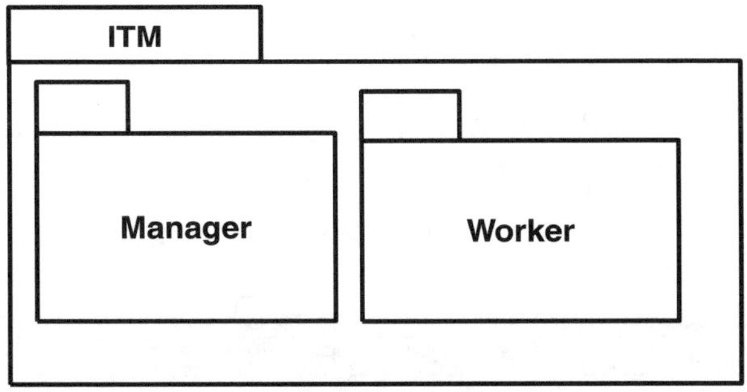

BASIC USE CASE DIAGRAM

They then create another diagram, showing each package inside the ITM system, with its functionality:

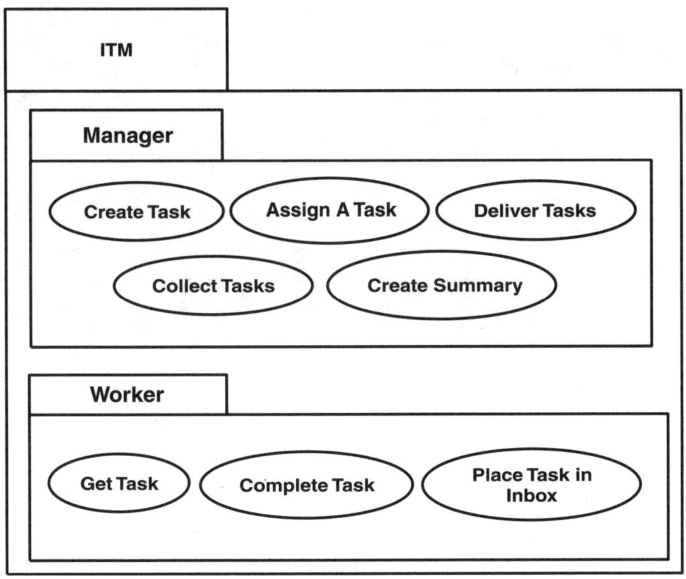

USE CASE ANALYSIS DIAGRAM

Use Case Analysis Process: Manager

The group then creates **Use Case Analysis** for each case in the packages. A Use Case Analysis further describes the Use Case, allowing the programmer to see if there are any cases that overlap, or are common.

Manager Use Case Analysis

Use Case:	**CREATE A TASK**
Description:	Create a new task.
Assumptions:	
Preconditions:	Manager has logged into the system
Steps:	1. Manager selects the "create task" form from list of options. 2. Manager fills in title, description, start

	date, end date. 3. Manager presses create task button.
Benefitting Actor:	Manager

Next we create a **User Interaction Sequence Diagram**. It has an Analysis Document like this:

Model: USER INTERACTION SEQUENCE DIAGRAMS
What They Provide: 1. A general visual representation of objects within the system and a users interactions with those objects. 2. A visual sequence of events from user action to system reaction. 3. A use case combined with a sequence diagram.
Scope: 1. This diagram should limit itself to high level objects within the system. The most common of these are the user, browser, application and storage objects, such as a database, text file, or memory object. 2. For brevity, only memory objects that are imperative to showing top level functionality should be shown.
Format: 1. This diagram can be expressed via a standard UML Sequence Diagram.
Refines: Activity, and Class Diagrams
Refined By:
Notes:

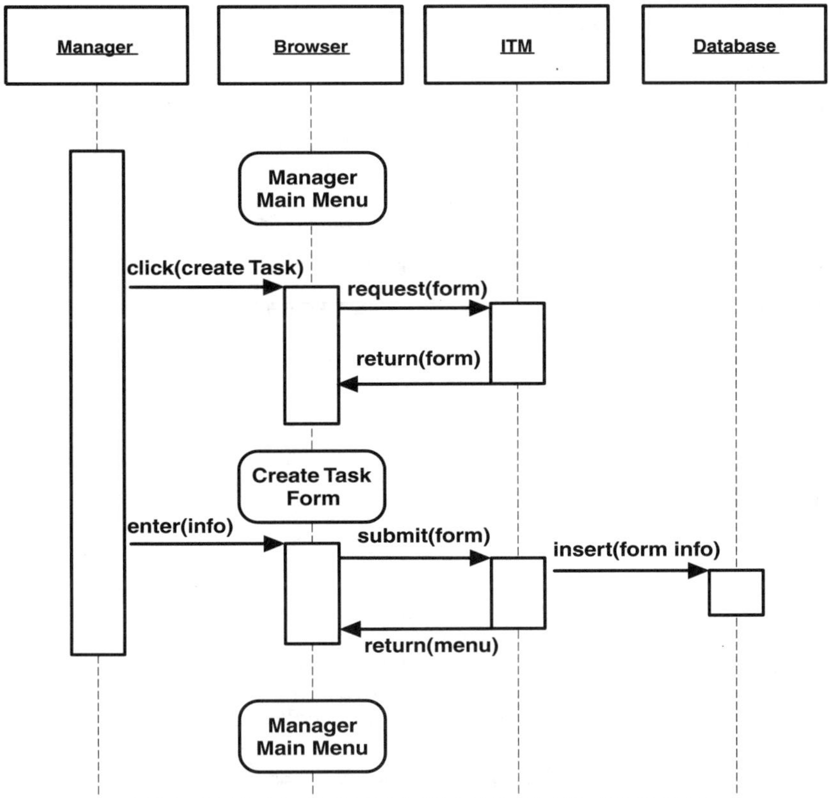

USER INTERACTION SEQUENCE DIAGRAM: MANAGER

User Interaction Sequence Diagrams are represented as a UML Sequence Diagram. Simply stated, Sequence Diagrams show the interactions between objects over time. Most of our diagrams include user objects, browser objects, application objects, persistent variable objects, and data source objects.

Although these diagrams are created during the specification phase, they could be considered part of the design phase, as they start to describe the application itself and its reactions to user input, albeit at a high level.

We begin the diagrams with a user interaction with the browser, which is in some given state. The browser will then make its request of the application, which will then interact with any data sources and variables it needs, and then return a page back to the browser, allowing the user further opportunities for interaction, if required by the diagram.

Use Case:	**VIEW COMPLETED TASKS**
Description:	View list of completed tasks.
Assumptions:	
Preconditions:	1. Manager has logged into the system. 2. Tasks have been assigned
Steps:	1. Manager selects the "view completed tasks" option from the main menu. 2. System displays list of completed tasks.
Benefitting Actor:	Manager

Use Case:	**CREATE SUMMARY**
Description:	Creates a weekly summary for each employee, displays all the tasks completed for the week by them.
Assumptions:	
Preconditions:	Manager has logged into the system Tasks have been assigned
Steps:	1. Manager selects the "view summary" option from the main menu. 2. System display list of employees. 3. Manager chooses employee. 4. System displays weekly summary.
Benefitting Actor:	Manager

Use Case Analysis Process: Worker

The group then creates a Use Case Analysis for each case in the packages.

Worker Use Case Analysis

Use Case:	**LOGIN**
Description:	User login to the system.
Assumptions:	
Preconditions:	
Steps:	1. User enters username/password. 2. System checks username/password. 3. If accepted user is logged in. 4. If rejected user is brought back to the login page.
Benefitting Actor:	Manager/Worker

Use Case:	**VIEW TASK**
Description:	View tasks assigned to self.
Assumptions:	Worker has logged into the system
Preconditions:	
Steps:	1. Worker selects the "view tasks" option from the main menu. 2. System displays list of tasks. 3. Worker selects task s/he wishes to view.
Benefitting Actor:	Worker

Use Case:	**COMPLETE TASK**
Description:	Log task as having been completed.
Assumptions:	
Preconditions	Worker has logged into the system
Steps:	1. Worker selects the "view tasks" option from the main menu. 2. System displays list of tasks. 3. Worker selects task he or she wishes to view. 4. Worker selects the "task completed" option from the menu. 5. System updates this task as completed.
Benefitting Actor:	Worker

Use Case Sequence Diagrams: Manager

The specification phase has now been completed. The analysts have fully documented ABC's business process, defined what IK's application will do, and developed Use Case Analysis and Interaction Diagrams to help the programmers to understand how the application should work.

The programmers begin by studying all the class diagrams they have been given. This gives them a quick look at the objects, both physical and nonphysical, that are involved in the system. It also allows them to see what actions those objects are capable of performing.

After studying all the diagrams, the programmers begin to turn all these pictures into code. Since this is a web application, they will be working with file directories. They begin to decide what directories will be needed. They create what is called a "Directory Structure Diagram" a directory structure diagram has the following analysis document:

Model:	**DIRECTORY STRUCTURE DIAGRAM**
Stage:	Design
What They Provide:	1. A visual representation of the directory structure of the application. 2. A base document to begin creating Fusebox, Fuseaction and file diagrams. 3. A tree-form view of the application.
Scope:	1. Fusebox directories with a stereotypical "Fusebox" structure. 2. Image directories 3. Query directories 4. Other pertinent directories
Constraints:	1. No attributes 2. No Fuseactions
Format:	1. The UML Class Diagram. 2. Directories are class elements.
Validates:	Analysis Phase: Class Diagram
Validated By:	Fusebox/Fuseaction Diagram
Notes:	

This diagram is relatively straight-forward, looking very much like a normal directory structure.

Directory Structure Diagram

The programmers, looking at the specification diagrams, come to realize that what they need is a set of directories for a Task Manager. The manager and worker are users of the system, tracked in a user directory, developed elsewhere. The actions that the employees could perform would need to be built into the system but would not require actual employee directories.

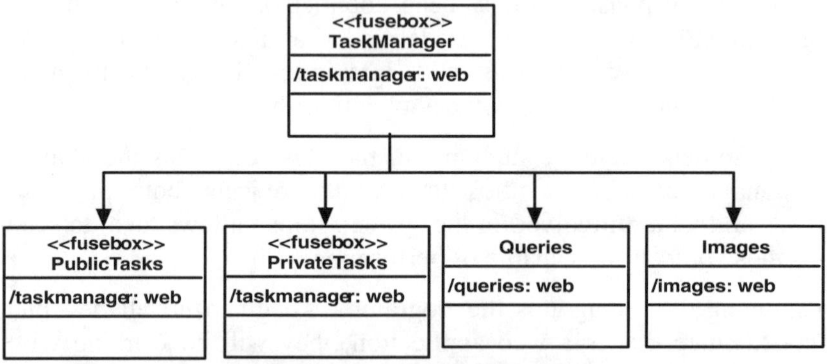

DIRECTORY STRUCTURE DIAGRAM

There are two sets of actions that can take place within the ITM: Manager actions and worker actions. To add a little more security, the actions have been separated into directories for public and private tasks. Both directories extend the functionality of the Task Manager and are placed underneath the

TaskManager directory. All three directories, TaskManager, PublicTasks and PrivateTasks have the stereotypical characteristics of "Fusebox". This indicates that the directory is not only a directory in the application, but a Fusebox as well.

The TaskManager Fusebox has an attribute of */taskmanager:web*. This indicates to the programmer that it will have a virtual mapping named "*taskmanager*", mapped by the web server. (Note: The mapping could have also been a ColdFusion mapping and would then have been labeled */taskmanager:cf*.)

Fusebox/Fuseaction Diagrams: Worker

After the directory structure diagram comes the Fusebox/Fuseaction diagram, which will expand the model and validate the directory structure. (In UML, every diagram should validate the one before.)

The Fusebox/Fuseaction diagram dives further into the application and helps us to see what Fuseactions each Fusebox needs to perform.

Fusebox/Fuseaction diagrams have the following analysis documents:

Model:	**FUSEBOX/FUSEACTION DIAGRAM**
Stage:	Design
Purpose:	Diagram the Fusebox and each of its Fuseactions.
Scope:	1. Fusebox being diagramed 2. Fusebox's local variables 3. Fuseactions of that Fusebox 4. Each Fuseaction's attributes 5. Each Fuseaction's files 6. Each Fuseaction's required parameters
Constraints:	1. Files do not show their input and output parameters
Format:	1. The UML Class Diagram 2. Fuseboxs and Fuseactions are displayed as classes.
Validates:	Analysis Phase: Class Diagram; Analysis Phase: Use Case Interaction Diagrams; Directory Structure Diagram
Validated By:	Fuseaction Sequence Diagram, File Diagram
Notes:	

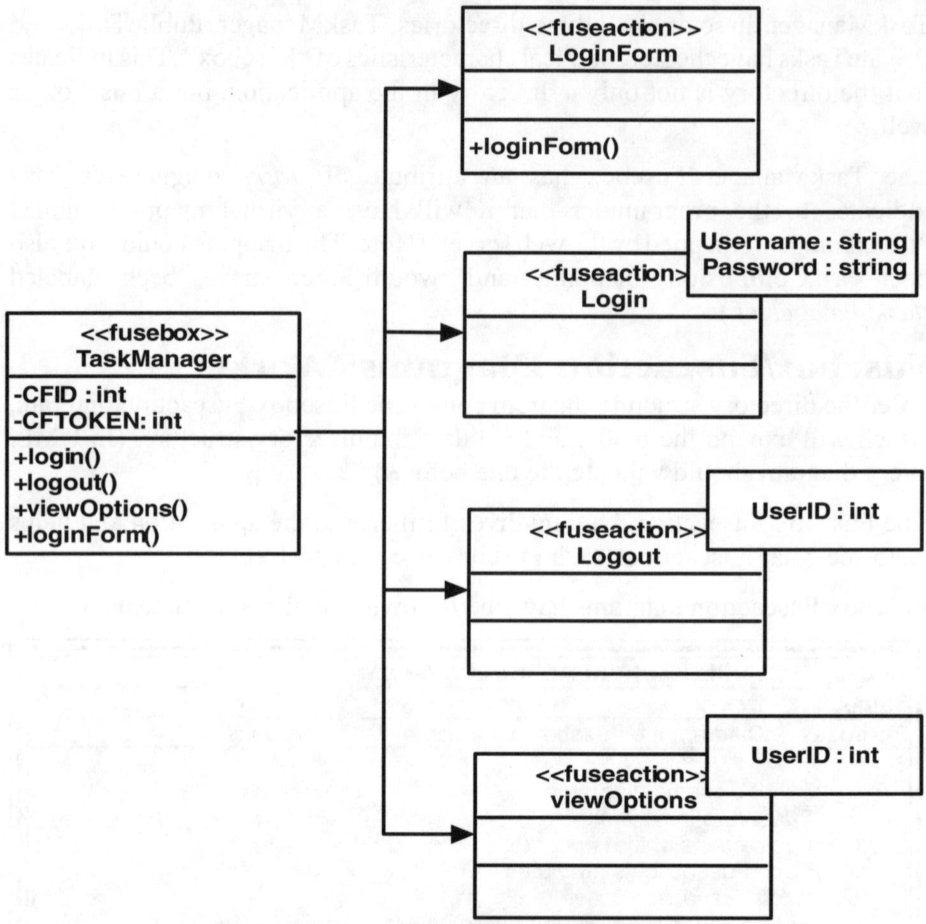

FUSEBOX AND FUSEACTION DIAGRAM

This is the first version of the Fusebox/Fuseaction diagram. It allows us to see a Fusebox and all of its Fuseactions in one shot. The Fuseactions are then created by evaluating the Use Case Interaction Diagrams from the Analysis Phase.

In this situation, this diagram has two versions. The programmer can create the Fuseactions needed by looking at Class and Use Case Diagrams, but also creates a Fuseaction Sequence Diagram to gain a better understanding of the files needed by each Fuseaction. Fuseaction Sequence Diagrams are used to give the programmer a better understanding of the flow of the Fuseaction and clarifies which files are needed by the application.

Fuseaction Sequence Diagrams: Worker

The programmer decides he has gotten as far as he can with the Fusebox/Fuseaction Diagrams and needs to dive further into the Fuseaction before finishing that diagram up. He creates a Fuseaction Sequence Diagram to map out the flow. A Fuseaction Sequence Diagram has the following Analysis Document:

Model:	**FUSEACTION SEQUENCE DIAGRAM**
Stage:	Design
Purpose:	To portray the interactions between objects and changes in state within a Fuseaction.
Scope:	Objects used in a Fuseaction, i.e., file, database.
Constraints:	
Format:	The UML Sequence Diagram
Validates:	Analysis Phase: User Interaction Sequence Diagram; Fusebox/Fuseaction Diagram
Validated By:	File Diagram
Notes:	

Fuseaction Sequence Diagram
Fuseaction: Login

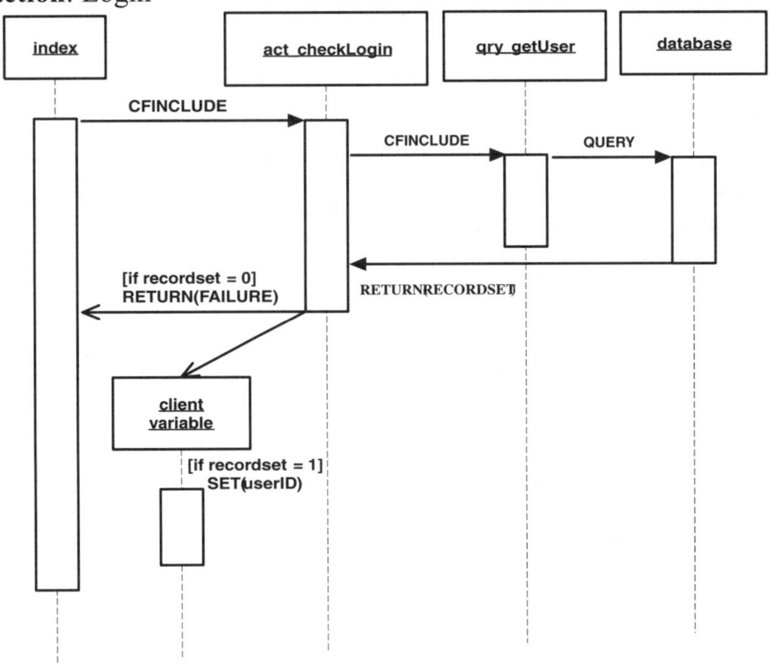

LOGIN

The following additional diagrams are created, using the same methods:

Fuseaction Sequence Diagram
Fuseaction: Logout

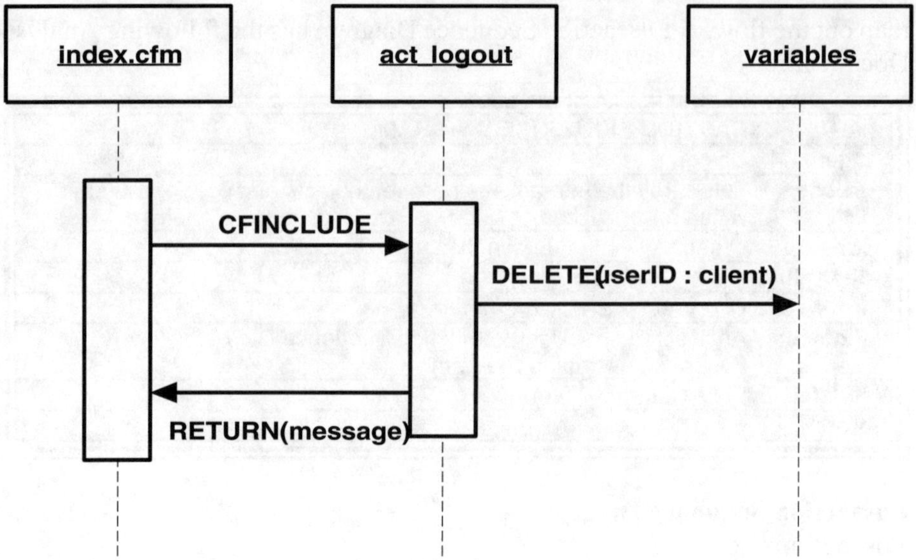

LOGOUT

Fuseaction Sequence Diagram
Fuseaction: viewOptions

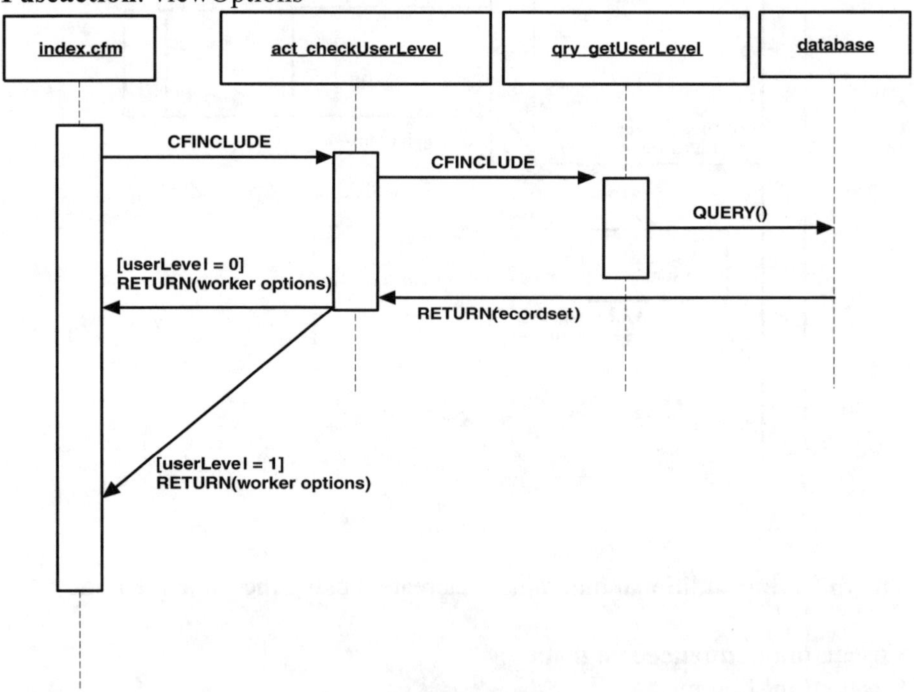

ViewOptions

Evaluating the User Interaction Sequence Diagram from the Analysis Phase and the Fusebox/Fuseaction diagrams, the programmer creates the above diagrams.

It is now clear which what files are needed to complete each Fuseaction. With these preliminary diagrams in hand, the programmer completes the Fusebox/Fuseaction Diagram.

Fusebox/Fuseaction Diagram Version 2: Worker

Using the newly-created Fuseaction Sequence Diagrams, the programmer now goes back to the Fusebox/Fuseaction diagrams and adds the necessary files.

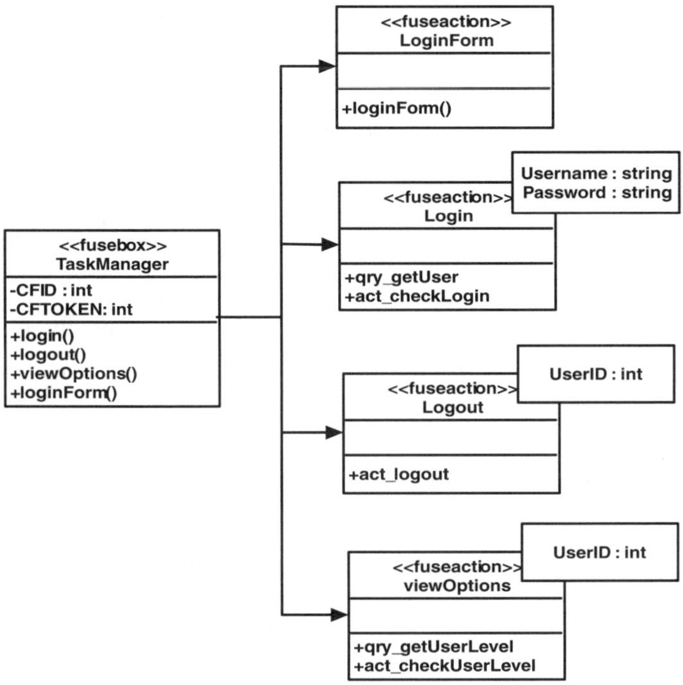

FUSEBOX/FUSEACTION DIAGRAM V.2: WORKER

File Diagrams: Worker

Once the Fusebox/Fuseaction and Fuseaction Sequence diagrams have been completed, the programmer concentrates on the files.

Model:	**FILE DIAGRAM**
Stage:	Design
Purpose:	Define each file used within a Fuseaction.
Scope: 1. Filename 2. Input parameters 3. Output parameters	
Constraints:	
Format: 1. Visio Static Structure Diagram 2. Files as classes with a 'file" stereotype.	

Validates: Fusebox/Fuseaction Diagram
Validated By: File Activity Diagram
Notes:

Fuseaction File Diagram
Fusebox: TaskManager
Fuseaction: Login Form

<<file>>
dsp_loginForm
<--- loginForm : form
[responsibility] - Display alogin form

LOGIN FORM

Fuseaction File Diagram
Fusebox: TaskManager
Fuseaction: Login

<<file>>
qry_getUser
---> username : string
---> password : string
<--- getUser : query
[responsibility] - query the database for a user with the supplied username/password combination

GET USER

<<file>>
act_checkLogin
---> getUser : query
<--- relocate : cflocation
[responsibility] - CheckgetUser query, if 1, relocate to options, if 0 relocate to error page

LOGIN

Fuseaction File Diagram
Fusebox: TaskManager
Fuseaction: Logout

<<file>>
act_logout
---> userID : client
<--- relocate : cflocation
[responsibility] - delete user©sCFID and CFTOKEN

LOGOUT

Fuseaction File Diagram
Fusebox: TaskManager
Fuseaction: ViewOptions

<<file>>
qry_getUserLevel
---> userID : client
<--- getUserLevel : query
[responsibility] - query for the user©s security level

GET USER LEVEL

<<file>>
qry_checkUserLevel
---> getUserLevel : query
<--- userOptions : display
[responsibility] - test the getUserLevel qry;display full options if they are a manager; partial if a worker

TEST USER LEVEL

Conclusion

The PRIVATETASKS and PUBLICTASKS Fuseboxes flow much the same as the TASKMANAGER does. To keep from repeating ourselves, we are only showing the one Fusebox. That is sufficient to show how fUseMl can be extremely helpful in specifying and designing your web applications.

Fusebox helps you maximize your code and get the most out of your development time. Using the UML in conjunction with Fusebox can help you get the most out of your Specification and Design phases, as well.

APPENDIX C: How to Make Fusebox and Frames Get Along

Frames are a programming device that places specific text and graphics in adjustable boxes, called "frames". Usually, each box is adjustable in size and may scroll independently of each other, but are held in the same relative positions to one another. In some cases, one or another frame may be closed while leaving the other(s) open. This is an excellent technique to present independent but related material, i.e., a table of contents bar beside the text being viewed, or a site navigation bar above a product presentation.

Web-based applications oftentimes are the best place to use frames. A web application is a collection of scripts, run from a web server, designed to perform a specific function directly for the user or, in some cases, for another application. Examples of Web applications include e-mail programs such as Hotmail® (*http://www.hotmail.com*), communication programs such as CFBoard's discussion forum software (*http://www.cfboards.com*), contact manager systems like a Yahoo!® address book (*http://address.yahoo.com*), and stock trading tools like Datek (*http://www.datek.com*).

If you can visualize these tools, you might agree that using frames can be a good idea. In case you aren't convinced why the use of frames is a good thing, here are some reasons why frames are good.

Use Frames to:

Display Updates

Hidden frames and meta-refresh tags allow the browser to retrieve new data without the user feeling like they have lost control of the entire page, if the whole page needs to reload. Users no longer feel, "My browser got hijacked!"

Run Multiple Processes

Along with controlling parts of a page, individual frames can control different aspects of the user interface and perform different actions for the user. Multiple requests can be sent to the server with a single click, making the user feel "in control". Without frames, the entire display page has to reload before the user can begin another process, or multiple processes must be submitted at a single click, which present user interface dilemmas and ColdFusion Markup Language logic trickeries.

Enable Faster Client Loads

The client only has to download the specific individual pieces that need to be changed or updated. Fewer packets back and forth across the Internet mean less chance for error, and better performance for slower connection speeds.

Reduce Server Load

The server must retrieve all new information and instantiate all the variables every time the screen reloads in a non-framed environment. That left-hand navigation menu that never changes does not need to be rebuilt every time. Using frames lightens the load on the server.

Improve Session Management

Using hidden frames and client variables (which you should be doing anyway), you can flawlessly tell whether a user is still using the system. Here's how: Set up a hidden frame to meta-refresh every sixty seconds or few minutes. Place the following code in between the <HEAD> and </HEAD> tags in your page:

```
<meta http-equiv="Refresh" content="60;url='index.cfm?fuseaction=Hidden'">
```

Make sure that this frame source reads a client variable. It can be any variable – even CFID/CFTOKEN. This will update the "LVISIT" column in the CGLOBALS table of the client variable database. You can build a query that shows whether a given user is still on the system by comparing their last page hit (LVISIT) with the current date/time. You can also remove the client record associated with that CFID/CFTOKEN, freeing memory, and giving client variables the low-timeout benefit of session variables. Without frames, you're reliant on the long timeout values or sloppy JavaScript onUnLoad() functions.

Better Manage Targets

Admittedly, keeping your <HREF> and form action targets sorted out can be tricky. But, a clear, obvious frame naming scheme from the outset reduces the headaches here.

Building the Frameset

Loading the Frameset

As we know, the only page that should ever be called by the browser is *index.cfm*. Therefore, we should not allow the frameset page to be called by the browser. The default Fuseaction of the circuit's *index.cfm* page will call the frameset page:

```
<!--- index.cfm --->
...
<CFPARAM name="attributes.fuseaction" default="main">
<CFSWITCH expression="#attributes.fuseaction#">
    <CFCASE value="main">
        <CFINCLUDE template="fra_main.cfm">
```

```
    </CFCASE>
    ...
</CFSWITCH>
```

The Frameset Page

Because all form and URL links in a Fusebox application go through the *index.cfm* (the Fusebox), we should call frame sources via *index.cfm* as well. Each frame source should call *index.cfm* with a Fuseaction requesting the output of the page. Here's an example of the frameset page:

```
<!--- fra_main.cfm --->
...
<frameset cols="137,*" frameborder="0" framespacing="0" border="0">
    <frame name="Left" src="index.cfm?fuseaction=NavBar&#URLToken#"
        marginwidth="0" marginheight="0"
        scrolling="no" frameborder="0" framespacing="0">
    <frame name="Center" src="index.cfm?fuseaction=Body&#URLToken#"
        marginwidth="0" marginheight="0"
        scrolling="auto" frameborder="0" framespacing="0">
    </frameset>
    ...
```

You may notice that the name of the file is "*fra_main.cfm*". This prefix seems to contradict the Fusebox file naming scheme.

But herein lies the beauty of Fusebox – it's flexibility. If you are only using one or two frameset pages in your application, we recommend sticking to the standard "*dsp_*" prefix. However, if your application contains many frameset pages, use the "*fra_*" prefix. That will allow you to keep straight which HTML pages are the frame **sources** and which are the frameset **pages**.

Calling the Frames

The above frameset call uses *index.cfm* to load the frame contents. Let's take a look at the Fuseactions for loading the contents of the frames:

```
<!--- index.cfm --->
...
<CFCASE value="NavBar">
    <CFINCLUDE template="dsp_NavBar.cfm">
</CFCASE>

<CFCASE value="Body">
    <CFINCLUDE template="dsp_DefaultBody.cfm">
</cfcase>
...
```

That's all there is to it! Using this flexible, modular and powerful method of Fusebox and frames together will allow you to nest multiple framesets and call frame sources across Fuseboxes.

Nested Framesets and Multiple Fuseboxes

Here's a code example on nesting multiple framesets, and filling the frame contents across multiple Fuseboxes. First, an example of the *fra_main.cfm*, in this case calling two nested framesets and four frame sources.

```
<!--- fra_main.cfm --->
...
<frameset rows="*,0" frameborder="0" framespacing="0" border="0">
    <frameset cols="137,*" frameborder="0" framespacing="0" border="0">
        <frame name="Left" src="index.cfm?fuseaction=
        NavBar&#URLToken#"
            marginwidth="0" marginheight="0"
            scrolling="no" frameborder="0" framespacing="0">
        <frameset rows="64,*" frameborder="0" framespacing="0"
        border="0">
            <frame name="Top" src="index.cfm?fuseaction=
            TopBar&#URLToken#"
                marginwidth="0" marginheight="0"
                scrolling="no" frameborder="0" framespacing="0">
            <frame name="Center"
                src="center/index.cfm?fuseaction=Main&#URLToken#"
                marginwidth="0" marginheight="0"
                scrolling="auto" frameborder="0" framespacing="0">
        </frameset>
    </frameset>
    <frame name="Hidden"
src="index.cfm?fuseaction=Hidden&#URLToken#"
        marginwidth="0" marginheight="0"
        scrolling="no" frameborder="0" framespacing="0">
</frameset>
...
```

You can nest framesets as deeply as you want. There is no practical limitation. On the other hand, to keep the user interface pleasant, make sure you can completely justify every frame on the display page.

The above example is four frames. Notice that the frame named "Center" (middle of the code block) calls a separate Fusebox to retrieve its contents. Let's take a peek at *center/index.cfm*:

```
<!--- index.cfm --->
...
<CFSWITCH expression="#attributes.fuseaction#">
    <CFCASE value="Main">
        <CFINCLUDE template="fra_main.cfm">
    </CFCASE>
...
</CFSWITCH>
```

Remember, every frameset call or frame source load requires *index.cfm* to tell it what to do. The above-nested circuit's *index.cfm* is no different. This Fuseaction is quite simple, but requires us to check out the *fra_main.cfm* file in this circuit:

```
<!--- fra_main.cfm in "center" circuit --->
...
<frameset rows="280,*" frameborder="0" framespacing="0" border="0">
    <frameset cols="182,*" frameborder="0" framespacing="0" border="0">
        <frame name="QuoteChart"
            src="index.cfm?fuseaction=QuoteChart&#URLToken#"
            marginwidth="0" marginheight="3"
            scrolling="no" frameborder="0" topmargin="3">
        <frame name="CustomGraph"
            src="index.cfm?fuseaction=CustomGraph&#URLToken#"
            marginwidth="0" marginheight="3"
            scrolling="no" frameborder="0" topmargin="3">
    </frameset>
        <frame name="NewsTicker"
src="/service/index.cfm?fuseaction=Note&#URLToken#"
        marginwidth="0" marginheight="0"
        scrolling="auto" frameborder="no">
</frameset>
...
```

This frameset page calls yet another Fusebox to supply the contents of the frame named "*NewsTicker*" (bottom of the code). There's no need to show you the *index.cfm* and the subsequent pages that are included to fulfill the action "*/service/index.cfm?fuseaction=Note*". It could contain an HTML page, some complex CFML, another frameset page, or, even a <CFMODULE> to another Fusebox.

Fusebox and Frames, Pretty as a Picture

As you can see, Fusebox works well with frames to give you optimal performance in a manner that is both attractive and practical from the user's viewpoint. It can also improve the application's overall functionality by helping keep track of user status, among other internal niceties. And of course, the very use of Fusebox, with its self-sustaining nomenclature, can add longevity to the application's life cycle.

APPENDIX D: Before and After: A Case Study in Fusebox Development

JazzLoft.com, Some Background

No computer book is complete without code, and lots of it. It's even better when included code actually makes up a complete application. Many technical books, conferences and seminars show you lots of cool code or applications but never tell you how/why to use them. Many of us walk away thinking "That was interesting, but why do I need it?"

In this book, we strove to supply great ideas and code snippets. Now we will show you the "how" and "why" of using Fusebox in your applications. There is no better way to do this than with a live site.

We have made arrangements with Alan Lawrence of **JazzLoft.com**, the leader in independent jazz CD commerce, to take the site's existing ColdFusion application and convert it into Fusebox, giving you a before-and-after look at a real-life application. The JazzLoft.com site was already coded and functioning using ColdFusion, so the challenge was "Can we make it **better** using Fusebox?"

We think Fusebox passes the test and will prove it here. The code for the site in question is fully available at SecretAgents.com. Yes, that's right, every line is included for you to view. All we ask is if anything slips past our editor – perish the thought – let us know. We are providing a bug site on SecretAgents.com to allow people to report bugs in the application and thus keep every person who spent their hard-earned money on this book up-to-date. The code is and remains the copyright of JazzLoft, with limited copy permission granted.

The Challenge for Us

The challenge for us was to "Fusebox-ize" JazzLoft.com. With that in mind, the intention was not to add to the site, but make it work exactly as it did before, except make the code easier to understand, debug, maintain and integrate with new code. With that said, we did not perform a specification and design analysis with the customer and instead simply gathered all functionality from the existing code.

This appendix is broken into four sections.

1. **Side by Side**: What was old is new again. We show the old CF code and map it to its corresponding Fusebox/Fuseactions.
2. **Database Normalization**: When converting the database, a few tables were updated to make it "normal." (Ok, so we had to add SOME functionality.)
3. **Site-Wide Optimization**: A listing of ideas/code we used to get the most out of our code.
4. **Challenge**: Our challenge to YOU, the reader, to make this site the best it can be, now and forever.

Side By Side: A Comparison

Sorting Out the Pieces

The original JazzLoft.com site consisted of static HTML files and only the following ten ColdFusion files:

1. basket.cfm
2. basket2.cfm
3. basket3.cfm
4. basket4.cfm
5. bioscatalog.cfm
6. bios.cfm
7. catalog.cfm
8. pos.cfm
9. search.cfm
10. action.cfm

These, combined with HTML files, comprise JazzLoft.com.

It is pretty easy to see what Fuseboxes will be needed just by looking at the file names, except maybe "*pos.cfm*". This clear naming scheme is a credit to the original coder and will help make our job easier as we go along.

After looking at each file (we'll look into them in more detail shortly), we came up with the following list of Fuseboxes.

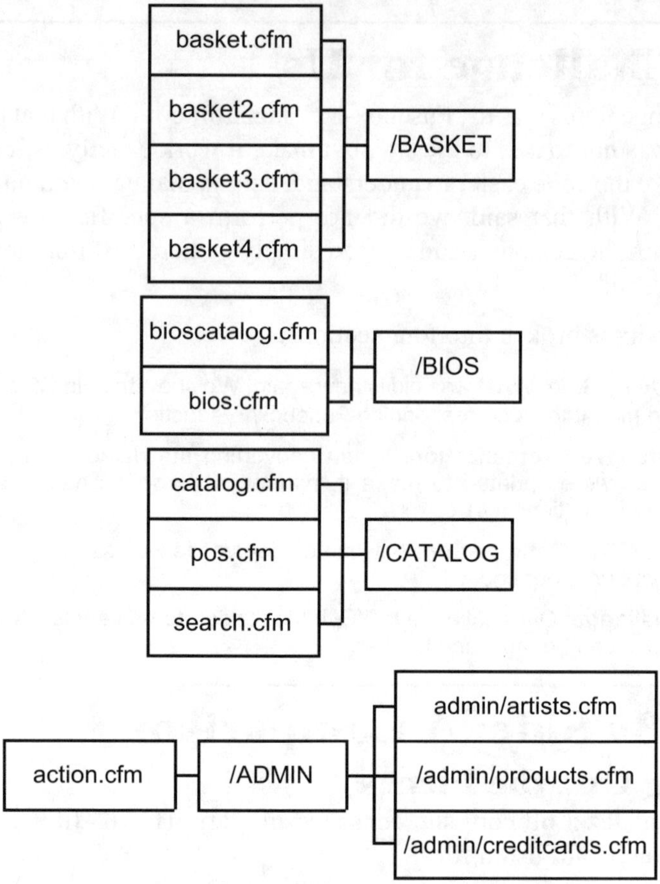

Take It From the Top with "BASKET"

Breaking Out the Fuseactions

The next step was to break each step down into needed Fuseactions. For that we need to review the code. This section is interactive, so you may want to follow along with the code you downloaded from SecretAgents.com.

A bit of background first: JazzLoft calls a series of variables called "*Steps*". These tell the application where the user is in the checkout process: Step 1 adds an item to the cart, Step 2 enters the user's information, Step 3 adds credit card information, and Step 4 completes the transaction.

Basket.cfm

We started by writing down a brief explanation of what the file does. Then we created a list of exactly what each file does.

Basket.cfm is Step 1 in the checkout. It will create a new cart as necessary, making sure that it is empty, and display the cart to the user. From this page, the user will be able to update his/her quantities or proceed to the next page in the checkout process.

1. Check for a *cookie.custid*, which stores the customer ID. If "*notfound*" (there was no *cookie.custid*), go to 3. (Line 21)
2. If found, search the database for the customer's information. (Line 23)
3. If the query does not return a record, insert the customer and create a new cookie with the new *customerid*. (Lines 27-40)
4. If the variable STEP = 1 (the user is just starting the purchase process), then empty the shopping basket. (Line 58)
5. Perform a check to see whether the item is currently in the user's shopping cart. If the item is not in the cart, insert a record into the database, thus putting the item in the cart. If the item is already in the cart, update the quantity of the item by one. (Line 66)
6. Obtain appropriate shipping cost. (Lines 107–127)
7. Display basket. (Lines 129–end of file (EOF))

The "actions" that this file performs can then be broken into Fuseactions for the /Basket Fusebox:

1. checkCustomer
2. getCustomerInfo
3. updateCustomer
4. emptyBasket
5. updateBasket
6. getShippingCost
7. viewBasket

Basket2.cfm

Basket2.cfm contains actions for emptying the user's basket and also contains a form for entering the user's billing and shipping addresses.

Existing Actions:

1. If Step = 1 (user has just started the purchase process), delete any existing items from basket. (Line 15)
2. If Step = 2 (order is being placed),: (Line 21 – EOF)
3. Get customer information; (Line 94)
4. Display form with customer billing and shipping information. (Line 98)

Converted Fuseactions/Fuses:

1. emptyBasket
2. getCustomerInfo
3. editBillingAndShipping

Basket3.cfm

Basket3.cfm deals with obtaining a user's credit card information. It also works in conjunction with *basket2.cfm* by updating the user's address information.

Existing Actions:

1. Update customer information supplied from *basket2.cfm*. (Line 45)
2. Get additional customer information. (Line 69)
3. Display billing and shipping information. (Line 72)
4. Get shipping cost. (Lines 116–145)
5. Display basket. (Line 147)
6. Display credit card form. (Line 215)

Converted Fuseactions/Fuses:

1. updateCustomer
2. getCustomerInfo
3. viewBillingAndShipping
4. getShippingCost
5. viewBasket
6. editCreditCard

Basket4.cfm

Basket4.cfm deals with doing the final calculation of the order and capturing the actual payment of the order.

Existing Actions:

1. Insert payment information from *basket3.cfm*. (Line 23)
2. Obtain the order information. (Lines 25-40)
3. Display customer information. (Line 44)
4. Get shipping cost. (Lines 87–108)
5. Display shopping basket. (Line 110)
6. Display order ID. (Line 172)

Converted Fuseactions/Fuses:

1. addOrder
2. getOrder
3. viewCustomerInfo
4. getShippingCost
5. viewBasket
6. viewOrder

Coordinating the Pieces

Creating this list has helped us to understand how the basket currently works. We now have a list of all the Fuseactions our /BASKET Fusebox needs to perform (with all the duplicates taken out):

1. checkCustomer
2. getCustomerInfo
3. viewCustomerInfo
4. updateCustomer
5. viewBasket
6. emptyBasket
7. updateBasket
8. getShippingCost
9. editBillingAndShipping
10. viewBillingAndShipping
11. editCreditCard
12. addOrder
13. getOrder
14. viewOrder

The Resulting Fusebox: /BASKET

FUSEBOX: /BASKET

Fuseaction: *UpdateBasket*

General Comments: This updates the quantity of the products in a user's basket. If the quantity is set to zero, it removes the product from the user's basket.

Fuse: *act_updateBasket*

File Comments: This will update the quantity field in the *tblbaskets* table.

Fuseaction: *EmptyBasket*

General Comments: This removes all items from a basket.

Fuse: *qry_emptyBasket*

File Comments: This will remove all the items from a user's basket.

Fuseaction: *ViewBasket*

Next Action: *UpdateBasket*
Next Action: *EmptyBasket*
Next Action: *CheckoutForm*

General Comments: This lists all the products a user has added to their basket and totals up the price.

Fuse: *dsp_viewBasket*

File Comments: This will list all the items a user is planning on purchasing and select the data from the *tblbaskets* table associated with the user.

Fuseaction: *CheckoutForm*

Next Action: *UpdateCustomer*

General Comments: This is a form for a user to enter shipping and billing information. If they have cookies turned on, the information will "automagically" be filled in.

Fuse: *dsp_checkoutForm*

File Comments: This will display a form for the user to enter personal information: where to send the products, billing address, and credit card information.

Fuseaction: *UpdateCustomer*

Next Action: *PreviewCheckout*

General Comments: If the user's CFID/CFTOKEN are already in the database, this updates his/her record; if CFID/CFTOKEN are not in the database, it inserts a new record.

Fuse: *act_updateCustomer*

File Comments: This will update the customer information in the *tblcustomers* table

---

Fuseaction: *Preview Checkout*

Next Action: *CompleteCheckout*

General Comments: This gives the user one last chance to change his/her shipping/billing and credit card information.

Fuse: *act_remember*

File Comments: This sets the CFID/CFTOKEN cookies.

Fuse: *dsp_previewCheckout*

File Comments: This will display the order for the user to review.

Fuseaction: *Complete Checkout*

Next Action: *Receipt*

General Comments: This saves the order into the database

Fuse: *act_addOrder*

File Comments: This will insert a record into the *tblorders* table and associated *tblorder_products* table connected with the user.

Fuseaction: *Receipt*

General Comments: This displays the order to the user.

Fuse: *dsp_receipt*

File Comments: This will display the user's order, including shipping address.

Fuseaction: *Add Product*

Next Action: *ViewBasket*

General Comments: This adds a product to the user's basket and assigns the product to the user's CFID/CFTOKEN.

Fuse: *act_addProduct*

File Comments: This will insert a new product into the *tblbaskets* table.

Summary

These are all the Fuseactions we need to make a complete shopping basket.

Now for /BIOS and /CATALOG

We then performed the same operations on both the /BIOS and /CATALOG Fuseboxes, simply listing what the file does, then creating a list of possible Fuseactions.

/BIOS

bioscatalog.cfm

Existing Actions:

1. Select artists with bios
2. Display artist name

Converted Fuseactions/Fuses:

1. viewBios

bios.cfm

Existing Actions:

1. Select an artist's bio
2. Display artist's bio

Converted Fuseactions/Fuses:

1. viewBio

The Resulting Fusebox: /BIOS:

FUSEBOX: /BIOS

Fuseaction: *ViewBios*

Next Action: *ViewBio*

General Comments: This displays a listing of artists that have biographical information in the database. It is linked to view the individual "bio".

Fuse: *dsp_viewBios*

File Comments: This will list all of the artists for whom the site has bios.

Fuseaction: *ViewBio*

General Comments: This displays an artist's biographical information.

Fuse: *dsp_viewBio*

File Comments: This will display a single artist's bio.

/CATALOG

catalog.cfm

Existing Actions:

1. Display alpha-filter list
2. Select non-CD products
3. Display non-CD products
4. Select artists matching keyword/alpha character
5. Display matching artists
6. Display alpha-filter list

Converted Fuseaction/Fuses:

1. viewProducts

pos.cfm

Existing Actions:

1. Select product info
2. Display product info

Converted Fuseactions/Fuses:

1. viewProduct

search.cfm

Search.cfm is a way for a user to run a text search on the CDs on JazzLoft. Not much was changed when moving to Fusebox; in fact the Fuseactions hold the csame names.

The Resulting Fusebox: /CATALOG

FUSEBOX: /CATALOG

Fuseaction: *ViewProducts*

Next Action: *ViewProduct*

General Comments: This lists artists and their products, allowing the user to filter the artist alphabetically and by keyword.

Fuse: *dsp_viewProducts*

File Comments: This will select from the *tblproducts* table and list products and their prices.

Fuseaction: *ViewProduct*

Next Action: *AddProduct*

General Comments: This displays a product's information.

Fuse: *dsp_viewProduct*

File Comments: This will select a single product from the *tblproducts* table and display all the information on it.

And Finally: /ADMIN

The existing *action.cfm* file shows how the original programmer had progressed in his own professional development. It was actually very much like a Fusebox *index.cfm* file, in that it took an "action" attribute, which would determine what user was attempting to do, and then displayed the appropriate code.

The main difference between this *action.cfm* file and a Fusebox *index.cfm* file is that it contained actual CFML/HTML code instead of calls to modules. This meant the file was incredibly long and hard to follow. It also contained administrative actions for dealing with ALL the various admin tasks. Many of these tasks could be broken out into smaller sections.

FUSEBOX: /ADMIN/PRODUCTS

Fuseaction: *EditProduct*

Next Action: *UpdateProduct*
Next Action: *EditTracks*
Next Action: *AddProduct*
Next Action: *DeleteProduct*
Next Action: *ViewFirst*
Next Action: *ViewLast*
Next Action: *ViewNext*
Next Action: *ViewPrevious*

General Comments: This form will be used for editing/adding a product.

Fuse: *dsp_editProduct*

File Comments: This form will select a single product and fill in the fields with the existing data.

Fuseaction: *UpdateProduct*

General Comments: This will update the product data in the database.

Fuse: *act_updateProduct*

File Comments: This will run an update statement on the *tblproducts* table.

Fuseaction: *EditTracks*

Next Action: Update Tracks

General Comments: This form is for editing tracks on a CD.

Fuse: *dsp_editRealAudio*

File Comments: This will allow a user to upload a Real Audio (.ram) file, using the type=file input field.

Fuseaction: *UpdateTracks*

General Comments: This will update the tracks in the database.

Fuse: *act_updateTracks*

File Comments: This will update the tracks in the *tbltracks* table.

Fuseaction: *AddProduct*

General Comments: This will insert a new product into the database.

Fuse: *act_updateProduct*

File Comments: This will run an update statement on the *tblproducts* table.

Fuseaction: *DeleteProduct*

General Comments: This will delete a product from the database.

Fuse: *qry_getArtistProducts*

File Comments: This will select all the products associated with an artist.

Fuse: *qry_deleteCD*

File Comments: This will run a delete statement on the tracks table.

Fuseaction: *ViewFirst*

General Comments: This will go to the first product in the database.

Fuseaction: *ViewLast*

General Comments: This will go to the last product in the database.

Fuseaction: *ViewNext*

General Comments: This will go to the next product in the database.

Fuseaction: *ViewPrevious*

General Comments: This will go to the previous product.

FUSEBOX: /ADMIN/CREDIT CARDS

Fuseaction: *ViewOrders*

Next Action: *ViewOrder*
Next Action: *ConfirmOrder*

General Comments: This will list out all the current orders.

Fuse: *dsp_viewOrders*

File Comments: This will select all the orders that have not been confirmed yet.

Fuseaction: *ViewOrder*

General Comments: This will display full order information.

Fuse: *dsp_viewOrder*

File Comments: This will select a single order, allowing an administrator to mark the order as being confirmed.

Fuseaction: *ConfirmOrder*

General Comments: This will confirm whether a credit card was valid or not.

Fuse: *qry_confirmOrder*

File Comments: This will update the "confirmed" bit field in the *tblorders* table to 1.

FUSEBOX: /ADMIN/ARTIST

Fuseaction: *ArtistForm*

Next Action: *AddArtist*

General Comments: This will be a form for adding an artist.

Fuse: *dsp_artistForm*

File Comments: This is a form for adding a new artist to the database.

Fuseaction: *LabelForm*

Next Action: AddLabel

General Comments: This form will be for adding a label.

Fuseaction: *Add Artist*

General Comments: This will add an artist to the database.

Fuse: *qry_insertArtist*

File Comments: This inserts an artist into the database.

Fuseaction: *AddLabel*

General Comments: This will insert a label into the database.

Fuseaction: *Search Form*

Next Action: *Search*

General Comments: This will give the user a method of searching for an artist, searching by artist name or label.

Fuse: *dsp_searchForm*

File Comments: This gives a form for searching for an artist.

Fuseaction: *Search*

Next Action: *EditProduct*
Next Action: *EditBio*

General Comments: This will run the query, filtering out the appropriate artists, then listing the artists, linking to products/bios.

Fuse: *dsp_search*

File Comments: This displays the search results.

Fuseaction: *EditBio*

Next Action: *UpdateBio*
Next Action: *DeleteBio*

General Comments: This will display a form for editing biographical information.

Fuse: *dsp_editBio*

File Comments: This will give an administrator a form for editing an artist's bio.

Fuseaction: *UpdateBio*

General Comments: This will update the bio in the database.

Fuse: *act_updateBio*

File Comments: This will update an artist's bio.

Fuseaction: *Delete Bio*

General Comments: This will delete a bio from the database.

Fuse: *qry_deleteBio*

File Comments: This will delete a bio from the database.

Database Normalization

Normalization refers to applying a set of rules to a database design to increase its efficiency, reduce errors, and eliminate potential problems before they start. There are three basic normalization "forms", referred to as first, second, and third normal forms. There is also a fourth normal form, and several other types of normalization, but the three basic levels are what are most often encountered.

First Normal Form (1NF): Each field in a table contains different information. For example, in an employee list, each table would contain only one birthdate field.

Second Normal Form (2NF): No field values can be derived from another field. For example, if a table already included a birthdate field, it could not also include a birth year field, since this information would be redundant.

Third Normal Form (3NF): No duplicate information is permitted. So, for example, if two tables both require a birthdate field, the birthdate information would be separated into a separate table, and the two other tables would then access the birthdate information via an *<index.htm>* field in the birthdate table. Any change to a birthdate would automatically be reflected in all tables that link to the birthdate table.

You should always be attempting to achieve Third Normal form, although, sometimes it will be necessary to "denormalize" your database. Denormalizing is commonly done for speed purposes, but it can cause serious problems with inconsistent data in your database.

For example, look at the definition of Second Normal Form, above. The database in the example should only have a single "birthdate" field, without a "birth-year" field. Imagine if you had both of these fields, then one of the people in the database realizes his/her birthdate was incorrect. If s/he changes it, but does not realize s/he should also change the birth-year record, how will you know which field is correct?

Much of the original JazzLoft database was denormalized, so on this version our goal was to redesign the structure of the database so that it was in Third Normal form. To normalize a database, each table must be analyzed to identify the fields that are redundant.

The new database schema appears on the next page.

The new database may look a little more complex, but managing it will be much easier. Many of the fields which are duplicated in the first database will quickly get out of sync. Below is a comparison of the existing table with the new tables that are replacing it.

Customers Tables

CUSTOMERS: OLD TABLE
which becomes:

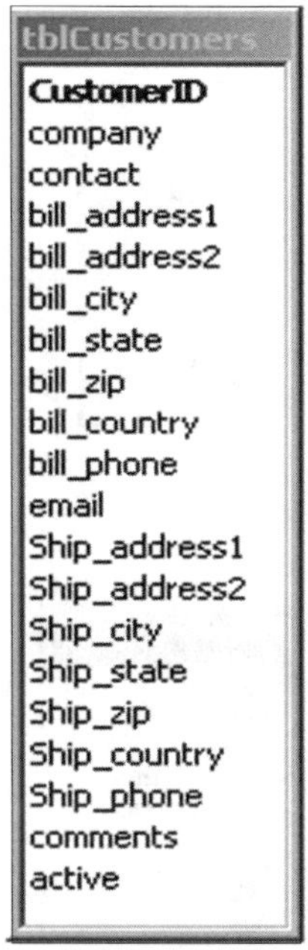

CUSTOMERS: NEW TABLE

The Customers Table actually grew slightly in size. The original Customers Table was incomplete, since it did not allow a customer's *shipping address* to be different from the *billing address*. We have added the ability to have two different addresses.

You will notice that the new Customers Table is also "denormalized", in that the addresses are denormalized. A *billing address* might be the same as the *shipping address*, thus having what is effectively duplicate data.

Products Tables

A diagram of these tables appears on the next page.

How did one table suddenly become six tables? This happens by normalizing the data. Normalizing your database will mean you commonly have more tables, but it also means your data will not be duplicated, which ensures cleaner data.

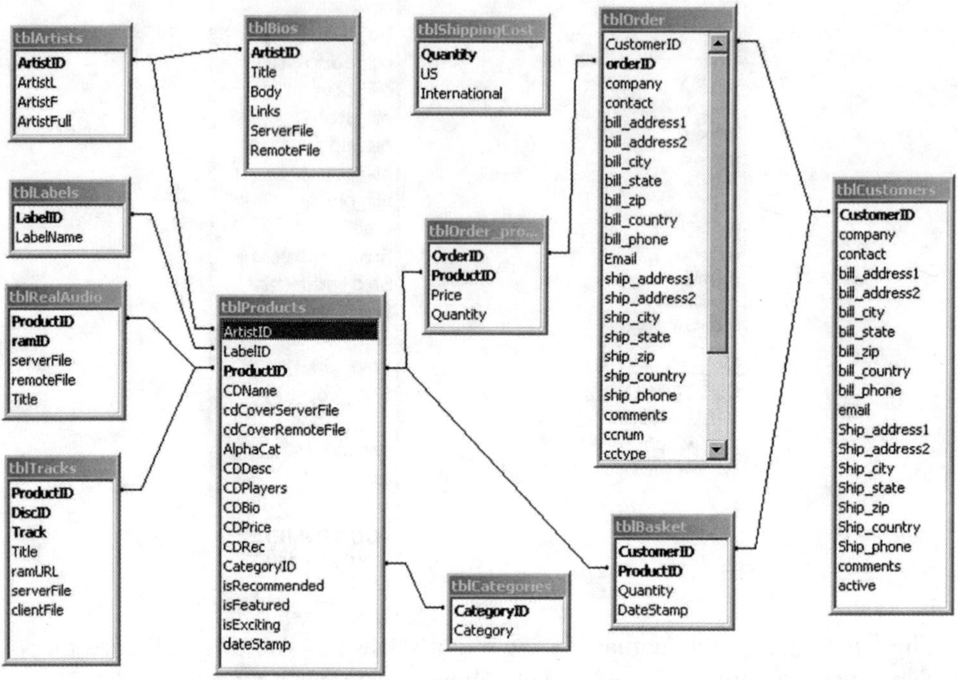

NEW DATABASE SCHEMA

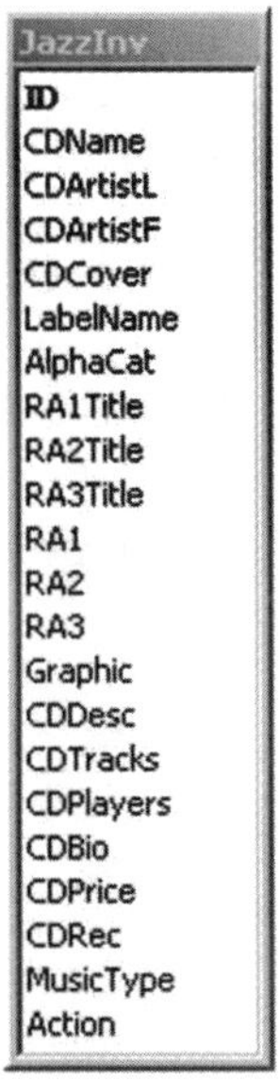

PRODUCTS: OLD TABLE
which becomes:

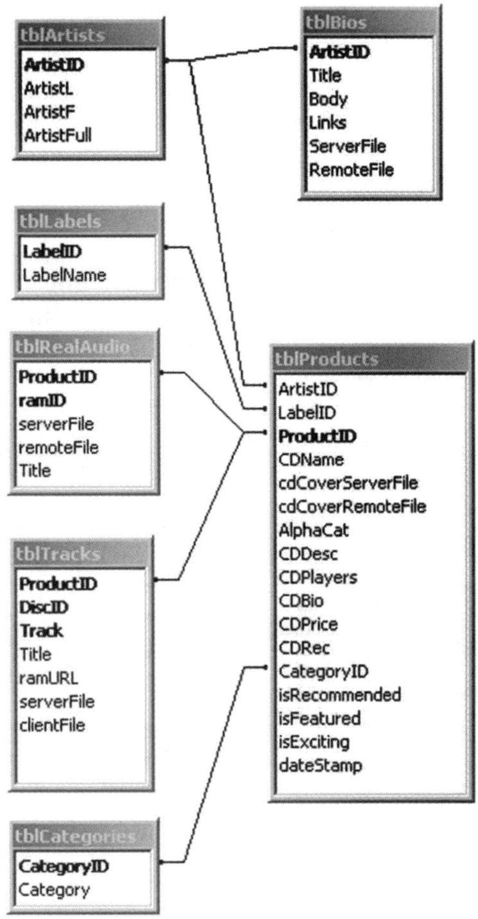

PRODUCTS: NEW TABLE

- In the original table, an artist's name would be duplicated if that artist had more than one CD. In the new tables, an artist would contain a single record in the *tblartists* table and have as many products as we would like. We also added the *tblbios* to keep more detailed information about the artists.
- In the original, a product had a one-to-one relationship with the labels. This means that any time a label changes its name, such as when one company buys another company, all the records with the old name would need to be updated to reflect this change. Now, in the new table group, a table named *tblLabels* is created which has a one-to-many relationship with products.
- In the original table, the RA (RealAudio) fields could cause confusion and very easily get out of sync, meaning a *RA1* could have a value without *RA1Title* having a value. In addition, in the old table, a CD could only have three real audio files associated with it. In the new schema, *tblrealaudio*

was created to store those values and associate them with the correct product. This way, a product can have as many or as few RealAudio clips as are available, and the data can be more easily error checked. For instance, we can now verify that the "*serverfile*" and "*title*" fields are not null.

- We have added a new amenity, "*tbltracks*", to list each of the many tracks on a single CD.
- The Categories Table was split off because categories are not directly associated with products. One category may contain many products.

Orders Tables

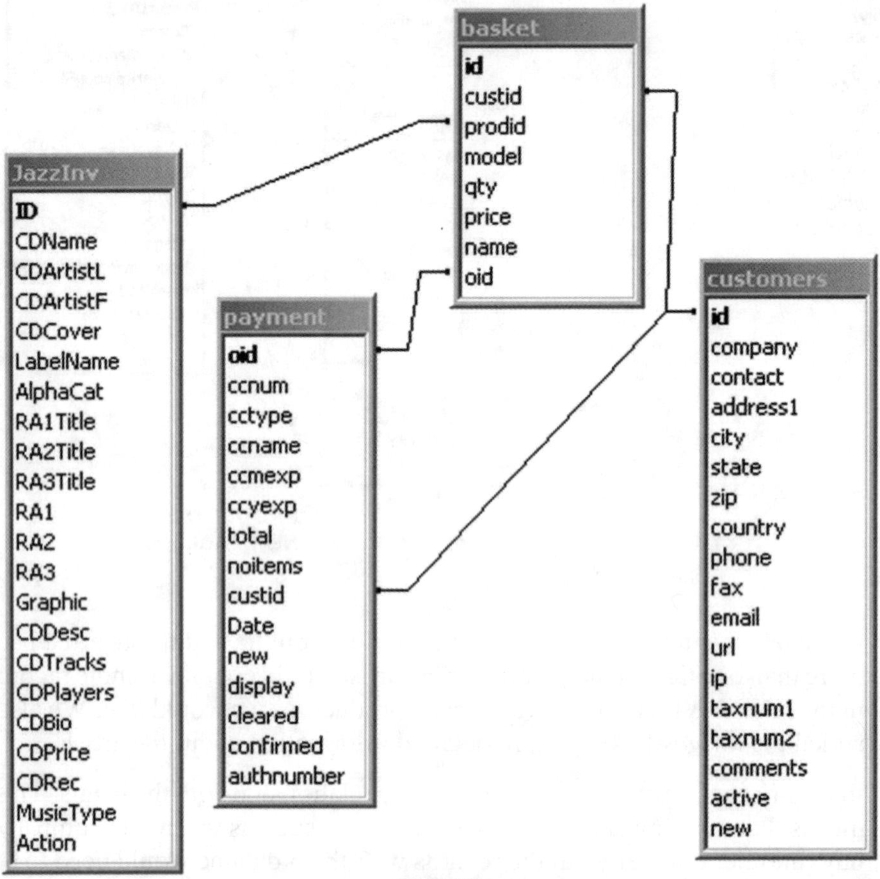

ORDERS:
OLD TABLE
which becomes:

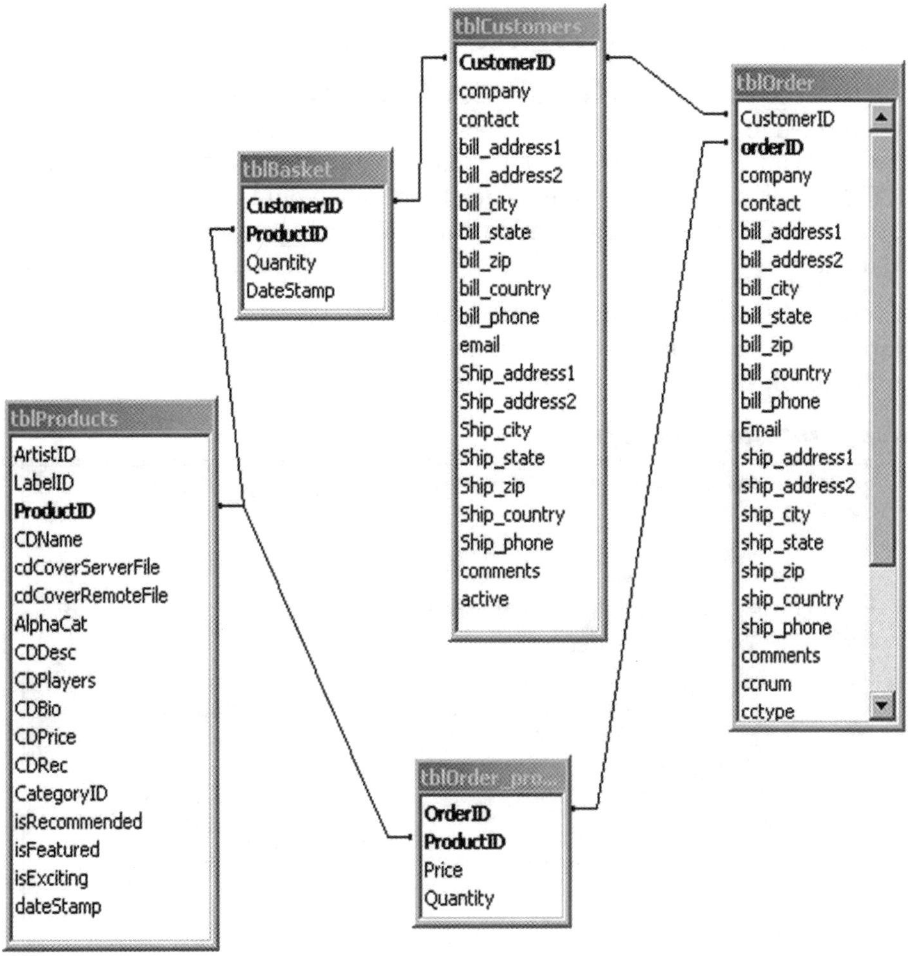

ORDERS:
NEW TABLE

The Orders Tables did not change as dramatically as the other schemas. The main difference between these two are the Baskets Tables.

In the original set up, JazzLoft stored detailed information about the product in the Baskets Table, which can also be obtained from the Products Table. By duplicating it in the Baskets Table, the data could quickly get out of sync. For example, if someone has an item in their basket and then an administrator changes the price of the product, all the records in all the baskets must be updated with that new value.

Under Fusebox, we used a pointer to the Products Table. If we need to display information, we can get the latest value from there.

Site Wide Optimization

Common Link Reuse on HTML Pages

We needed to turn these HTML pages into ColdFusion pages in order to track the user using CFID/CFTOKEN without cookies. Had we left them as straight HTML files, any link from them back to the site would result in the issue of a new CFID/CFTOKEN combination, thus losing any previous relations we had to the user.

These HTML files all use a common set of links back to the site, just different variations of those links. Updating/maintaining a set of links for each page is not optimal, so we developed *dsp_commonlinks.cfm*:

dsp_commonlinks.cfm

```
<CFPARAM name="attributes.linkList" default="">
<CFOUTPUT>
<FONT SIZE=2>
<CFSET counter = 1>
<CFLOOP list="#attributes.linkList#" index="ListElement">
    <CFSWITCH expression="#ListElement#">
        <CFCASE value="1">
            <a href="#request.site.webroot#/index.cfm?fuseAction=
            main">HOME</A>
        </CFCASE>
        <CFCASE value="2">
            <a href="#request.site.webRoot#/catalog/index.cfm?
            #urlToken#">CATALOG</A>
        </CFCASE>
        <CFCASE value="3">

<a href="#request.site.webRoot#/catalog/index.cfm?categoryID
            =3">SteepleChase Records</A>
        </CFCASE>
        <CFCASE value="4">
            <a href="##search">SEARCH</A>
        </CFCASE>
        <CFCASE value="5">
            <a href="#request.site.webRoot#/basket/index.cfm?
            #urlToken#" target="main">CHECKOUT</a>
        </CFCASE>
        <CFCASE value="6">
            <a href="#request.site.webRoot#/links.html">LINKS</a>
        </CFCASE>
        <CFCASE value="7">
            <a href="#request.site.webRoot#/bios/index.cfm?
            #urlToken#">BIOS</a>
        </CFCASE>
```

```
            <CFCASE value="8">
                <a href="#request.site.webRoot#/contact2.html">CONTACT
                </A>
            </CFCASE>
            <CFCASE value="9">
                <a href="#request.site.webRoot#/index.cfm?fuseAction=
                shipping">SHIPPING</A>
            </CFCASE>
            <CFCASE value="10">

<a href="#request.site.webRoot#/catalog/index.cfm?categoryID
                =3"><b>Go to SteepleChase Catalog</A>
            </CFCASE>
            <CFCASE value="11">
                <a href="mailto:alawrence@jazzloft.com">E-MAIL</a></B>
            </CFCASE>
            <CFCASE value="12">
                <a href="#request.site.webRoot#/catalog/index.cfm"><b>Jazz
                Catalog</A>
            </CFCASE>
            <CFCASE value="13">
                <a href="#request.site.webRoot#/catalog/index.cfm?
                CategoryID=6"><b>Other Genres</A>
            </CFCASE>
            <CFCASE value="14">

<a href="#request.site.webRoot#/catalog/index.cfm?categoryID
                =3">STEEPLCHASE </A>
            </CFCASE>
            <CFCASE value="<br>">
                <br>
            </CFCASE>
        </CFSWITCH>
        <CFIF NOT counter is ListLen(attributes.linkList) and NOT ListElement
        is "<br>">
            |
        </CFIF>
        <CFSET counter = counter + 1>
</CFLOOP>
</FONT>
</CFOUTPUT>
```

Dsp_commonlinks.cfm is called from almost every page. In order to have the links output in the desired order, the programmer supplies a list of numbers corresponding to the links s/he wishes to ouput and the order in which they are to be displayed, like so:

```
<CFMODULE template="dsp_commonlinks.cfm" linkList="1,2,4,6,7,8,9,<br>,10,11">
```

If a break in the display is required, the programmer simply adds <br> to the list. This allows the programmer to update/maintain just one file, eliminating many headaches.

Header/Footer Reuse (ALL FILES)

All of the files use common HTML headers and footers, That is, they have the same HTML tags at the beginning and ending of each page:

Sample HTML Header

```
<HTML>
<HEAD>
<TITLE>The Jazz Loft</TITLE>
      <META NAME="DESCRIPTION" CONTENT="Hard to find CDs from
      independent jazz musicians from all over the world. Specializes in small
      labels and hard-to-find jazz recordings.">
      <META NAME="AUTHOR" CONTENT="Alan Lawrence">
      <META NAME="ROBOTS" CONTENT="all">
      <META NAME="ABSTRACT" CONTENT="The Jazz Loft, an online
      store for serious jazz fans by a serious jazz fan. The premier Jazz site
      on the Web for the discovery and purchase of independently produced
      jazz compact discs and discs from small jazz labels. There's some
great
      music here waiting to be discovered.">
      <META NAME="KEYWORDS" CONTENT="jazz, Jazz, music,
      shopping, compact disc, CD, records, jazz music, jazz cds,
      entertainment, discs, cd's, cd, cds, music, compact discs, Palmetto,
      Songlines, Screwgun, Songlines, Jazz Focus, Nine Winds, Anthony
      Braxton, Nimbus, Horace Tapscott">
</HEAD>
<BODY bgcolor="FFFFFF" text="FFFFFF" link="FFFFFF" vlink="FFFFFF"
alink="FFFFFF">
<DIV align="center">
<FONT face="Georgia,Arial,Helvetica" color="white">
<a name="top"></a>
```

This code was reused again and again in each file. Not wanting to maintain this code for every file, we placed this code into *dsp_header.cfm* and then call it from each file. If any changes occur, we can update the one file, and every page will be updated automatically.

Normally, a programmer would place a <CFINCLUDE> tag on every page, calling *dsp_header*. This technique is not wrong, but if we were to change the name of the header file we were using, we would then need to open every file containing the <CFINCLUDE> and update them by hand.

Fusebox provides powerful tools to help us maximize our code reuse. Used in conjunction with <CF_BODYCONTENT> and *app_layout*, our header file can be declared and managed from one central place.

<CF_BODYCONTENT>

This tag, explained more fully in Chapter 5, is used by wrapping it around your *index.cfm* file. It will capture any output generated by your *index.cfm* file and place it into a variable named *request.bodycontent*.

index.cfm with <CF_BODYCONTENT>

```
<CF_BODYCONTENT>
<CFSWITCH expression="attributes.fuseaction">
    <--- CFCASES go here --->
</CFSWITCH>
</CF_BODYCONTENT>
```

app_layout.cfm

Finally, we complete our header/footer reuse process with the *app_layout.cfm* file. This file basically outputs *request.bodycontent*, with *request.headerfile* before and *request.footerfile* after it.

Used together, these tags give us a powerful tool for code reuse.

Global Customer Information (Basket Fusebox)

JazzLoft.com tracks a user throughout the site. In order to do this, it uses client variables and tracks CFID/CFTOKEN combinations, through the following code in the *app_model.cfm* file (which we will discuss shortly):

```
<!--- User Variables --->
<CFIF not isdefined("client.customerid")>
    <CFSET client.customerid= "#CFID#_#CFTOKEN#">
    <CFINCLUDE template="queries/qry_getuserinfo.cfm">
    <CFIF len(getuserinfo.customerid)>
        <CFIF len(getuserinfo.country)>
            <CFSET client.country = getuserinfo.country>
        <CFELSE>
            <CFSET client.country = "us">
        </CFIF>
    </CFIF>
</CFIF>
```

This first checks to see if the variable *client.customerID* exists. If it doesn't, it runs the query *getUserInfo*, then places the resulting *customerID* into *client.customerid*. *Client.customerid* is then used throughout the site when referencing that customer.

If the customer purchases an item, the CFID/CFTOKEN combination is stored on the customer's computer as cookie variables. This allows a customer to be remembered the next time s/he visits the site.

app_model.cfm/dsp_header

App_model.cfm is an idea first proposed by Gabe Roffman at the September 2000 Fusebox Developer Conference in Charlottesville, VA. Future editions of this book may contain a chapter on this concept, for now, we will explain the basics here. In creating JazzLoft.com, *app_model.cfm* has proven invaluable in allowing us to reuse code.

App_model. cfm is an Application Object Model for Cold Fusion/Fusebox development, similar in concept to the Document Object Model for Javascript. It uses standardized structures for storing commonly-used variables. These variables can then be referenced anywhere in the application.

The *app_model.cfm* uses **request scope variables**. The request scope is available both locally and globally within custom and nested custom tags. The *app_model.cfm* for JazzLoft.com is given here:

```
<!--- Site DSN variable --->
<CFPARAM name="request.site.mainDSN" default="jazzloft">

<!--- Page display variables --->
<CFPARAM name="request.page.headerfile" default="">
<CFPARAM name="request.page.footerfile" default="">
<CFPARAM name="request.page.title" default="The Jazz Loft">
<CFPARAM name="request.page.bgcolor" default="800000">
<CFPARAM name="request.page.font.color" default="FFFFFF">
<CFPARAM name="request.page.link.color" default="FFCC66">
<CFPARAM name="request.page.vlink.color" default="FFCC66">
<CFPARAM name="request.page.alink.color" default="FFCC66">

<!--- Path variables --->
<CFPARAM name="request.site.cfroot" default="/jazzloft">
<CFPARAM name="request.site.webRoot" default="/jazzloft">
<CFSET request.site.imagePath = "/jazzloft/graphics">
<CFSET request.site.imageHardPath =
"c:\webshare\wwwroot\jazzloft\graphics">
<CFSET request.site.realAudioPath = "/jazzloft/realAudio">
<CFSET request.site.realAudioHardPath =
"c:\webshare\wwwroot\jazzloft\realAudio">

<!--- User Variables --->
<CFIF not isdefined("client.customerid")>
    <CFSET client.customerid= "#CFID#_#CFTOKEN#">
    <CFINCLUDE template="queries/qry_getuserinfo.cfm">
    <CFIF len(getuserinfo.customerid)>
        <CFIF len(getuserinfo.country)>
            <CFSET client.country = getuserinfo.country>
        <CFELSE>
            <CFSET client.country = "us">
```

```
        </CFIF>
    </CFIF>
</CFIF>
```

As you can see, this stores all the variables we commonly need throughout the site. That means that programmers working on different sections of code don't need to worry about what the name of the variable would be and can concentrate instead on writing good code.

Let's run through each section, giving examples of how the variables are used, and why they are powerful when placed in *app_model.cfm*:

The first is relatively self-explanatory: The DSN is stored and used globally whenever a query is run. Since the DSN effects the site as a whole, it is prefixed "*request.site*"

The second section is titled "*page display variables*". As indicated, these variables modify a page's display and have the prefix "*request.page*". This section contains some of the most powerful variables in the *app_model.cfm*.

```
<!--- Page display variables --->
<CFPARAM name="request.page.headerfile"
default="#request.site.CFRoot#/dsp_header.cfm">
<CFPARAM name="request.page.footerfile"
default="#request.site.CFRoot#/dsp_footer.cfm">
<CFPARAM name="request.page.title" default="The Jazz Loft">
<CFPARAM name="request.page.bgcolor" default="800000">
<CFPARAM name="request.page.font.color" default="FFFFFF">
<CFPARAM name="request.page.link.color" default="FFCC66">
<CFPARAM name="request.page.vlink.color" default="FFCC66">
<CFPARAM name="request.page.alink.color" default="FFCC66">
```

There are two variables that need extra special attention and show the power of *app_model.cfm* used with <CF_BODYCONTENT> and *app_layout.cfm*: *Request.page.headerfile* and *request.page.footerfile*. These two files are used in conjunction with <CF_BODYCONTENT> and *app_layout.cfm* to specify which header and footer file the programmer desires at any point in the coding, before *app_layout.cfm* takes effect.

<CF_BODYCONTENT> will capture all of the output from a Fuseaction and store it in *request.bodycontent*. *App_layout.cfm* will then put out *request.bodycontent*, wrapped in between *request.site.headerfile* and *request.site.footerfile*.

These files become even more powerful after we modify *app_layout.cfm*.

app_layout.cfm

```
<CFPARAM name="request.bodycontent">
<CFPARAM name="attributes.showbody" default="yes">

<CFIF len(request.page.headerfile)>
    <CFLOOP list="#request.page.headerfile#" index="listelement">
        <CFINCLUDE template="#ListElement#">
    </CFLOOP>
</CFIF>

<CFIF attributes.showbody>
    <CFOUTPUT>#request.bodycontent#</CFOUTPUT>
</CFIF>

<CFIF len(request.page.footerfile)>
    <CFLOOP list="#request.page.footerfile#" index="listelement">
        <CFINCLUDE template="#ListElement#">
    </CFLOOP>
</CFIF>
```

Here we have changed *app_layout.cfm* to loop over a list of header file and footer files. This allows any Fusebox to set its own header/footer files and also contain any header/footer files from its parent Fusebox.

A good example of this is in the "admin" directory of JazzLoft.com. Admin is the parent application for all the circuit applications below it.

Every section in the administrator needs to have common navigation, found in /admin/*dsp_header.cfm*. Each also uses the global header file found in /jazzloft/*dsp_header.cfm*:

/jazzloft/*dsp_header.cfm*

```
<CFPARAM name="request.page.title" default="The Jazz Loft">

<CFOUTPUT>
<HTML>
<HEAD>
<TITLE>#request.page.title#</TITLE>
    <META NAME="DESCRIPTION" CONTENT="Hard to find CD's from
    independent jazz musicians from all over the world. Specializes in small
    labels and hard-to-find jazz recordings.">
    <META NAME="AUTHOR" CONTENT="Alan Lawrence">
    <META NAME="ROBOTS" CONTENT="all">
    <META NAME="ABSTRACT" CONTENT="The Jazz Loft, an online
    store for serious jazz fans by a serious jazz fan. The premier Jazz site
    on the Web for the discovery and purchase of independently produced
    jazz compact discs and discs from small jazz labels. There's some
great
```

```
    music here waiting to be discovered.">
    <META NAME="KEYWORDS" CONTENT="jazz, Jazz, music,
    shopping, compact disc, CD, records, jazz music, jazz cds,
    entertainment, discs, cd's, cd, cds, music, compact discs, Palmetto,
    Songlines, Screwgun, Songlines, Jazz Focus, Nine Winds, Anthony
    Braxton, Nimbus, Horace Tapscott">
</HEAD>
<BODY BGCOLOR="#request.page.bgcolor#"
TEXT="#request.page.font.color#" LINK="#request.page.link.color#"
VLINK="#request.page.vlink.color#" alink="#request.page.vlink.color#">
<DIV align="center">
<FONT face="Georgia,Arial,Helvetica" color="white">
<a name="top"></a>
</CFOUTPUT>
```

The first line sets the title for the page, which is held in "*request.page.title*". The last part simply outputs the HTML with the values of the "*request.page*" variables.

```
/jazzloft/admin/dsp_header.cfm

<CFOUTPUT>
<TABLE>
    <tr><td align="center"><b>Administration Options</b></td></tr>
    <tr>
        <td>
            [<a href="#request.site.webRoot#/admin/artists/index.cfm?
            fuseaction=artistForm">Add Artists</a>]
            [<a href="#request.site.webRoot#/admin/index.cfm?fuseaction
            =labelForm">Add Labels</a>]
            [<a href="#request.site.webRoot#/admin/artists/index.cfm">
            Manage Artists</a>]

[<a href="#request.site.webRoot#/admin/creditcards/index.cfm"
            >Manage Credit Cards</a>]
        </td>
    </tr>
</TABLE>
</CFOUTPUT>
```

This is the header file needed by all files.

The *app_globals.cfm* file calls the *app_globals.cfm* of its parent, the root JazzLoft directory, which in turn calls *app_model.cfm*, which sets up our global variables. The administrator does not need the same color scheme as our root directory, therefore the *app_globals.cfm* file for "admin" writes over the values of some of the "*request.page*" variables given to it by its parent.

```
<CFSET request.page.bgcolor = "FFFFFF">
<CFSET request.page.link.color = "">
<CFSET request.page.vlink.color = "">
<CFSET request.page.headerfile=ListAppend(request.page.headerfile,
"#request.site.cfRoot#/admin/dsp_header.cfm")>
```

/ADMIN changes the values set by *app_model.cfm*; here, it basically changes the color of the page from red to white. It also adds the header above to the list of headers output by the use of *app_layout.cfm,* using the CF ListAppend function to append the admin *dsp_header* file to the end of the global "*request.page.headerfile*" variable. The output for the administrator page will look like this:

```
<HTML>
<HEAD>
<TITLE>The Jazz Loft</TITLE>
    <META NAME="DESCRIPTION" CONTENT="Hard to find CD's from
    independent jazz musicians from all over the world. Specializes in small
    labels and hard-to-find jazz recordings.">
    <META NAME="AUTHOR" CONTENT="Alan Lawrence">
    <META NAME="ROBOTS" CONTENT="all">
    <META NAME="ABSTRACT" CONTENT="The Jazz Loft, an online
    store for serious jazz fans by a serious jazz fan. The premier Jazz site
    on the Web for the discovery and purchase of independently produced
    jazz compact discs and discs from small jazz labels. There's some
great
    music here waiting to be discovered.">
    <META NAME="KEYWORDS" CONTENT="jazz, Jazz, music,
    shopping, compact disc, CD, records, jazz music, jazz cds,
    entertainment, discs, cd's, cd, cds, music, compact discs, Palmetto,
    Songlines, Screwgun, Songlines, Jazz Focus, Nine Winds, Anthony
    Braxton, Nimbus, Horace Tapscott">
</HEAD>
<BODY bgcolor="FFFFFF" text="" link="" vlink="" alink="">
<DIV align="center">
<FONT face="Georgia,Arial,Helvetica" color="white">
<a name="top"></a>

<TABLE>
    <tr><td align="center"><b>Administration Options</b></td></tr>
    <tr>
        <td>
            [<a href="/jazzloft/admin/artists/index.cfm?fuseaction=
            artistForm">Add Artists</a>]
            [<a href="/jazzloft/admin/index.cfm?fuseaction=labelForm">
            Add Labels</a>]
            [<a href="/jazzloft/admin/artists/index.cfm">Manage
            Artists</a>]
```

```
            [<a href="/jazzloft/admin/creditcards/index.cfm">Manage
Credit
            Cards</a>]
        </td>
    </tr>
</TABLE>
```

After the script is run, we now have the header information from both the root Fusebox and the admin Fusebox at the beginning of our file. This can continue as long as needed.

The credit card Fusebox also has a header file that is necessary. It includes this file, the same way as the other two Fuseboxes do, and the result is then:

```
<HTML>
<HEAD>
<TITLE>The Jazz Loft</TITLE>
    <META NAME="DESCRIPTION" CONTENT="Hard to find CD's from
    independent jazz musicians from all over the world. Specializes in small
    labels and hard-to-find jazz recordings.">
    <META NAME="AUTHOR" CONTENT="Alan Lawrence">
    <META NAME="ROBOTS" CONTENT="all">
    <META NAME="ABSTRACT" CONTENT="The Jazz Loft, an online
    store for serious jazz fans by a serious jazz fan. The premier Jazz site
    on the Web for the discovery and purchase of independently produced
    jazz compact discs and discs from small jazz labels. There's some
great
    music here waiting to be discovered.">
    <META NAME="KEYWORDS" CONTENT="jazz, Jazz, music,
    shopping, compact disc, CD, records, jazz music, jazz cds,
    entertainment, discs, cd's, cd, cds, music, compact discs, Palmetto,
    Songlines, Screwgun, Songlines, Jazz Focus, Nine Winds, Anthony
    Braxton, Nimbus, Horace Tapscott">
</HEAD>
<BODY bgcolor="FFFFFF" text="" link="" vlink="" alink="">
<DIV align="center">
<FONT face="Georgia,Arial,Helvetica" color="white">
<a name="top"></a>

<TABLE>
    <tr><td align="center"><b>Administration Options</b></td></tr>
    <tr>
        <td>
            [<a href="/jazzloft/admin/artists/index.cfm?fuseaction=
            artistForm">Add Artists</a>]
            [<a href="/jazzloft/admin/index.cfm?fuseaction=labelForm"
            >Add Labels</a>]
            [<a href="/jazzloft/admin/artists/index.cfm">Manage
            Artists</a>]
```

```
                [<a href="/jazzloft/admin/creditcards/index.cfm">Manage
Credit
                Cards</a>]
            </td>
        </tr>
</TABLE>

<TABLE>
        <tr><td> </td></tr>
        <tr><td align="center"><b>Credit Card Options</b></td></tr>
        <tr>
            <td>
                [<a href="index.cfm?fuseaction=vieworders">All orders</a>]
                [<a href="index.cfm?fuseaction=view orders&confirmed=0">
                Unconfirmed orders</a>]
                [<a href="index.cfm?fuseaction=view orders&confirmed=1">
                Confirmed orders</a>]
            </td>
        </tr>
        <tr>
            <td align="center">34 orders, 1 confirmed</td>
        </tr>
</TABLE>
```

NOTE: When using multiple footer files, remember to use the *List**Pre**pend* function instead of the *List**App**end* function. Using *ListPrepend* will make sure your file comes out in the proper order.

```
<CFSET request.page.footerfile=ListPrepend(request.page.footerfile,
        "#request.site.cfRoot#/admin/dsp_footer.cfm")>
```

The third section in this *app_model.cfm* is user information. This information is needed for almost every page and therefore is tracked using client variables. Unfortunately, client variables cannot be structures, so we simply make the client variables as descriptive as possible.

```
<!--- User Variables --->
<CFIF not isdefined("client.customerid")>
    <CFSET client.customerid= "#CFID#_#CFTOKEN#">
    <CFINCLUDE template="queries/qry_getuserinfo.cfm">
    <CFIF len(getuserinfo.customerid)>
        <CFIF len(getuserinfo.country)>
            <CFSET client.country = getuserinfo.country>
        <CFELSE>
            <CFSET client.country = "us">
        </CFIF>
    </CFIF>
</CFIF>
```

In this particular case, we have used *client.customerID* and *client.country*.

Using <CFLOCATION> in Fuseactions

As stated in Chapter 4, using <CFLOCATION> inside of your Fuseactions can save you from unnecessary execution of code. Take the shopping cart, for instance: the Fuseactions *addProduct*, *updateBasket* and *emptyBasket* all relocate back to *viewBasket*. This is done because the end result of all these Fuseactions is the *dsp_viewBasket* Fuse. If the user refreshes his/her browser, this action will not continue to add items into their shopping cart, but simply refresh the *viewBasket* Fuseaction.

```
<CFINCLUDE template="../app_globals.cfm">

<CFPARAM name="attributes.fuseaction" default="viewBasket">

<CF_BODYCONTENT>
    <CFSWITCH expression="#attributes.fuseaction#">
        <CFCASE value="viewBasket">
            <CFINCLUDE template="dsp_viewBasket.cfm">
        </CFCASE>
        <CFCASE value="addProduct">
            <CFINCLUDE template="act_addProduct.cfm">
            <CFLOCATION url="index.cfm?fuseaction=viewBasket"
            addtoken="Yes">
        </CFCASE>
        <CFCASE value="updateBasket">
            <CFINCLUDE template="act_updateBasket.cfm">
            <CFLOCATION url="index.cfm?fuseaction=viewBasket"
            addtoken="Yes">
        </CFCASE>
        <CFCASE value="emptyBasket">
            <CFINCLUDE template="queries/qry_emptyBasket.cfm">
            <CFLOCATION url="index.cfm?fuseaction=viewBasket"
            addtoken="Yes">
        </CFCASE>
        <CFCASE value="checkoutForm">
            <CFINCLUDE template="dsp_checkoutForm.cfm">
        </CFCASE>
        <CFCASE value="updateCustomer">
            <CFINCLUDE template="act_updateCustomer.cfm">
            <CFLOCATION url="index.cfm?fuseaction=
            previewCheckout&remember=1" addtoken="Yes">
        </CFCASE>
        <CFCASE value="previewCheckout">
            <CFINCLUDE template="act_remember.cfm">
            <CFINCLUDE template="dsp_previewCheckout.cfm">
        </CFCASE>
        <CFCASE value="completeCheckout">
```

```
            <CFINCLUDE template="act_addOrder.cfm">
            <CFLOCATION url="index.cfm?fuseaction=receipt&orderID=
            #max_id#" addtoken="Yes">
        </CFCASE>
        <CFCASE value="receipt">
            <CFINCLUDE template="dsp_receipt.cfm">
        </CFCASE>
    </CFSWITCH>
</CF_BODYCONTENT>

<CFINCLUDE template="../app_layout.cfm">
```

Now, a Challenge for YOU

We believe you have learned some very useful tips and techniques in this book. We believe that so much in fact that, in conclusion, we are issuing a challenge to you, the reader. The challenge, if you choose to accept it, is to **add/edit JazzLoft.com**.

That's right – JazzLoft.com is the first **Fusebox Community Open Source Application** (FCOSA – pronounced fu-coh-sa).

Have an idea? Need some practice? Think you could have done something better? Prove it. Add or update anything on this site, submit it to the SecretAgents.com site and both Steve Nelson and Craig Girard will evaluate it. If approved, it will be added to the site. Everyone who has code that is approved and used will have their name listed on the site.

Why do this?

This site will help further the use of Fusebox and help support the Fusebox community. It will stand as a living example of how Fusebox can be used. Since the code will always be freely downloadable, anyone wishing to learn how to develop a medium-large scale application now has the means.

- **Hone your skills!** Learn to work within the Fusebox methodology. Use the provided code to practice.
- **Get your name out!** Everyone coming to the site will know you are a Fusebox aficionado by looking at the ABOUT page of JazzLoft.com.
- **Support our sponsor!** Help JazzLoft have the best site around, and thus say thanks for allowing us to use them as a case study.

– HAPPY FUSEBOXING! –

APPENDIX E: The Fusebox Custom Tags

These are the major Fusebox tags (available on ***Fusebox.org***.) Text files with further documentation are also available on Fusebox.org, but we have decided not to include them here.

App_layout.cfm

You will note that this is not a tag, but an included file. The <CF_BODYCONTENT> tag requires this as a secondary file, in order to display the header, body and footer. *App_layout.cfm* needs to be called from <CFINCLUDE>, rather than as a custom tag. This way, the variables in your header and footer do not require the use of the "caller" scope.

```
<CFPARAM name="request.headerfile">
<CFPARAM name="request.footerfile">
<CFPARAM name="request.bodycontent">
<CFPARAM name="attributes.showbody" default="yes">
<CFIF len(request.headerfile)>
    <CFINCLUDE template="#request.headerfile#">
</CFIF>
<CFIF attributes.showbody>
    <CFOUTPUT>#request.bodycontent#</CFOUTPUT>
</CFIF>
<CFIF len(request.footerfile)>
    <CFINCLUDE template="#request.footerfile#">
</CFIF>
```

<CF_BODYCONTENT>

```
<CFIF not thistag.HasEndTag>
    <CFSET thistag.generatedcontent="">
    You must have an end Tag
    <CFABORT>
</CFIF>

<CFPARAM name="attributes.name" default="bodycontent">

<CFIF thistag.executionmode is "end">
    <CFSET "request.#attributes.name#"=thistag.generatedcontent>
```

```
	<CFSET thistag.generatedcontent="">
</CFIF>
```

<CF_FORMURL2ATTRIBUTES>

```
<CFSETTING enablecfoutputonly="yes">

<!--- This tag will turn all 'Form' and 'URL' scoped variables into 'Attributes'
scoped variables. This allows you to have a common scope of variables,
thus allowing you to call the entire application, i.e., index.cfm, as a
<CFMODULE> or as a regular application.
Designed for: CF 4.01+ --->

<CFPARAM name="request.attributeslist" default="">
<CFPARAM name="setfuseaction" default="">
<CFPARAM name="attributes.displaybase" default="yes">
<CFPARAM name="caller.id" default="">

<!--- This will convert URL variables to attribute variables --->

<CFIF isdefined("cgi.query_string") and isdefined("cgi.path_info")>
	<CFIF not len(cgi.query_string)>

		<!--- This will support Search Engine capable URLs ex:
		http://127.0.0.1/index.cfm/fuseaction/shoppingcart/additems/
		127,88/myvar/hello+world --->

		<CFPARAM name="cleanpathinfo" default="#cgi.path_info#">

		<CFSET findindex=findnocase("index.cfm",cleanpathinfo)>
		<CFIF findindex>
			<CFSET cleanpathinfo=RemoveChars(cleanpathinfo, 1,
			findindex+9)>
		</CFIF>

		<CFIF len(cleanpathinfo)>

			<!--- If you want to append .htm onto the end of your URL, this
			will clean it so it doesn't affect your variables --->

			<CFIF len(cleanpathinfo) gte 4 and right(cleanpathinfo,4) is
			".htm">
				<CFSET cleanpathinfo=RemoveChars(cleanpathinfo,
				len(cleanpathinfo)-3, 4)>
			</CFIF>

			<CFSET cleanpathinfo=replace(cleanpathinfo,"&","/","all")>
```

```
        <CFSET cleanpathinfo=replace(cleanpathinfo,"=","/","all")>

        <CFLOOP index="i" from="1" to="#listlen(cleanpathinfo, "/")#"
        step="2">
            <CFSET urlname = listgetat(cleanpathinfo, i, "/")>
            <CFIF listlen(cleanpathinfo,"/") gte i+1>
                <CFSET urlvalue = listgetat(cleanpathinfo, i + 1, "/")>

                <!--- This will allow you to pass slashes in your
values,
                escape your / with a slash_ --->

                <CFSET urlvalue=replacenocase(urlvalue,
                "slash_","/","all")>
                <CFIF refindnocase("[[:alpha:]]",left(trim(urlname),1))
                and NOT ISDEFINED( 'caller.ATTRIBUTES.' &
                urlname )>
                    <CFSWITCH expression="#urlname#">
                        <CFCASE value="cfid">
                            <CFPARAM name="url.cfid"
                            default="#urlvalue#">
                        </CFCASE>
                        <CFCASE value="cftoken">
                            <CFPARAM name="url.cftoken"
                            default="#urlvalue#">
                        </CFCASE>
                        <CFDEFAULTCASE>
                            <CFIF urlvalue is "null">
                                <CFSET "caller.attributes.
                                #urlname#" = "">
                            <CFELSE>
                                <CFSET "caller.attributes.
                                #urlname#" = urlvalue>
                            </CFIF>
                            <CFSET request.attributeslist =
                            listappend(request.attributeslist,
                            urlname,"&")>
                            <CFSET request.attributeslist =
                            listappend(request.attributeslist,
                            urlencodedformat(evaluate("caller.
                            attributes.#urlname#")),"=")>
                        </CFDEFAULTCASE>
                    </CFSWITCH>
                </CFIF>
            </CFIF>
        </CFLOOP>
    </CFIF>
```

```
<!--- This is for converting URL fields to attributes scoped variables. ---
>
	<CFELSE>
		<CFLOOP list="#cgi.query_string#" delimiters="&"
		index="valuepair">
			<CFSET URLName = "#ListGetAt(valuepair, 1, "=")#">
			<CFIF refindnocase("[[:alpha:]]",left(trim(urlname),1)) and NOT
			ISDEFINED( 'caller.ATTRIBUTES.' & urlname )>
				<CFSET "caller.attributes.#urlname#" =
				"#evaluate("url."&"#urlname#")#">

				<!--- Remove these next 2 lines if you don't want a list of
				all attributes. It'll speed up processing by about 0.15
				millisecond.--->
				<CFSET request.attributeslist =
				listappend(request.attributeslist,urlname,"&")>
				<CFSET request.attributeslist =
				listappend(request.attributeslist,urlencodedformat
				(evaluate("url.#urlname#")),"=")>
			</CFIF>
		</CFLOOP>
	</CFIF>
</CFIF>

<!--- This is for converting form fields to attributes scoped variables. --->
<CFIF isdefined("form.fieldnames")>
	<CFLOOP list="#form.fieldnames#" index="field">
		<CFIF refindnocase("[[:alpha:]]",left(trim(field),1)) and NOT
		ISDEFINED( 'Caller.ATTRIBUTES.' & trim(field) )>
			<CFSET "caller.attributes.#trim(field)#" =
			"#evaluate("form.#trim(field)#")#">

			<!--- This is so that you can have multiple type="image"
buttons
			on the same page. If you name the button
			name="fuseaction_[the value you want]" it will set the
			fuseaction to that value--->
			<CFIF findnocase("fuseaction_",field) and
			findnocase(".x",field)>
				<CFSET setfuseaction=replacenocase
				(field,"fuseaction_","")>
				<CFSET setfuseaction=replacenocase
				(setfuseaction,".x","")>
				<CFIF refind("[0-9]",setfuseaction)>

<!--- This is so you can associate an "ID" with an image button (optional)
like this:
	<INPUT type="Image" src="/IMAGES/MYIMAGE.GIF"
```

```
    NAME="fuseaction_addthisaddress56">
This would return ID=56. That way you can have a bunch of image buttons
in the same form that all do the same thing, but each one has an ID
associated with it. --->
    <CFSET thisid=val(mid(setfuseaction,refind("[0-9]",setfuseaction),
    len(setfuseaction)))>
        <CFIF thisid>
            <CFSET caller.ID=thisid>
        </CFIF>
    </CFIF>

</CFIF>
            <!--- Remove these next 2 lines if you don't want a list of all
            attributes. That will speed up processing by about 0.15
            millisecond--->
            <CFSET request.attributeslist =
            listappend(request.attributeslist,trim(field),"&")>
            <CFSET request.attributeslist = list
            append(request.attributeslist,
            urlencodedformat(evaluate("form.#trim(field)#")),"=")>
        </CFIF>
    </CFLOOP>
</CFIF>
<CFIF len(setfuseaction)>
    <CFSET caller.attributes.fuseaction=setfuseaction>
    <CFIF len(caller.id)>
        <CFSET caller.attributes.fuseaction=
        replace(setfuseaction,caller.id,"")>
    </CFIF>
</CFIF>

<!--- This is so that your relative images will work; this is only needed if
you're using search engine URLs. --->
<CFIF attributes.displaybase>
    <CFSET script = REReplace(CGI.SCRIPT_NAME, "[^/]+\.cfm.*", "")>

    <CFSET caller.Base= "http://#CGI.SERVER_NAME##script#/">
    <CFIF CGI.SERVER_PORT NEQ 80>
        <CFSET caller.Base= "https://#CGI.SERVER_NAME##script#/">
    </CFIF>

    <CFHTMLHEAD text="<base href=""#caller.Base#"">">
</CFIF>
<CFSETTING enablecfoutputonly="No">
```

<CF_HTMLHEAD>

```
<CFSWITCH expression="#thistag.executionmode#">
    <CFCASE value="start">

    </CFCASE>
    <CFCASE value="end">
        <CFHTMLHEAD text="#thistag.generatedcontent#">
        <CFSET thistag.generatedcontent="">
    </CFCASE>
</CFSWITCH>
```

<CF_MAKETREE>

```
<CFSETTING ENABLECFOUTPUTONLY="yes">

<!--- Defaults and data checkers--->
<CFPARAM NAME="Attributes.getchildren" DEFAULT="no"
type="boolean">
<CFPARAM NAME="Attributes.Variable" DEFAULT="MakeTree">
<CFPARAM name="Attributes.Query" type="Query">
<CFPARAM name="Attributes.rootparent" default="0">

<!--- Set base worklist. This is the loop we will use to extract the tree. We
need to use a list instead of a structure because structures have no
particular order. --->
<CFSET WorkList="">

<!--- Set New Query --->
<CFSET tempQuery =
QueryNew("Indent,Parentlist,ChildList,#attributes.query.columnlist#")>

<!--- These three fields are keywords, so it will overwrite them if you pass in
the following fieldnames--->
<CFSET columnlist=attributes.query.columnlist>
<CFSET columnlist=replacenocase(columnlist,"ParentItemid","")>
<CFSET columnlist=replacenocase(columnlist,"Itemid","")>
<CFSET columnlist=replacenocase(columnlist,"description","")>

<!--- If the query has no records, exit, but still return a blank recordset. --->
<CFIF not Attributes.Query.recordcount>
    <CFSET "Caller.#Attributes.variable#"=tempQuery>
    <CFSETTING ENABLECFOUTPUTONLY="no">
    <CFEXIT>
</CFIF>
```

```
<!--- This structure is so that we can add additional columns to the query.
--->
<CFSET extrafieldstruct=structnew()>

<!--- Sets the initial values for the worklist. This loop also allows us to have
additional fields above and beyond the 'standard'. --->
<CFLOOP QUERY="Attributes.Query">
    <!--- Note the space before the : after the description.  This is so that if
    the description is blank, the code will still work. --->
    <CFSET WorkList = Variables.WorkList&"|
    "&Attributes.Query.Description&"
:"&Attributes.Query.ParentItemID&":"&Attributes.Query.ItemID>
    <CFSET extrafieldstruct["itemid[#itemid#]"]=StructNew()>
    <CFLOOP list="#columnlist#" index="column">
        <CFSET extrafieldstruct["itemid[#itemid#][#column#]"]
        =evaluate("Attributes.Query.#column#")>
    </CFLOOP>
</CFLOOP>

<CFSET WorkList = RemoveChars(Variables.WorkList, 1, 1)>

<!--- The rootparent allows the tree to work even if the root doesn't start with
0, although 0 is the default. --->
<CFSET Current=attributes.rootparent>

<CFSET Path=0>
<CFSET indent=0>
<CFSET countstruct=structnew()>

<!--- Loop over Query list and order in a tree ---->
<CFLOOP INDEX="Index" FROM="1"
TO=#Attributes.Query.RecordCount#>

    <!--- Sets the new row to the value for the list--->
    <CFSET Position = ListContains(Variables.WorkList,
    ":"&Variables.Current&":","|")>
    <CFIF position>
        <CFSET indent=indent+1>
    </CFIF>

    <!--- If the current ID has no children, drop down the path and try
    again --->
    <CFSET counter=0>
    <CFLOOP CONDITION="NOT Variables.Position">
        <!--- This will catch errors from items that don't belong in the tree.
        --->
        <CFIF not len(variables.path)>
            <CFBREAK>
```

```
        </CFIF>
        <CFSET Path=ListRest(variables.Path)>
        <CFSET Current=ListFirst(variables.Path)>
        <CFSET Position = ListContains(variables.WorkList,
        ":"&variables.Current&":","|")>
        <CFSET counter=counter+1>

        <!--- This will subtract from the indent when a node goes back up
        the tree. --->
        <CFIF counter gt 1>
            <CFSET indent=indent-1>
            <CFSET parentlist=listdeleteat(parentlist,listlen(parentlist))>
        </CFIF>
    </CFLOOP>
    <CFIF not len(variables.path)>
        <CFBREAK>
    </CFIF>

    <!--- Adds a new row--->
    <CFSET QueryAddRow(tempQuery)>

    <CFSET Sub = ListGetAt(Variables.WorkList, Variables.Position, "|")>
    <CFSET QuerySetCell(tempQuery, 'Description',
    ListGetAt(Variables.Sub, 1, ":"))>
    <CFSET tempparent=ListGetAt(Variables.Sub, 2, ":")>
    <CFSET QuerySetCell(tempQuery, 'ParentItemID', tempparent)>
    <CFSET QuerySetCell(tempQuery, 'ItemID', ListGetAt(Variables.Sub, 3,
    ":"))>

    <!--- This will add additional columns to the query. --->
    <CFLOOP list="#columnlist#" index="column">
        <CFSET QuerySetCell(tempQuery, column,
        extrafieldstruct["itemid[#ListGetAt(Variables.Sub, 3,
        ":")#][#column#]"])>
    </CFLOOP>

    <!--- If the parentItemID is the same as the rootparent, we want to
set
    the indenting to 0. --->
    <CFIF tempparent is attributes.rootparent>
        <CFSET indent=0>
        <CFSET parentlist=attributes.rootparent>
    <CFELSEIF not listfind(parentlist,tempparent)>
        <CFSET parentlist=listappend(parentlist,tempparent)>
    </CFIF>

    <CFSET QuerySetCell(tempQuery, 'parentlist', parentlist)>
```

```
    <CFSET QuerySetCell(tempQuery, 'Indent', indent)>
    <CFSET WorkList=ListDeleteAt(Variables.WorkList, Variables.Position
    ,"|")>
    <CFSET Current=ListGetAt(Variables.Sub, 3, ":")>
    <CFSET Path=ListPrepend(Variables.Path, Variables.Current)>

    <CFSET countstruct[ListGetAt(Variables.Sub, 3, ":")]=index>
</CFLOOP>

<!--- This is for returning a value in the query that lists all the children
under that category. --->
<CFIF Attributes.getchildren>
    <CFLOOP query="tempQuery">
        <CFLOOP list="#parentlist#" index="thisparent">
            <CFIF listfind(valuelist(tempquery.itemid),thisparent)>
                <CFSET tempquery.childlist[countstruct[thisparent]]
                =listappend(tempquery.childlist[countstruct[thisparent]],
                itemid)>
            </CFIF>
        </CFLOOP>
    </CFLOOP>
</CFIF>
<CFSET "Caller.#Attributes.variable#"=tempQuery>
<CFSETTING ENABLECFOUTPUTONLY="NO">
```

<CF_MAX_ID>

```
<!--- required attributes --->
<CFPARAM name="attributes.datasource">
<CFPARAM name="attributes.tablename">
<CFPARAM name="attributes.primarykey">

<CFQUERY name="getmaxID" datasource="#attributes.datasource#">
    select max(#attributes.PrimaryKEY#) as Max_ID from
    #attributes.tablename#
</CFQUERY>

<CFIF len(getmaxID.Max_ID)>
    <CFSET caller.Max_ID = getmaxID.Max_ID + 1>
<CFELSE>
    <CFSET caller.Max_ID = "1">
</CFIF>
```

<CF_REUSEFORM>

```
<CFPARAM name="attributes.fieldlist" default="">
<CFSWITCH expression="#attributes.action#">
    <CFCASE value="new">
        <CFLOOP LIST="#attributes.fieldlist#" INDEX="counter">
            <CFIF listlen(counter,";") gt 1>
                <CFSET defaultvalue="#listgetat(counter,2,";")#">
            <CFELSE>
                <CFSET defaultvalue="">
            </CFIF>
            <CFSET "caller.#listgetat(counter,1,";")#" = "#defaultvalue#">
        </CFLOOP>
    </CFCASE>
    <CFCASE value="query">
        <CFPARAM name="attributes.fieldlist" default="">
        <CFPARAM name="attributes.queryname" default="">
        <CFLOOP LIST="#attributes.fieldlist#" INDEX="counter">
            <CFSET "caller.#listgetat(counter,1,";")#" =
            "#evaluate("caller.#attributes.queryname#.#listgetat
            (counter,1,";")#")#">
        </CFLOOP>
    </CFCASE>
    <CFCASE value="form">
        <CFLOOP LIST="#attributes.fieldlist#" INDEX="counter">
            <CFSET "caller.#listgetat(counter,1,";")#" =
            "#evaluate("FORM." & "#listgetat(counter,1,";")#")#">
        </CFLOOP>
    </CFCASE>
    <CFCASE value="url">
        <CFLOOP LIST="#attributes.fieldlist#" INDEX="counter">
            <CFSET "caller.#listgetat(counter,1,";")#" = "#evaluate("URL."
            & "#listgetat(counter,1,";")#")#">
        </CFLOOP>
    </CFCASE>
</CFSWITCH>
```

<CF_RETURNFUSEACTION>

```
<!---
<CFIF isdefined("client.fusetoken")>
    <CFSET token=client.fusetoken>
<CFELSE>
    <CFSET token = "CFID/#client.cfid#/CFTOKEN/#client.cftoken#">
    <!--- <CFSET token=client.urltoken> --->
```

```
</CFIF> --->

<CFPARAM name="request.urltoken" default="">
<CFPARAM name="attributes.defaultURL" default="/index.cfm?rfa=null">
<CFPARAM name="request.skiplist" default="">
<CFPARAM name="attributes.action">
<CFPARAM name="attributes.Returnurl" default="">
<CFPARAM name="attributes.gotourl" default="">
<CFPARAM name="request.listofattributes" default="">
<CFPARAM name="client.returnfuseaction" default="">

<CFSWITCH expression="#attributes.action#">
	<CFCASE value="set">
		<!--- remove CFID and CFTOKEN from the gotoURL and returnurl
		using regular notation and search engine notation --->
		<CFSET attributes.gotourl=rereplacenocase(attributes.gotourl,"
		cfid=[0-9]*&cftoken=[0-9]*","","all")>
		<CFSET attributes.returnurl=rereplacenocase(attributes.returnurl,"
		cfid=[0-9]*&cftoken=[0-9]*","","all")>

		<!--- delimiting with a chr(13) (return character) because you can't
		have a chr(13) in a url --->
		<CFSET cleanreturnurl=trim(replace(attributes.returnurl,
		chr(13),"+","all"))>

		<CFIF
listfindnocase(client.returnfuseaction,cleanreturnurl,chr(13))>
			<CFSET client.returnfuseaction=replacenocase
			(client.returnfuseaction,cleanreturnurl,"","all")>
		<CFELSE>
			<CFLOOP list="#request.skiplist#" index="skip" delimiters="|">
				<CFIF findnocase(skip,cleanreturnurl)>
					<CFSET cleanreturnurl=" ">
				</CFIF>
			</CFLOOP>
		</CFIF>

		<CFSET client.returnfuseaction=listappend
		(client.returnfuseaction,cleanreturnurl,chr(13))>

		<CFIF len(attributes.gotourl)>
			<CFIF find("?",attributes.gotourl)>
				<CFLOCATION url="#attributes.gotoURL#&inside=
				yes&#request.urltoken#" addtoken="No">
			<CFELSE>
				<CFLOCATION url="#attributes.gotoURL#?inside=
				yes&#request.urltoken#" addtoken="No">
			</CFIF>
```

```
        </CFIF>

    </CFCASE>
    <CFCASE value="return">
        <CFIF listlen(client.returnfuseaction,chr(13))>
            <CFSET returnurl=listlast(client.returnfuseaction,chr(13))>
            <!--- This will delete the last URL in client.returnfuseaction --->
            <CFSET client.returnfuseaction=listdeleteat
            (client.returnfuseaction,listlen(client.returnfuseaction,
            chr(13)),chr(13))>
            <CFIF len(trim(returnurl))>
                <CFIF not findnocase("index.cfm",returnurl)>
                    <CFSET returnurl="#returnurl#index.cfm">
                </CFIF>
                <CFIF find("?",returnurl)>
                    <CFLOCATION url="#returnurl#&#request.
                    listofattributes#&#request.urltoken#" addtoken="No">
                <CFELSE>
                    <CFLOCATION url="#returnurl#?#request.
                    listofattributes#&#request.urltoken#" addtoken="No">
                </CFIF>
            <CFELSE>
                <CFIF find("?",attributes.defaulturl)>
                    <CFLOCATION url="#attributes.defaulturl#&
                    #request.urltoken#" addtoken="No">
                <CFELSE>
                    <CFLOCATION url="#attributes.defaulturl#?
                    #request.urltoken#" addtoken="No">
                </CFIF>
            </CFIF>
        <CFELSE>
            <CFIF find("?",attributes.defaulturl)>
                <CFLOCATION url="#attributes.defaulturl#&
                #request.urltoken#" addtoken="No">
            <CFELSE>
                <CFLOCATION url="#attributes.defaulturl#?
                #request.urltoken#" addtoken="No">
            </CFIF>
        </CFIF>
    </CFCASE>
</CFSWITCH>
```

APPENDIX F: Fusebox and ColdFusion Online Resources

Fusebox

Fusebox.org (***http://www.fusebox.org/***): Fusebox community site. Here you will find all of the latest on the Fusebox specs, white papers, and other Fusebox community initiatives.

Hal Helms' Site (***http://www.teamallaire.com/hal***): Hal has a lot of good information online, including his papers and articles about Fusebox.

Fusebox Mailing List (***http://www.houseoffusion.com***): A good way to network with other Fusebox programmers and catch the latest on what's happening.

SecretAgents.com (***http://www.secretagents.com***): Steve Nelson's tools for Fusebox developers; useful tools and services, reasonably priced.

ColdFusion

ColdFusion Sites

House of Fusion (***http://www.houseoffusion.com***): Articles, experiments and insights, pushing ColdFusion to the edge, by Michael Dinowitz, ColdFusion guru. Also the home base for the ColdFusion community lists and other resources.

TeamAllaire.com (***http://www.teamallaire.com***): Hal Helms' site, full of ColdFusion tricks, tips and information.

Forta.com (***http://www.forta.com/cf/***): Ben Forta, Allaire's Product Evangelist, with his views and information on ColdFusion.

ColdCuts (***http://www.teratech.com/coldcuts***): Lots of neat ColdFusion tricks, organized by subject matter and date, courtesy of TeraTech, Inc.

Allaire Forums (***http://forums.allaire.com/***): Allaire's web-based forums, organized by subject.

ColdFusion Magazines

Fusion Authority (***http://www.fusionauthority.com***): Weekly online news alert, with all the latest news, articles, tips and reviews, published by Michael and Judith Dinowitz.

CFAdvisor (***http://www.cfadvisor.com***): An online ColdFusion magazine, with articles, reviews and other useful features. Subscriber-based.

ColdFusion Developer's Journal (***http://www.sys-con.com/coldfusion/***): ColdFusion's major print magazine (ColdFusion Developer's Journal) online.

Defusion (***http://www.defusion.com***): An online magazine and resource run by Duncan Campbell, another major ColdFusion developer.

CFTIPSPLUS! (***http://www.cftipsplus.com***): A lot of good community resources, including a CFTIPS ezine, compiled and published by Nathan Stanford.

CF_Newbie.com (***http://www.cfnewbie.com***): A good beginner's magazine, with resources and insights, run by Rey Bango, another major ColdFusion developer.

ColdFusion Community

ColdFusion Community Lists (***http://www.houseoffusion.com***): CF-Talk, CF-Community, Spectra-Talk, JRun-Talk, and a plethora of other lists for the ColdFusion community. A good place to get answers to your urgent ColdFusion questions, or to "hang" with other members of the ColdFusion community.

ColdFusion User Groups (***http://devex.allaire.com/developer/usergroups/***) Allaire's listing of ColdFusion user groups by area.

GLOSSARY

Absolute Format URLs: When a mapping is added to a web server, an <a href> tag can access a URL without the http:// prefix. This is done like this:

<a href="/products/index.cfm">

where "/" is the same as: "http://www.secretagents.com/".

Access Database: A file-based database that is commonly used by new programmers because it is inexpensive and easy to learn.

Action Blocks: Used to manipulate data or insert records into a datasource, they do not display anything to the user. They are also used for tasks not requiring output to a user.

Active Server Pages: A scripting language created by Microsoft used for creating web applications. ASP works much like ColdFusion, although its syntax is a little more complex to master.

Allaire™ Corporation: Creators of ColdFusion®.

App_Globals.cfm: Used in the Fusebox Method to initiate applications and set up global variables and settings. This replaces the standard practices of calling these items from within the *Application.cfm* template, which goes against the portability goals of Fusebox.

App_Locals.cfm: Similar in use to *app_globals.cfm* except that it is used to define local application settings for individual Fuses. While you will have only one *app_globals.cfm* files, you may have several *app_locals.cfm* files for the main application and subsequent sub-applications (Fuses).

App_login.cfm: This is the script run after a user enters in their login information. Login information is usually either email/password or username/password. This script will verify the user is who they say they are. Then set two variables: *#client.user_id#* and *#client.user_groups#.*

App_logout.cfm: This script is run to log a user out. It will delete their client variables and any associated cookies assigned to that user.

App_secure.cfm: Used to verify a user is either logged in and/or belongs to the appropriate groups. It is called through <CFMODULE> in either *app_globals.cfm,* which will secure every circuit application, in *app_locals.cfm,* which will secure every Fuseaction in a single circuit application, or at the top of a <CFCASE> statement, which will secure a single Fuseaction.

Application: A computer program that performs a specific task, such as word processing or database creation/manipulation, often made up of several smaller programs and designed for commercial or internal use.

Application Files: These are application-wide files that are used in multiple areas of your applications. Commonly called on all page requests.

Application.cfm: A ColdFusion template that is always called at the beginning of every page request. The ColdFusion server will recursively move back up the directory structure until it finds one.

ASP: See Active Server Pages

Attributes.fuseaction: This is "what" the user is attempting to do in a circuit application. A single circuit application will have many Fuseactions. Each of these Fuseactions will call the necessary files to run that action.

Autonumber Field/Identity Key: This is an integer datatype in a database which will auto-increment. This means it will add 1 to the last value in that field. The autonumber field is commonly used as a primary key in a table. It is difficult to transfer from one database to another because there is no standard on how the various databases use autonumber fields.

Bug: *(AKA "software bug")* An error in an application. Some will cause your application to stop working; others will be small and while they won't break the application, they may cause data to be displayed incorrectly. The term was started at either MIT or Harvard (depending on the report you believe) when a moth trapped between two electrical relays on a Mark II Aiken Relay Calculator caused the whole machine to shut down. Hence the term "A Bug in The System"

Circuit Application: This is a directory of .cfm files. A circuit application is a group of tasks (Fuseactions) that the user may perform. A home application is made up of many circuit applications.

CF: See ColdFusion.

<CFAPPLICATION>: This tag is used to turn on application, session and client variables. It also allows for automatically setting CFID/CFTOKEN cookies in a user's browser.

<CF_BodyContent>: This is a custom tag used in *index.cfm* files that allows for nesting Fusebox circuit applications together. It allows for the body of the page to be processed before the header/footer so that the header and footer can be manipulated.

CFID/CFTOKEN: These are variables set by the CF server to identify a user's session. CFID is an incrementing value and CFTOKEN is a randomly generated value. These variables are used to associate server side variables such as client and session variables.

<CFINCLUDE>: This tag allows for dynamically adding the CFML code from one file in another. Useful for reusing code.

<CFLOOP>: This is the ColdFusion tag for looping. It can do "for" loops, "while" loops, and loop over recordsets, lists, COM objects, etc.

<CFMODULE>: ColdFusion code written up as a separate file and called using a special interface. This code is run as a separate operation and will send back results to the "calling page". ColdFusion modules can be called either by using the ColdFusion tag of the same name or a shorthand prefix of "CF_". This tag is similar to <CFINCLUDE>, except that it allows local scoped variables. That simply means that variables can exist inside the template being included that do not exist in the parent template.

<CFOBJECT>: A ColdFusion tag that calls component code (COM, CORBA, etc.) from inside a ColdFusion template.

<CFPARAM>: This is used for setting default values for a variable. These values can be overridden if the variable is set before the call to this tag. This makes sure that a variable exists.

<CFQUERY>: This tag is used to connect to ODBC databases. ColdFusion can connect to almost all of the major database software on the market. This tag allows SQL to be written directly into the tag and returns a record set of the result given by the database.

<CFSTOREDPROC>: Used for running stored procedures on the database. It allows for multiple recordsets to be returned by the database.

<CFSWITCH> / **<CFCASE>** / **<CFDEFAULTCASE>**: This is very much like a *if/elseif* statement, except that it only looks at a single variable. The <CFSWITCH> statement is used in the *index.cfm* of a Fusebox application to determine what Fuseaction the user is attempting to run.

CFX: General term used by Allaire for all extensions to ColdFusion. Originally reserved for the VC++ custom tags. Additionally, this is the prefix for all VC++ based custom tags.

<CFX_J>: CFX Tag that allows the inclusion of Java Classes into ColdFusion code. This tag will be phased out and included into the <CFOBJECT> tag in a future release.

Coding Phase: This is the phase in the spiral method when the application is actually written. It is important to plan out what needs to be written before moving into this phase, otherwise time will be wasted.

ColdFusion®: A product created by Allaire™ Corporation (located in Cambridge, Mass.) It includes an Application Server and a development tool set designed to create applications using data from almost any source. (See ColdFusion Markup Language (CFML).)

ColdFusion Custom Tags: A custom tag is simply a file called as <CFMODULE> or with the <CF_FILENAME_WITHOUT_EXTENSION> syntax. A custom tag is much like a <CFINCLUDE>, except that it allows for variables to be passed in (attributes scope) and out (caller scope).

ColdFusion Markup Language (CFML): A tag-based language created and developed by Allaire Corporation and used by ColdFusion programmers all over the world.

ColdFusion Template: The actual page containing ColdFusion code to be processed. Uses the .cfm or .cfml extensions (.dbm and .dbml in older editions).

COM: A proposed component technology used by Microsoft. Based on OLE, it is also known as server side ACTIVEX or Microsoft DNA.

Cookies: These are variables that exist in a user's browser. The only variables that "should" be stored as cookies are session identifier variables. In ColdFusion, this is CFID/CFTOKEN. All other variables should be stored on the server through client variables. This allows for the best security.

CORBA: A proposed component technology. Usually written in Java, it is a must for many enterprise level products.

Custom Tag: See <CFMODULE>

Deployment Phase: This is the phase in the spiral method when code is moved from the development servers to the production servers. An application should not be deployed unless it has gone through the testing phase.

Design Phase: This is the phase in the spiral method of determining how the specification will technically work. It generally means explaining each of the Fuses in each of the Fuseactions described in the specification.

Different Server Absolute Format: To access a URL on another server it is necessary to add the http:// prefix to the URL, like this:

```
<a href="http://www.secretagents.com/products/index.cfm?fuseaction=product&product_id=1">
Testing Tool</a>
```

Display Blocks: Small files of text and HTML code used to display information to the user. Information displayed is sometimes static and sometimes called from Query Blocks.

Display Files: This is a Fuse that contains some type of output that the user will see. A display file will never change any information on the server, in case the user reloads their browser. It is important that data does not get duplicated on the server. Fusebox is not specific to HTML; display files can contain other display types like WML.

Dot Notation: This is used in CFML structures, like this:
somevariable.variable1.name="joe"

Emergent Behavior: *(See "Bug")*

Form Field Variable: A variable contained in a <FORM> tag, such as:

```
<input type=""text"" name=""Fuseaction"" value=""affiliate"">
```

Fuse: Basically the same as a Fusebox; the main difference is that it's being called as a sub-application through the main Fusebox.

Fuseaction: Set of instructions to be taken when called by a user. Typically used to set parameters, variables, and necessary includes of query blocks, action blocks, and display blocks. It is called through either the main Fusebox or a Fuse.

Fusebox: Central point for all applications using the Fusebox Method. It is typically called *index.cfm*. Actions are called from within the Fusebox using Fuseactions.

Fusebox Method: A methodology of "Best Programming Practices". It's based on the goal of maximizing code re-use by coding all applications to be run as both stand-alone applications and as custom tags. Uses a "wheel-and-spoke" architecture, with all actions returning to the Fusebox.

Fusebox Organization: The international organization of developers who have contributed to the growth and development of the Fusebox Methodology (**www.fusebox.org**)

Fusebox Process: The process of developing a Fusebox application using the spiral method.

fUseML: A new proposal to Fusebox for describing Fusebox graphically.

Global Navigation: This is navigation which exists on every page of an application.

Global Variables: Variables accessible from anywhere in the application.

Home Application: This is the application as a whole, such as SecretAgents.com. A home application is made up of many circuit applications.

House of Fusion: A site dedicated to assisting ColdFusion developers improve their knowledge of the ColdFusion language

Index.cfm: Main "switchboard" of a Fusebox styled application.

Interface: A "middle layer" that exists between two applications or pieces of code that allows information from one to be moved over to the other. This allows the writer of one "object" to send data to the other without knowing anything about how the data will be used or where it's going.

Java Applet: Small client side Java applications used within web pages.

Java Servlets: A server side JAVA program that integrates into a webserver for dynamic page content generation. Seen by many as one of the few "true" uses of Java.

JRun: A product that allows a programmer to use Java servlet technology on "standard" webservers.

LDAP: Short for "**L**ightweight **D**irectory **A**ccess **P**rotocol", a set of protocols for accessing information directories. LDAP is based on the standards contained within the X.500 standard, but is significantly simpler. This is commonly used for storing security information such as user and group data.

Lightweight Directory Access Protocol (LDAP): This is commonly used for storing security information such as user and group data.

Methodology: A body of practices, procedures and rules used by those who work in a discipline or engage in an inquiry; a set of working methods.

Modules: Code which is written separated so it can be used in multiple areas. This allows for managing less code.

Normalization refers to applying a set of rules to a database design to increase its efficiency, reduce errors, and eliminate potential problems before they start. There are three basic normalization "forms", referred to as first, second, and third normal forms. There is also a fourth normal form, and several other types of normalization, but the three basic levels are what are most often encountered.

Each form is more restrictive in design requirements than the previous one, but provides a better database design in most cases. In each successive level of normalization, redundant data is eliminated, moving toward the eventual goal of never repeating any information. The database design can become more complex with higher normalization levels because there are more tables to keep track of.

For example, if you have a database in which you wish to track customer orders and address information, a completely non-normalized design would have only a single table. If a customer wished to order three parts, the table would require three columns: Part1, Part2, and Part3. This obviously would be a problem if you wished to let your customers order more than three parts at a time. In addition, repeat customers would have their address and other contact data repeated for each order. Obviously this is not an efficient design.

The same database in a fully normalized (3rd normal form) database would have a customer table, a parts table, an invoices table, and a parts_to_invoices table to connect invoices to parts. These tables would be linked to one another through columns called "primary" and "foreign" keys. Data is never repeated in this design. For example, an invoice would contain a reference to a customer in the customer table and would contain links to each part the customer wanted through the parts_to_invoices table. The actual invoice record itself would be little more than a number and some IDs to point to values in other tables. When you wish to look at the data, it is assembled by a database query into a coherent format.

Novice Method, The: A method of development which consists of only two phases, requirements phase and coding phase.

Oracle Database: A powerful database server produced by Oracle. Commonly used in companies with large budgets, Oracle is one of the leading database servers.

Perl: A free open-source scripting language used for creating web applications. Perl works much like ColdFusion, although its syntax is a little more complex to master.

PHP: A free open-source scripting language used for creating web applications. PHP works much like ColdFusion, although its syntax is a little more complex to master.

Query Blocks: These pull information from a datasource for either display or data manipulation; they are never used to display information. They are also commonly used by Action Blocks.

Query Caching: The ability to store data retrieved from the database in RAM on the CF server.

Query Files: These files have a prefix of *"qry_"* and contain one or more <CFQUERY> statements in them. They are useful in reusing Queries in various areas of your application.

Redirection Files: These are files which contain a <CFLOCATION> tag in them. They are used after an action file updates data on the server to send a user to a display Fuseaction. This will ensure that, if the user hits "reload" on their browser, it doesn't continue to change data on the server.

Relative Format: If a link has no "/" or http:// on the beginning of it, the browser will assume to look in the current directory, i.e., <a href="products/index.cfm">

Request Scope: This type of variable exists at all levels of nested custom tags. It is a true global variable, but does not remain in memory like an application variable.

Request.CFRoot: This is the ColdFusion mapping to the root directory of your Fusebox application. It is used for <CFINCLUDE> and <CFMODULE>. Generally looks like: "/secretagents".

Request.ImagesRoot: This is the mapping for the images in your Fusebox application. It is used so that images can be stored on separate web servers from your ColdFusion server. This improves scalability and speed. Generally looks like:

"#request.protocol#images.secretagents.com".

Request.MainDSN: This is the main datasource used for your Fusebox application. Storing this in a variable allows for easily switching to other datasources.

Request.Protocol: This is used so that the *request.imagesroot* will also be *https://* when a user goes to a secured page. This will ensure that the user does not get the message that there are unsecured items on the page.

Request.SSLRoot: This is the mapping to the SSL URL for your site. It is useful when moving from development server to production server. Generally development servers do not have SSL keys on them, so simply changing this variable will allow for mimicking a production server. Generally looks like: "https://www.secretagents.com".

Request.Timespan: This is used for the *"cachedwithin"* attribute in <CFQUERY> when doing query caching and also used in the *"applicationtimeout"* attributes in <CFAPPLICATION>. This is useful for refreshing the CF server, to get the most recent data from the database.

Request.URLToken: This is simply *client. URLtoken* in request scope. It was found to be slightly faster than using the client scope.

Request.WebRoot: This is the web server mapping to the root directory of your Fusebox application. It is used for global navigation in <a href> <form action> and <CFLOCATION URL>. Generally looks like: "http://www.secretagents.com".

Scriptlet: A quasi-COM object created using the Windows Scripting Host. This allows vb-script, j-script and other languages to be wrapped up and used within ColdFusion using the <CFOBJECT> tag.

Servlet: See Java Servlets.

Scoping: See **variable scoping**.

SDLC: A **S**ystem **D**evelopment **L**ife **C**ycle is a logical process by which systems analysts, software engineers, programmers, and end-users build information systems and computer applications to solve business problems and needs. It is sometimes called an "application development life cycle".

SecretAgents.com: An Application Service Provider that offers web based tools for improving your Fusebox development.

Secured Sockets Layer: Transfers sensitive data thru the net. A lock and key at bottom of browser in checkout at an ecommerce site indicates that this is in effect. Allows for encrypting between browser and server.

Software Development Life Cycle: The process, from start to finish, of dreaming up and creating a piece of software.

Spiral Method, The: The spiral method consists of five phases: Specification, Design, Coding, Testing, and Deployment.

Specification: This is "what" the application needs to do. The specification describes in English (or your native tongue) each of the circuits and Fuseactions of an application.

Specification Phase: The specification phase is the first step in the spiral method, when the client and the developer discuss what the application needs to do.

SQL: *(also* **Structured Query Language**.) This is a programming language to interact with a relational database.

SSL: Secured Sockets Layer *(see above)*

Standalone Application: An application that works by itself and does not require being called from within another application.

Team Allaire:A group of professional web developers recognized by Allaire whom assist other developers with writing CFML.

Testing Phase: The phase in the spiral design when the application is verified that it is working correctly.

UML: *See* **Unified Modeling Language**

Unified Modeling Language: A modeling language for diagraming software systems designed by Grady Booch, James Rumbaugh and Ivar Jacobson.

Universal Format: A format for the URL in links and forms that will work both when called as a standalone application and when called the circuit application is called as a <CFMODULE>. Looks like: <a href="index.cfm"> or <form action="index.cfm">.

URL Parameter: This is a variable which is passed in the URL. Looks like: http://www.secretagents.com/content/index.cfm?fuseaction=Affiliate.

URLTOKEN: A combination of CFID and CFTOKEN. Looks like: CFID=32934 & CFTOKEN=2834759.

Visio-Type Modeling Tool: A tool used for drawing UML and flowchart diagrams

Waterfall Method, The: A software development process where one area of the software design must be complete before the next one can begin. This is less superior than the spiral method, in which multiple areas can be worked on at the same time and are revised for each version. The waterfall method is essentially a single-pass version of the spiral method.

Web Application: A web application is software that can be accessed through a web browser.

Web Application Development Language: A programming language used to create a web application.

www.fusebox.org: The Fusebox Organization *(see above)*

WYSIWYG: What You See Is What You Get

Please Note: Much of this list was originally published in **Fusion Authority**, Issue 31:

(www.fusionauthority.com/alert/index.cfm?alertid=31#tech3)

as the Fusebox Definition List by Fred T. Sanders, and further developed by him and others specifically for this book. We appreciate their contributions.

INDEX